ROBERT LIDDELL ON THE NOVEL

ROBERT LIDDELL ON THE NOVEL

WITH AN INTRODUCTION BY

Wayne C. Booth

THE UNIVERSITY OF CHICAGO PRESS

Originally published by Jonathan Cape as *A Treatise on the Novel* and *Some Principles of Fiction,* protected under the International Copyright Convention 1947, 1953 by Robert Liddell

Library of Congress Catalog Card Number: 78-76204
THE UNIVERSITY OF CHICAGO PRESS, CHICAGO 60637

Published 1969
Printed in the United States of America

CONTENTS

CONTENTS

CONTENTS

PUBLISHER'S NOTE

This volume is a combination of two books by Robert Liddell, *A Treatise on the Novel* and *Some Principles of Fiction.* In the preliminary pages of *A Treatise on the Novel,* which is dedicated to Olivia Manning, the author says: "I wish to thank Mr. P. H. Newby for reading the manuscript of this book, and for making several valuable suggestions.

"Thanks are also due to Mr. T. S. Eliot and Messrs. Faber & Faber for permission to use extracts from *Second Thoughts on Humanism,* to the executors of Henry James for permission to quote from *The Art of the Novel,* to Librarie Gallimard for permission to quote from the works of Marcel Proust, and to Miss I. Compton-Burnett for permission to use illustrative passages from her works."

The author also states: "For the translations from the French I am generally responsible. Those from Madame Bovary, however, are taken from the *Everyman* translation. The edition of Flaubert's letters used is that of Bibliothèque-Charpentier (Paris 1920)."

INTRODUCTION

THROUGHOUT the first half of this century, critics often complained that criticism of fiction was still in its infancy. A commonplace of prefaces to books about novelists held that Aristotle had established a long and healthy critical tradition for drama, but that the novel, through its very novelty, had suffered from neglect and confusion. It was sometimes said, during the thirties and forties, that Percy Lubbock, following Henry James, had at last filled this cultural lacuna with his discovery that systematic attention to point of view was the whole art of novel-writing and the whole science of criticism. But complaints about poverty of terms and inadequacy of theory continued, and they continue even today.

Whatever may now be said about the adequacy of our criticism, no one can any longer complain about its scarcity. In 1947, when Robert Liddell's *A Treatise on the Novel* was published, there were scarcely a half dozen books about the novel that could be recommended honestly to the novelist or his reader. Now there are so many useful works available that winnowing will forevermore be required: no man will ever again read, unless he is mad, all that might be worth reading about the art of the novel.

The reprinting of these two short books by Liddell can be seen as one significant move in the Great Sifting. They have never, I think, been given the attention they deserve, overshadowed on the one hand by the more systematic Percy Lubbock and on the other by the wittier E. M. Forster. Why our seemingly insatiable appetite for good talk about novels should have put Liddell to one side is not easy to determine. We might blame it on his aggressive lack of system, his casual way of ignoring problems of logic and method that many

American critics would worry over for hundreds of pages. No coherent theory of the novel is stated openly in these books, and I doubt that one could be extracted. No rules of technique are here, and if there is something like an implied great tradition of Novelists Who Matter, it is so broad and eclectic as to disappoint those who have found the simple canon of Leavis reassuring. He oversimplifies shamelessly, as in his fumbling attempts to get into his subject through two abstractions, "Academic" and "Practical" criticism. But the fact is that Forster is twice as brazen about skirting issues, twice as resistant to anyone seriously interested in theory, twice as haphazard—and yet we have taken him to our hearts.

Whatever the reason for the neglect, it is a pity, because few pages ever written about fiction are so stimulating as these. Liddell's mind, like Forster's, is richer than its overt categories; his very willingness to range over various topics without pushing openly for full coherence or completeness frees him to express a more comprehensive view than seems to be available to most of us—witness the many recent reductive efforts at constructing a "poetics of fiction," especially in the pages of the fine new journal, *Novel.* By refusing to pin himself down prematurely, by refusing to be this kind of critic or that, by a steady habit of looking at his own experience as novelist and reader rather than at abstract rules about what a novel ought to be, he produces an astonishingly concentrated list of provocations to thought about fiction. His is by no means a complete survey of critical problems or technical advice, and he hardly ever carries a topic far enough to suit me (which may be to say that if I had been doing it I would have produced several longer and stodgier books). But if there are any discussions of fiction with more individual thought per line, more real meat per bite, I am unaware of them.

I shall return to some of Liddell's limitations later on. But it is important first to dwell on his powers, if only because they seem to have been overlooked.

INTRODUCTION

I

There are two kinds of critics of "the novel" — those who are ashamed of the fact that novels tell stories and those who, like Liddell, help us understand how it is done. E. M. Forster placed himself — only half playfully — among the first kind when he wrote that the novel "tells a story." "Yes — oh, dear, yes — the novel tells a story," and his book *Aspects of the Novel,* though it deserves its fame for other reasons, is not of much use to anyone — author or reader — who is curious about how good stories, especially good *long* stories, work as stories. Robert Liddell never forgets that novels are good long stories that work. His two short books provide more useful talk about *how* they work than Forster would have believed possible.

II

There are two kinds of critics who believe that novels tell stories — those who reduce plot to adventure or intrigue (and thus play into the hands of critics who want to dismiss plot as trivial) and those who, like Liddell, know that all good long stories are "representations of characters in action" and that something important happening *in* a character is as much "plot" as something happening *to* a character. His analyses, brief as they are, cover a wide range of actions, and they are full of hints for both critics and novelists about what makes the difference between successful plotting and mere manipulation.

III

There are two kinds of critics who object to mere manipulation and artificially imposed intrigue — those who, like Liddell, know how much a good plot depends on the novelist's basic values and those who do not. Significant plots are built against a backdrop of values more or less openly espoused by the novelist's "writing self." Liddell stands as far as possible from those who would say that it does not matter what a novelist attempts to do, so long as he does it well. Some such critics say that we should not talk about beliefs and values because they are mere "content," and we should be concerned only with form. Others say that we should ignore them because if we once risk taking them seriously, we are in danger of deciding between the good guys and the bad guys according to whether *their* values are *our* values, and soon Catholic critics will be refusing to read non-Catholic novelists, and agnostic critics will be banning Mauriac. Robert Liddell knows the dangers, but he also knows that a critic should take fiction, a serious art, seriously. He often refers to Jane Austen's words of praise: the novel "conveys to the world in the best chosen language the most thorough knowledge of human nature, the happiest delineation of its varieties, and the liveliest effusions of wit and humor." He is quite clear that the word "knowledge" is crucial here. Though a novelist may be "protestant, Catholic, agnostic or atheist . . . imperialist, pacifist, conservative, liberal or socialist, independent or apolitical," he cannot afford to be *wrong* about "personal values." What he knows about "character in action" is what various actions *mean,* in human terms, and the critic who refuses to talk about how the novelist *means* would be as deficient, for Liddell, as the critic who refuses to talk about how the novelist *forms.* In fact, under close analysis they became the same thing. Just as plot is nothing different from character in action, so it is not different, except in analysis, from action judged in a context of values.

IV

There are two kinds of critics who take the central values or truths of a work of fiction seriously — those who, like Liddell, respect the rich and recalcitrant facts of the individual novel, with its unique plot and characters and style, and those who like to crowd as many novels as possible under one symbolic or metaphorical umbrella, regardless of how much of each one is left out in the rain. Liddell is not afraid to be commonsensical and literal; there is no hint here of an effort to discover a formula for "*the* quest" of all fictional heroes, or *the* proper relation of symbol and action. What this amounts to is that he respects the works of art more than his own desire for pattern or originality, and he is thus a splendid antidote to the improvising original critics who flood us with startling new interpretations that have nothing to recommend them except their lack of paternity. Even when he is not as painstaking in pursuing the grounds of a controversial reading as one would like, he gives us readings that in almost every case have permanent value: the interpretation offered is so well grounded in the details of the novel that no critic can easily dismiss it. Thus it is that his essay on "The Turn of the Screw" is still one of the best on the much-vexed subject of the governess and of James's intentions about her. No conscientious critic can reject Liddell's reading without rejecting most traditional assumptions about what a critic does and how literature works. If a critic decides to refute Liddell, he will be required to move from the assumption that his own hypothesis is self-proving ("All good literature is interpretable in sexual terms; therefore *Turn* is. . . .") to grapple with the unique and recalcitrant details about *this* governess in *this* story, *as James wrote it,* not as it might have been if the critic had been in charge.

Though Liddell knows perfectly well that we care only about the values of the author's "writing self," not about what he says, does, or claims to believe outside his writing life, he is wise enough—one might almost say lucky enough, since he writes in 1947 and not in 1969—to take for granted what everyone knows unless it is artificially trained out of him: that one difference between good novelists and bad, or between great novelists and the merely competent, is the breadth or depth or significance or finally even the truth of what the novelist shows us. His demonstration of how wrong values can partially vitiate even the work of a fine novelist like E. M. Forster seems to me unanswerable; insofar as *The Longest Journey* or *A Room with a View* depends upon our believing that one "Great Refusal," one failure to value a "Noble Savage" properly, can permanently destroy a man's character, it is flawed. Some readers may be troubled by Liddell's use of religious labels for what is wrong with some novels: he speaks of heresy, of grace, even of God. But I find the religious terms especially economical: "Mr. Forster is being harder than God or Life would have been to Lucy – he wants to deny her another chance."

I cannot see how anyone can effectively reply to Liddell's charge without admitting his general case: even to defend Forster's view of his own characters would be to admit the importance of sharing such values as we read his fiction. Without falling into any of the traps that threaten the critic who dares to take novelists' beliefs seriously, Liddell shows us one highly successful and supple version of "doctrinal criticism."

V

There are two kinds of critics who do justice to the importance of ideas and beliefs in fiction – those who, like Liddell, understand the intricacies of fictional technique and those who dismiss technique as unimportant. Without immodesty, Liddell aspires to being useful to novelists by writing intimately, *as* a novelist, of plot and character, of background, of "summary" and dialogue, of the use of notebooks and the misuse of superfluous information. What he writes about technique could never constitute a "first course in writing the novel"; unlike most of the guides that take technique seriously, it assumes a good deal of sophistication and experience in the reader; its relatively unsystematic hints and aggressively personal list of "Terms and Topics" cannot be advertised as a vade mecum to successful writing. But I can think of no survey of the novelist's problems that touches on so many of the exasperating little matters that plague the real novelist as he writes. Almost every page suggests a subject for some lesser man's book. (How neatly he summarizes, eight years before me, the originating idea for my own book: "Fiction, which still has the resource of Summary undisguised, has very little excuse for employing Summary badly disguised as Scene, when it needs to 'hark back to make up.' ")

VI

Finally, there are two kinds of critics, or at least there used to be — those who, like Liddell, believe in form, in relevance, in the functional articulation of the parts of a work into a beautiful whole, and those who see the restraints of form and function as chains binding what should be the free artist. Another way of saying this is that some critics see the artist's self-expression as a supreme goal, while others see the making of a work of art as the point of supreme interest for the critic. Liddell views the act of composing, of making form where life was formless, in almost the same reverential light as does Henry James. Whether he is granting credit to the detective story as, after all, "one of the better-made things of our time," or praising George Eliot (whom he generally makes too little of, I think) for restoring "Unity of Action as a principle," he never forgets that the glory of the novel is its capacity to join together that which Life, in all its carelessness, had left asunder. His faith in the supremacy of the organic plot is only one aspect of his conviction that what the novelist does in detail must relate to what he is trying to do in the large; if it does not, he will not really improve his presentation of Life but rather destroy his proper form of life.

In 1969 it is not fashionable to worry about form, about relevance, about beauty of organization. Academic critics (now so different from the academic critics Liddell had in mind!) may say what they will, but simulated chaos is in vogue. There is no reason to believe that those who see genius in the absolute submission to chance or the cheerful embrace of tedium will be converted by Liddell. His quiet faith in the shaping power of the artist will, however, be useful to writers long after the present avant-garde has been epatéed in its turn.

VII

I have written almost as if I thought Liddell's books were to be placed among the great works of criticism, and I scarcely can mean that. Liddell is terribly handicapped by his lack of sophistication about theory and method—I almost write "by being an Englishman writing for Englishmen about English fiction." He often struggles unsuccessfully with a problem that other critics, past and present, can handle easily—for example, his difficulties with *Rasselas* "as a novel" (*Principles*, p. 188) disappear for anyone who has read carefully in Aristotle or Johnson or Coleridge, or for that matter in Sheldon Sacks. Perhaps most annoying, he worries far too much and too clumsily about evaluation. Although Northrop Frye and others seem to me quite wrong when they argue that reasoned defenses of critical judgments are impossible, it is equally dangerous to begin at the opposite extreme: "It is the function of literary criticism first to distinguish between those novels which call for serious criticism, and those which are beneath it (Categories I and II). The next task is to distinguish, among novels which call for serious criticism, between those which are good, and those which might have been good but are not (Categories I (*a*) and I (*b*))." The absurdity here is so obvious that one can simply urge readers to plow ahead in order to discover how far this is from what Liddell actually does. I would urge them, in fact, to skim chapter I of *A Treatise* very quickly (especially articles 2 through 6) and return to it only after reading carefully to the end. By then they will have discovered, if they have read with sympathy, a critic so shrewd that even what at first seems simple-minded is worth preserving. Whatever our next stage in criticism is to be, we shall be fortunate if it is as comprehensive, as free of crippling dogma, and as thoroughly embedded in literary experience as are these books.

WAYNE C. BOOTH

A Treatise on the Novel

Il y a autre chose à faire d'une belle oeuvre que de la copier, c'est de rivaliser avec elle. Ce n'est pas ses résultats qu'elle nous enseigne, ce sont ses moyens.

Claudel: *Le Soulier de Satin,*
deuxième journée, sc. v

CHAPTER I

AN APPROACH TO THE CRITICISM OF FICTION

§I THE DIGNITY OF THE NOVEL

THE Novel as a literary form has still a flavour of newness. It is true that it can trace its descent from Longus, Heliodorus and Petronius, and from medieval prose romances; it is true, but not very interesting, and more learning than thought has been employed to trace this descent, which is no uncommon thing in Genealogy. In a family that has in modern times produced great men, *they* are what we care about; we are impatient with long accounts of their remoter ancestors, though they must of course have had ancestors. In the same way prose fiction before the eighteenth century can only matter to us as scholars, not as critics or general readers.

When we remember what the romances of his time were like, we are not indignant with Bossuet for praising Henriette d'Angleterre, in his funeral oration upon her, because she did not care for novels. 'Our admirable princess studied the duties of those whose lives make up history; there she insensibly lost the taste for romances and for their insipid heroes, and, anxious to form herself upon truth, she despised those cold and dangerous fictions.'

Even in our own times the Novel is sometimes still attacked; but though we can readily pardon Bossuet, it is not so easy to pardon those who attack a form that has been used by Jane Austen, by Stendhal, by Tolstoy, by Flaubert, by Henry James and by Proust. Attacks upon the Novel as a form have adversely influenced both novelists and critics, many of whose worst errors can directly be traced to a low view of this form of art.

The case put forward against the novel by Mr. Montgomery

Belgion may be examined, although his book has perhaps been forgotten. His argument should be answered in case it is ever put forward again by anyone else.

Mr. Belgion says that there is no such thing as a creative artist; and, since a novelist is not a creative artist, there is only one thing he can be, a propagandist for his own particular view of life, and an irresponsible propagandist at that. The title of creative artist is denied to the novelist because 'to create' means 'to bring into existence out of nothing': characters in fiction have never been made out of nothing, but always out of some shreds of experience; and they never come into existence – we cannot take them by the hand.[1]

The answer is simple and obvious. We regard ourselves and our neighbours as individually created beings, although none of *us* was made out of nothing. And there is more than one way of existing: Wisdom and Virtue exist, although you cannot take either of them by the hand. Therefore although Falstaff or Mrs. Gamp may not belong to the same order of being as Napoleon, it is nevertheless not unreasonable to say that they exist, and that they have been created by their authors.

But even allowing the novelist to be a creative artist, some people think his art a very inferior one. Several novelists are unfortunately of this opinion. 'Oh dear, the novel tells a story,' says Mr. Forster regretfully,[2] and clearly wishes that it did not. Mr. Forster at least dwells with more complacency on the fact that the novel depicts character, but even that Mr. Aldous Huxley thinks a trivial thing to do. A character of his reflects (with his apparent approval) on 'the wearisomeness to an adult mind, of all those merely descriptive plays and novels which critics expected one to admire. All the innumerable, interminable anecdotes and romances and character-studies, but no general theory of anecdotes, no explanatory hypothesis of romance or character. Just a huge collection of facts about lust and greed, fear and ambition, duty and affection; just facts and imaginary facts at that, with no co-ordinating philosophy superior to common sense and the local system of conventions, no principle of arrangement more rational than simple aesthetic expediency.'[3]

It is very shocking to find that a novelist thinks facts about Human Nature so wearisome, when they should be his stock-in-trade. It is worse that he wishes for any arrangement of those facts other than 'simple aesthetic expediency' — what principle for an artist could be more rational? And his contempt for the imagination does not make things any better. We shall see, in a subsequent chapter, that for a novelist no philosophy is superior to common sense.

If we turn away from Mr. Huxley to a novelist of creative genius, who respected and loved her art, to Jane Austen, we shall find a character whom she wishes to ridicule expressing himself in terms very similar to those of Mr. Huxley's would-be intelligent character.

Sir Edward Denham in *Sanditon*, the fragment left unfinished by Miss Austen at her death, makes this boast: 'I am no indiscriminate Novel-Reader. The mere trash of the common Circulating-Library, I hold in the highest contempt. You will never hear me advocating those puerile Emanations which detail nothing but discordant Principles incapable of Amalgamation, or those vapid tissues of ordinary Occurrences from which no useful Deductions can be drawn. In vain may we put them into a literary Alembic; we distil nothing which can add to Science.'

Sir Edward's pomposity is a prophetic parody of that of Mr. Huxley and of all others who are not content that a novel should be a novel, but want it to be something else as well — as if to be a good novel were not enough. And it is just that Mr. Huxley should be rebuked out of the mouth of Miss Austen, for in depreciating the Novel, and thereby fouling his own nest, he is doing precisely the thing that she had condemned in a famous passage in *Northanger Abbey*.

'I will not adopt that ungenerous and impolitic custom, so common with novel writers, of degrading, by their contemptuous censure, the very performance to the number of which they are themselves adding; joining with their greatest enemies in bestowing the harshest epithets on such works, and scarcely ever permitting them to be read by their own heroine, who, if she accidentally take up a novel, is sure to turn over its insipid pages with disgust . . . There seems almost a general wish of decrying the capacity and undervaluing the labour of the novelist, and of slighting the performances which have only genius, wit, and taste to recommend them. "And what are you reading, Miss—?" "Oh, it is only a novel," replies the young lady; while she lays down her book with affected indifference or momentary shame. It is only *Cecilia*, or *Camilla*, or *Belinda*, or in short, only some work in which the most thorough knowledge of human nature, the happiest delineation of its varieties, the liveliest effusions of wit and humour are conveyed to the world in the best chosen language.'

There has not yet been made a more eloquent defence of the novel. No further apology is needed for asserting the dignity of that literary form which enables 'the most thorough knowledge of human nature, the happiest delineation of its varieties, the liveliest effusions of wit and humour' to be 'conveyed to the world in the best chosen language'.

§2 THE NOVEL, AND THE HERITAGE OF DRAMA

Saintsbury, the genealogist of the Novel, insisted on its ancient history, for its history was identical with that of the Romance, whether in prose or verse. He argued that it was unhistorical, and otherwise unexampled, for a literary genre to appear for the first time in the eighteenth century — when epic, tragedy, comedy, the essay and the epigram can all be traced back to the literatures of Greece and Rome. Moreover, he argued, if we are to call the Romance and the Novel different genres before the eighteenth century, then we must logically maintain this difference during and after the eighteenth century — which it would be difficult to do. Lastly he said that it was artificial to contrast the Romance, or story of incident, with the Novel, or story of character and motive — since every story with people in it is potentially a novel.

Without directly contesting Saintsbury's arguments, one may differ from him so completely in values that their force vanishes. Suppose that we grant that it is unhistorical to say that the first novel appeared about two hundred years ago, and that the literary genre must have a longer history — yet it is possible to maintain that a qualitative change occurred at some point, so great that in order to study the Novel after this development we get little help from examples of what (one may grant) was the same literary form before the development.

There are parallels enough for a change of this sort — in literature one may quote the development of Greek drama during the lifetime of Aeschylus, or of English drama during the lifetime of Marlowe. Outside literature, we know that music and wine were so much poorer and thinner things to the Ancient World than they are to-day, as hardly to be recognizable.

The danger of insisting too much on the long history of the Novel, the chief fault to be found with those many-volumed histories of fiction in which Richardson comes nearly half-way, is that we are thereby blinded to the important heritage which the modern novel has received — not from earlier novelists, but from the Drama. The relation between the Novel and the Drama should be understood, as a preliminary to criticism. The history of the Drama is the pre-history of the Novel.

It may be said, shortly and dogmatically, but with infinitely more truth than such statements in literary history are commonly made, that the English theatre died in 1700 — a glorious death, after its most brilliant comedy, *The Way of the World* — and that the English novel was born, with *Pamela*, in 1740. There must be some connection between these two events, and of course there is. Poetry, having separated from Drama, has led an independent life ever since, for the most part little concerned with the representation of character in action. As for the representation of character in action — here the Novel succeeded to the Play, and minds that in other ages would have been devoted to the Drama have been devoted to fiction. We may attribute much of the tedium of pre-Richardsonian fiction to the fact that it was the work of essentially uncreative minds, more creative minds being in the service of the stage. On the other hand, if the entire Drama of the western world written in the last two hundred years were to be lost, there would be very few masterpieces to grieve for — and among those few there would not be any English plays.

Although the Novel is the rightful heir to the Drama, and in England (at least) has been the natural prose form for a creative mind to adopt since the time of Richardson, this aspect of the situation was far from obvious to the earlier novelists, and has perhaps not yet been fully accepted. The English drama (with some interruptions) had had a life of such incomparable brilliance for a hundred and ten years, that it must have been hard in the eighteenth century to think of it as extinct or dormant. Fielding, an unsuccessful dramatist, thought that in *Joseph Andrews* he was attempting a different art, that of Comic Epic. His attitude to character and plot was therefore, deliberately, epic rather than dramatic. He was far too conscious an artist, far too well drilled in Aristotle, to be content with a plot that did not exhibit unity of action to some extent, though he allowed himself an epic poet's liberties in the introduction of episodes. Such liberties were extended by Smollett, and his admirer Dickens to the licence of the novel of 'the English school' — a 'prose romance' or 'comic epic' of a purely episodic nature, kept together only by unity of hero, and called by the hero's name: such as *The Adventures of Roderick Random* or *The Life and Adventures of Nicholas Nickleby*.

Until George Eliot restored Unity of Action as a principle, it was the exception in the English novel — to be found in the novels of Jane Austen, in *Vanity Fair* and *Esmond*, in *Wuthering Heights*, and in such uncharacteristic work of Scott and Dickens as *The Bride of Lammermoor* and *Great Expectations*. And only Jane Austen and Emily Brontë are insistent the whole time that their characters shall unremittingly contribute to the plot.

It was perhaps Henry James, another unsuccessful dramatist, who was the first to show us deliberately, in *The Awkward Age*, that the Novel could do everything that the Drama can — later, in *The Ambassadors*, he showed us how much it could do that the Drama cannot. Nevertheless a critic like Mr. Forster is still so much under the spell of the great name of Drama that he can write of 'a novel which ought to have been a play'[4] — though he does not tell us why any novel ought to have been a play, or what it would gain. It is hard to see what function prose Drama now retains that cannot be better performed by the Cinema or the Novel — and hard, with the best will in the world, to regard modern verse Drama as more than a picturesque revival of an ancient custom.

Aristotle is still worked far too hard as a literary critic, and it is little more than a waste of time to apply his generalizations about a literature with which he was thoroughly familiar, to a literature which he could not have foreseen. Nevertheless, without being pedantic about Unity of Action, without having what Jane Austen called 'starched notions' about the Novel, and while admitting a degree of legitimate difference in taste, it is reasonable to claim that such structurally perfect novels as *Emma*, *Madame Bovary* and *The Ambassadors*, whose underlying principle is dramatic rather than epic, belong to a higher artistic order than the more rambling of the Waverley novels or *Martin Chuzzlewit*.

With the rest of the heritage of the Drama, the Novel came into its position as the dominant literary form. The dangers to a literary form of dominance have been well set out by Mr. C. S. Lewis. 'Its characteristics are formalized. A stereotyped monotony unnoticed by contemporaries but cruelly apparent to posterity, begins to invade it . . . In the second place, a dominant form tends to attract to itself writers whose talents would have fitted them much better for work of some other kind . . . And thirdly — which is most disastrous — a dominant form attracts to itself those who ought not to have written at all;

it becomes a kind of trap or drain towards which bad work moves by a certain "kindly enclyning". Youthful vanity and dullness, determined to write, will almost certainly write in the dominant form of their epoch.'[5]

With these characteristics of a dominant form, the criticism of fiction must be equipped to deal.

§3 CATEGORIES OF THE NOVEL

The contemporary novel falls roughly into two main categories, each of which may be sub-divided into two sub-categories. (This classification is influenced by, though not directly derived from, *Fiction and the Reading Public* by Q. D. Leavis, a work which professes to be anthropological rather than critical, and therefore requires a different system of arrangement.)

I. Novels which call for serious literary criticism.

(*a*) Good novels.

Though the critic will refuse to establish any sort of examination-order of novelists, or to give marks to their work, yet he may properly speak of e.g. 'great novels', and of 'minor classics'. The terms have been abused, but they still have meaning; it is part of the critic's duty to restore value to such distinctions.

(*b*) Novels which might have been good.

The writers had minds of the necessary sensibility; but for some reason the books are bad, or uneven, or technical failures. In this class may be placed the failures of good novelists, and books by writers 'whose talents would have fitted them much better for work of some other kind'.

II. Novels which are beneath serious criticism.

(*a*) 'Middlebrow'.

(*b*) 'Lowbrow'.

From the point of view of literature it is of course not worth distinguishing between the two main categories of fiction regarded as beneath criticism. As Dr. Johnson would say, it is like establishing the precedence between a flea and a louse. But entomology may distinguish properly between a flea and a louse though it is not the business of etiquette to do so. From her own sociological or anthropological point of view Mrs. Leavis's distinction between what she calls 'middlebrow' and 'lowbrow' work is of value.[6] Her analysis ought to be used more than it is by reviewers, who seldom have the material offered to them upon which serious critical work can be done. Moreover, it is certainly the duty of reviewers to indicate those middlebrow writers who, in her words: 'are making for enlightenment and, in a confused way, for more desirable (but not finer) feeling . . . doing a very necessary work in a society of dwellers on a rising series of plateaux, the work of keeping the lower levels posted with news of what is stirring higher up.'[7]

It would also be worth while to point out such 'middlebrow' fiction as presents interest on account of its subject-matter, or its technical skill in managing some special device, or meeting some specific difficulty. Such reasons may make ephemeral work worth reading for some years after its publication; they do not confer on it the title of literature, which distinguishes only such reading-matter as is of permanent value.

§ 4 DEFECTS OF 'ACADEMIC' CRITICISM

It is the function of literary criticism first to distinguish between those novels which call for serious criticism, and those which are beneath it (Categories I and II). The next task is to distinguish, among novels which call for serious criticism, between those which are good, and those which might have been good but are not (Categories I(*a*) and I(*b*))

In the second task we may be helped by such technical apparatus as has been provided for us by Mr. Forster, by Percy Lubbock, by Lord David Cecil or by other academic critics.

In the first task, Mrs. Leavis is right in saying that such terms as Plot and Character, as academically applied, will not be much help in distinguishing those novels which are the fit subject for literary criticism from those which are beneath it. Such terms alone are too often used to assess the slickness of a writer's technique rather than the quality of his mind; and great technical accomplishment can coexist with a very inferior mind.

Mrs. Leavis commands our assent when she writes: 'the essential technique in an art that works by using words is the way in which words are used, and a method is only justified by the use that is made of it; a bad novel is ultimately seen to fail not because of its method but owing to a fatal inferiority in the author's make-up.'[8] She only accounts, however, for those novels which could not possibly, by any means, have been good — for the novels of Category II.

Mr. Denys Thompson puts the case against academic criticism in stronger words: 'Fiction . . . has been accorded little intelligent criticism, most critics being content to appraise the excellence of character-drawing or plot-making, an employment which does not further the business of criticism (to evaluate the quality of the mind to the influence of which we are submitting ourselves); by such tests Edgar Wallace will be as good or better than Shakespeare.'[9]

We shall have to find fault with this statement.

§5 INADEQUACY OF 'PRACTICAL' CRITICISM

In determining the quality of the mind of the novelist, Mr. Wyndham Lewis was one of the first in the field with the 'Cabman's test', demonstrating from the first page of Mr. Huxley's *Point Counterpoint* the kind of sensibility we were to expect in the rest of that novel. Mrs. Leavis (followed by Mr. Thompson) has also done a valuable work in showing how we may apply to passages from works of fiction the kind of analysis applied to poetry by Mr. I. A. Richards in *Practical Criticism.* She recommends as a method for the critic of the novel 'to reinforce a general impression by analysis of significant passages', warning us that sensibility as well as intelligence is required.

But to obtain such a general impression, a more 'academic'

and intellectual method is needed to reinforce the findings of 'Practical Criticism'. And such an impression should not only be an impression of the novelist's mind, but also of how it does its work. It is by no means the only business of criticism 'to evaluate the quality of the mind to the influence of which we are submitting ourselves'; such an evaluation is indeed a vital part of the business, and until it has been done we do not know whether a book is worth further criticism or no — but we have also to ask how such a mind has been used, and if its productions are successful or not. Here it is relevant to 'appraise the excellence of character-drawing or plot-making'. Such terms, even if academically applied, can yet yield some results in determining the difference between Categories I(*a*) and I(*b*).

At its worst, a strictly 'academic' method will only distinguish between degrees of competence; at its worst, 'Practical Criticism' will only be a sort of intelligence or sensibility test applied to writers, and will tell us nothing about their specific aptitude for the Novel, nor what they have made of this specific aptitude in particular cases.

It is being maintained that the Novel is a specific literary form, and as the dominant form we saw that it 'tends to attract to itself writers whose talents would have fitted them much better for work of some other kind'. We may say then of Hardy, for example, that he was a great writer but without great specific aptitude for that form which he chose to use for most of his work — not a great novelist. The admirers of his novels admit freely — they cannot avoid it — his failure over plot and character as we generally understand these things when we speak of fiction. They often say that he views the world as a lyric or tragic poet, not as a novelist; they generally imply that a lyric or a tragic poet is a greater thing to be.

Whether a lyric or tragic poet or a novelist be greater, is however a meaningless question. It would depend on the poet and the novelist, and between a great poet and a great novelist one could not determine — between Shelley, for instance, and Miss Austen. This however can, and should be said: Miss Austen's surviving verses (they are few) are not so good as Shelley's, and no one maintains that his novels are equal to hers. When you are writing poetry, it is better to be a poet than a novelist, and when you are writing a novel it is better to be a novelist than a poet.

We are still able to say that Hardy's novels contain great writing, or (if we wish) that they are great books, without having to say that they are great novels. We can say (for example) that *The Return of the Native* is a significant work of art, which *The Heir of Redclyffe* is not; but that *The Heir of Redclyffe* is better, technically, as a novel. Nor must we conclude that the good qualities in *The Heir of Redclyffe* (convincing characterization, and a plot which issues naturally from the characters) are negligible, even from an artistic point of view.

Charlotte Yonge had an immature mind, an undistinguished style, and the values of a pious schoolgirl — there are worse values — but an educated reader cannot now readily surrender his mind to her influence. Nevertheless, she had real literary gifts which anyone might envy, and which, if he possibly could, Hardy ought to have tried to cultivate, since he wished to be a novelist.

Our criticism of the Novel must account not only for cases like Hardy's, but also for the use made of their specific talents by novelists on particular occasions. 'Practical Criticism' alone, with its evaluation of the author's mind, will not provide us with principles on which we can condemn bad work by great writers, empty books on which often a great deal of beautiful work has been wasted — such as *The Outcry*, *The Other House*, and other failures of Henry James's.

Nor can we get on without the terms of Academic criticism when we are assessing novels read in translation — and Mrs. Leavis admits that novels can be translated. If 'the way in which words are used' is the only and final criterion, then English readers who do not know Russian have no right to praise the novels of Tolstoy or Dostoievsky, but only to praise the minds of Louise and Aylmer Maude, or of Constance

Garnett. Yet there is a sufficiently respectable consensus of English opinion that Tolstoy and Dostoievsky are indeed great novelists to have evidential value.[10]

We need not take up in detail Mr. Thompson's assertion that plot and character analysis would make out Edgar Wallace better than Shakespeare, until he provides us with such an analysis, exhibiting such a conclusion. Meanwhile, if his general meaning is that the contemporary detective-story would come out high on such an analysis, we need not be shocked. It deserves some credit, as one of the better-made things of our time. 'We see covering the earth,' writes M. Jean Paulhan, not without satisfaction, 'the one contemporary genre which obeys rules stricter than the tragedy of Voltaire, or the ode of Malherbe. I am thinking of that kind of novel which forbids itself, in the psychological order, dreams, reveries, presentiments; in the choice of personages, the metaphysician, the occultist, the member of a Secret Society, the Hindu, the Chinaman, the Malay Twins; in the explication, myths, allusions, symbols; in the figures of style, metaphor and ellipse — and follows, in its progress, an order rigorous to the point of offering, from the first chapter, *all* the elements — personages, places, objects — of a problem which will not be resolved before the last pages.'[11]

One can imagine not only Aristotle, but also Henry James, echoing this satisfaction.

§6 THE NECESSITY OF A COMBINATION OF THESE METHODS

If an analysis of their character-drawing or plot-making were to set Edgar Wallace above Shakespeare, then it could only be because such terms had been very crudely applied. Such absurd conclusions would no more invalidate the terms of 'Academic' criticism than a student's bungling attempts at 'Practical' criticism would invalidate the methods suggested by Mr. I. A. Richards.

In fact a sensitive and intelligent examination of a novel requires a combination of 'Academic' and 'Practical' criticism.

Analysis of selected passages, on Mr. Richards's lines, in terms of 'Sense, Feeling, Tone and Intention', is an invaluable test of the quality of the novelist's mind. Analysis of a novel in terms of plot and character, is an invaluable test of the writer's specific aptitude as a novelist, and of his achievement on this particular occasion – moreover it is by this form of analysis that passages are best selected for detailed analysis on Mr. Richards's lines. Analysis of such passages would then give greater depth and authority to the analysis of plot and character, and might tell us as much in the end about the structure and content of the book as about its texture. An adaptation of such a critical technique would enable us to make critical pronouncements on authors like Tolstoy or Dostoievsky, whose texture, if we do not know Russian, must remain hidden from us.

Mrs. Leavis, although she attacks the use of the term 'character', yet provides us with some help in restoring the currency of this term – if she were writing criticism she would find that she could not do without it.

Her objections may as well be set out here, and answered.

(1) Character is the creation of the reader, not of the writer. 'Apparently all a novelist need do is to provide bold outlines, and the reader will co-operate to persuade himself that he is in contact with "real people".'[12]

A little analysis here, directed to passages in which a character is established, would reveal in each case whether the author had given it vitality and idiosyncracy, or whether he had left that work to the reader.

(2) The demand on the part of the reader for plausible or likeable characters prevents enjoyment of such novelists as Jane Austen or Emily Brontë.

The vulgar demand for 'likeable' characters in no way invalidates the use of the term 'character', which by no means implies conventional pleasantness. Jane Austen in creating Emma, and consciously occupied with character-creation, was aware that she was making a character whom most of her readers might dislike.

While to the objection that characters need not be conventionally plausible, Mrs. Leavis has herself made the best possible answer: 'This is not to say that we do not — and rightly — require the author to preserve internal consistency (as in *Wuthering Heights*), so that Masson was perfectly justified in complaining in his *British Novelists and their Styles* (1859): "The very element in which the novelist works is human nature; yet what sort of Psychology have we in the ordinary run of novels? A Psychology, if the truth must be spoken, such as would not hold good in a world of imaginary cats".'[13]

We need no further admission to re-establish the term 'character'.

(3) Mrs. Leavis believes that an interest in 'character' contributes to the 'resentful bewilderment one notices in the objections to such novelists as Virginia Woolf and Henry James, who do not offer anything in the nature of "character".'[14]

Of the first-mentioned of these two novelists we must say boldly that, while a great artist, she was not a great novelist — and that precisely because she lacked the novelist's specific gifts. Moreover, her greatest achievement is *To the Lighthouse*, a book marked out from all her others by the magnificent characterization of Mr. and Mrs. Ramsay.

Of Henry James, we must deny that the creator of such figures as Mrs. Gereth, Fleda Vetch, Maisie, Mrs. Wix, Mrs. Beale, Sir Claude, Mrs. Brook or Strether — to name only a few — offers nothing in the way of character. How bitterly he would have resented such a charge!

A reason for the modern revulsion from that kind of criticism which is based on the study of plot and character, may be found in the present state of Shakespeare studies. There is a strong reaction from that kind of criticism of which Bradley's

Shakespearian Tragedy is the climax. A parallel reaction may be discovered in the criticism of the novel.

There are two reasons for resisting such a reaction in the criticism of the novel. In the first place the reaction against Bradley is largely due to the fact that he is so good: further work along his lines is apt to be unprofitable when Shakespeare is the subject[15] — this does not mean that this type of analysis is exhausted where fiction is concerned. In the second place, Shakespeare was not a nineteenth-century author — he is far away from us, we do not quite know what he was trying to do. Such theorists as Miss Spurgeon or Professor Wilson Knight will each have something to tell us about him: there must be much that escapes a nineteenth-century plot-character analysis. On the other hand, Jane Austen and Flaubert were nineteenth-century authors. A form of criticism derived from nineteenth-century novelists, though of doubtful applicability to Shakespeare, is of certain applicability to nineteenth-century novelists.

The fact remains that novelists have generally conceived it to be their business to draw characters, and to make them behave within the limits of some sort of plot. It is therefore temerarious in the extreme to reject these terms, and to put out of court all the evidence that can be collected about the way in which novelists have set about their business.

It is never the artist's purpose (if he is a good artist) to exhibit his exquisite sensibility, but always to *make* something. His sensibility cannot avoid showing itself in the thing made, and perhaps will be the source of that beauty which, as Mr. Forster has reminded us, is always to be found in a great novel, but can never be the object of the novelist's direct pursuit. The relation between the two is somewhat analogous to that between the tune and the words of 'Uncle's' song in *War and Peace*.

' "Uncle" sang as peasants sing, with full and naive conviction that the whole meaning of a song lies in the words, and that the tune comes of itself, and that apart from the words there is no tune, which exists only to give measure to the words. As a result of this, the unconsidered tune, like the song of a bird, was extraordinarily good.'[16]

Probably novelists most often work with the full and naive conviction that the whole meaning of a novel lies in the plot and characters; and probably those who no longer hold this full and naive conviction would do well to act as if they did.

§7 WHAT WRITERS HAVE TO TELL US ABOUT THEIR WORK

A further contribution to the criticism of fiction may be made by a study of the creative act in fiction, and of what novelists tell us about it. We may expect to know more about novels if we learn more about how they have been made.

It may seem like a presumptuous undertaking: there is some degree of mystery involved in creation. Are we making what Edith Wharton called: 'the fascinating but probably idle attempt to discover *how it is all done*, and exactly what happens at that "fine point of the soul" where the creative act, like the mystic's union with the unknowable, really seems to take place'?[17] Certainly novelists do not always know how they have done it;[18] their subsequent accounts of how they have written their books are not always perfectly convincing.

Nevertheless, even if everything cannot be known, something can be known. Even 'the mystic's union with the unknowable' is a subject about which there is a considerable body of literature, much of which is illuminating. And writers have in one way or another told us a good deal about their work; and about their aims, methods and inspiration. Even if the accounts they give are not always implicitly to be accepted, yet they remain the first and best authority.

It appears to be a popular fallacy that writers are not at all aware of what they are doing, and that the psycho-analyst knows better than they. An objection to psycho-analytical criticism is that it can only operate upon an author's written work: to be thorough, it would have to call him up for an oral examination. Dead authors are safe from this, and it is unlikely that any living author would submit to such impertinence. Moreover we shall see in the next chapter that an author's range may not be anything like so extensive as his experience. The psycho-analyst, confronted only with written work, will have a severely limited material to deal with.[19]

About the making of poetry we really know a great deal, and our knowledge might be further increased by a systematic study of what we already know. The creative act in fiction has been less studied, but, proportionately, there are even more documents for such a study. For more than two thousand six hundred years Poetry has been written that still matters to us; the prose fiction that matters to us has all been written in the last two hundred years. And it is in the last two hundred years that artists have been most self-conscious.

We need not hesitate to endorse these rather cautious words of Virginia Woolf: 'Nothing indeed was ever said by the artist himself about his state of mind till the eighteenth century perhaps. Rousseau perhaps began it. At any rate, by the nineteenth century self-consciousness had developed so far that it was the habit of men of letters to describe their minds in confessions and autobiographies. Their lives also were written, and their letters were printed after their deaths. Thus, though we do not know what Shakespeare went through when he wrote *Lear*, we do know what Carlyle went through when he wrote the *French Revolution*; what Flaubert went through when he wrote *Madame Bovary*; what Keats was going through when he tried to write poetry against the coming of death and the indifference of the world.'[20]

The present study aims at making some use of the information which many writers, great and small, have left us about their art, about the raw material presented to them by life, about the form they wished to impose on it, about their struggles with it, and about those gifts of inspiration which have seemed to come to them from nowhere.

NOTES

There is an intention of being useful. The critic and the general reader may hope to learn something about the novel from seeing how some novels have been made. A writer may hope to become less bad from a study of the procedure of good writers. And any attempt to treat the novelist seriously, as an artist, not as a medium or a reporter,[21] is at the present time a service, however humble, to literature.

NOTES

1. *Our Present Philosophy of Life*, p. 43.
2. *Aspects of the Novel*, p. 41.
3. *After Many a Summer*.
4. loc. cit., pp. 115-16.
5. *The Allegory of Love*, pp. 232-3.
6. The terms 'highbrow', 'middlebrow' and 'lowbrow' are not euphonious, but there are no exact synonyms for them. Their use in criticism is further sanctioned by Virginia Woolf, who has given a convenient definition of them, v. *The Death of the Moth*, pp. 113 ff.
7. *Fiction and the Reading Public*, p. 70 f.
8. ibid., p. 232 f.
9. *Reading and Discrimination*, p. 34. This is a useful, little book for school use; but the limitations of its form (as here) make it unfortunately dogmatic.
10. It is true that caution is always required in the judgment of translated literature. Those who support the inflated reputation of Thomas Mann would do well to reflect on the following 'great' English novels that have won serious consideration in France: *La Renarde*, by Mary Webb; *Contrepoint*, by Aldous Huxley; *Un Cyclone à la Jamaique*, by Richard Hughes; *Le Sombre Miroir*, by March Cost; *Intempéries*, by Rosamund Lehmann.
11. *Les Fleurs de Tarbes* (1941), pp. 167-8.
12. loc. cit., p. 59.
13. loc. cit., p. 324.
14. loc. cit., pp. 60-1.
15. e.g. such a book as the late Professor Gordon's *Shakespearian Comedy*, with its futile speculations about the mothers of Shakespeare's heroines.

16. Book VII, chapter vii.
17. *A Backward Glance* (1934), p. 121.
18. Evidence from two very different sources may here suffice. 'Blessed is the novelist who has no idea how he has done it', *Letters of J. M. Barrie*, December 25th, 1893.
'M.J. . . . "I like to know how people work."
I.C.B. "I daresay you do, but the people themselves are not always quite sure."'
A conversation between I. Compton-Burnett and M. Jourdain, Orion (1945), p. 26.
19. Literary research can sometimes refute the findings of psycho-analysis, as Professor Livingston Lowes in *The Road to Xanadu* has refuted Mr. Robert Graves's analysis of *Kubla Khan*. Appendix II of this book seeks to do the same thing for the 'Freudian' theory of *The Turn of the Screw*.
20. *A Room of One's Own*, pp. 77-8.
21. 'Ainsi vont les Lettres, balancées du journaliste au médium', Jean Paulhan, *Les Fleurs de Tarbes*, p. 39.

CHAPTER II

THE NOVELIST'S RANGE

§ I SELECTION: WHAT THE NOVELIST LEAVES OUT

THE word 'range' is here generally to be understood as it is understood in another modern art, photography. No two arts run parallel very far, and we shall drop the language of photography when it ceases to help us; but some thoughts will be suggested by it before we have to discard it.

Some novelists have borrowed this language. Mr. Christopher Isherwood writes: 'I am a camera with its shutter open, quite passive, recording not thinking. Recording the man shaving at the window opposite and the woman in the kimono washing her hair. Some day, all this will have to be developed, carefully fixed, printed.'[1]

Flaubert on one occasion seems to have become a camera fitted with a green or a yellow filter, for he writes: 'Do you know how I passed a whole afternoon the day before yesterday? In looking at the countryside through coloured glasses. I needed it for a page of my *Bovary*, which will not, I think, be one of the worse pages.'[2]

If some novelists have repudiated the suggestion that they were photographers, they have generally meant that they were not mere photographers, not merely turning a gaping lens uncritically upon life, and producing an uninspired copy of unselected material. This is what Hardy means. He writes: 'As in looking at a carpet, by following one colour a certain pattern is suggested, by following another colour, another: so in life the seer should watch the pattern among general things which his idiosyncracy moves him to observe, and describe that alone. This is quite accurately a going to Nature, yet the result is no mere photograph, but purely the product of the writer's own mind.'[3]

Photography considered as an art is, however, no longer *mere* photography, but also, like fiction, a search for significant form. Good photographers watch that pattern among general things which their idiosyncracy moves them to observe, and their work is as far from a cheap postcard street-scene as a great novelist's writing is from journalism, or from the dreary rapportage which has in England lately done duty for the short story.

The photographer has the same task of selection as Hardy himself had, and these words of Hardy's are true of both arts: 'The recent school of novel-writers forget in their insistence on life, and nothing but life, in a plain slice, that a story must be worth the telling, that a good deal of life is not worth any such thing, and that they must not occupy the reader's time with what he can get at first hand anywhere about him.'[4] The picture must be worth making, the story worth telling, and what makes them worth while is precisely the pattern or inscape.

When Hardy wrote his notes, some years ago, he probably intended such writers as Arnold Bennett when he spoke of 'the recent school'. With even more justice his words can be applied to a more recent school, to those writers who in the fourth decade of this century filled such periodicals as *New Writing* with purely documentary accounts of the lives of industrial workers, into which imagination seldom or never entered. It was claimed that they were extending the range of art to include sides of life in which other writers had not been interested, and that such writers had 'escaped' into art from life. Unfortunately, though new facts were piled up, the range of art was in no way extended; these story-writers failed to give them significant form. It was they who were escapers, but they had escaped from art into life — a much more suicidal flight for an artist.

If you go out with your camera, and open the shutter at random, you will not make beautiful or interesting photographs. You must carefully compose your picture. And quite as important a problem as the difficulty of getting in those objects which you wish to get in, is the difficulty of leaving out what you wish to leave out. So it is in the composition of a novel. 'Life', says Henry James, 'has no direct sense whatever for the subject, and is capable . . . of nothing but splendid waste.'[5]

Life gives the material, yes; but not when or how the artist wants it. Those who lie in wait for wild animals with their cameras have to wait long and patiently for results, and often never get the results they are waiting for.

Flaubert went to the funeral of the wife of a friend of his, like Charles Bovary a doctor; and, like Madame Bovary, the woman had died suddenly. 'Perhaps I shall get something for my *Bovary*,' he wrote to a friend before he went. 'This exploitation to which I shall give myself up would seem hateful if one owned to it; but what is there wrong in it? I hope to make the tears of others flow with the tears of one man, passed through the chemistry of style.'[6]

When he got there, all he met with was a bore, who asked him foolish questions about the public libraries of Egypt, a country which he had lately visited. The bereavement of his friend, which he had come to witness, was quite put in the background by the boringness of this bore. 'Decidedly, God is a romantic,' complained Flaubert of this mixture of the tragic and comic. 'He is continually mixing the genres.'[7]

The attitude of the real novelist, not the reporter or the propagandist, to his material, may be summed up in the words which Mark Twain humorously attributes to Herodotus: 'Many things do not happen as they ought, and most things do not happen at all. It is for the conscientious historian to correct these defects.'

The large, the obvious subject is not necessarily that which most appeals to the trained eye. Catherine Morland in *Northanger Abbey* was astonished and upset to learn this, when she was first introduced to the laws of composition and of the picturesque. 'The little she could understand . . . appeared to contradict the very few notions she had entertained on the matter before. It seemed as if a good view were no longer to be taken from the top of a high hill, and that a clear blue sky was no longer a proof of a fine day.' But presently she learned so fast that 'she voluntarily rejected the whole city of Bath as unworthy to make part of a landscape'.

Similarly Jane Austen voluntarily rejected the Napoleonic wars as unworthy to enter into her picture of contemporary life. She has often, and very foolishly, been condemned for this. On the other hand in our dreary fiction of the 'thirties the mere shadow of a coming war is all-important: many writers were constantly saying that they felt it a duty to express the contemporary situation. Had they left this aspect of the situation to statesmen, and had statesmen been equally enthusiastic about dealing with it, we might be happier to-day, and we might have pleasanter books to read.

To return to Jane Austen, it is not easy to see how the Napoleonic Wars could be fitted into the plot of *Emma*; there are however readers who have felt that they could be taken out of *War and Peace* or *La Chartreuse de Parme* with some advantage.

§2 WHAT THE NOVELIST LEAVES IN: CHOICE OF SUBJECT

After speaking of what the novelist leaves out, we must now look at what he leaves in — what he chooses as his subject. Inevitably this means another return to Flaubert, the 'true Penelope', as Ezra Pound calls him.

> His true Penelope was Flaubert,
> He fished by obstinate isles;
> Observed the elegance of Circe's hair
> Rather than the mottoes on sundials.

He says of himself, comparing himself with Ulysses the wanderer. The 'obstinate isles' may represent the snares of public life, and 'Circe's hair' those of private life: at all events he did not heed 'the mottoes on sundials', which generally remind us, in one language or another, that time is short. But as Ulysses always tended towards Penelope, his faithful wife, who at home in rocky Ithaca rejected the blandishments of her suitors, and occupied herself with weaving a shroud for her father-in-law Laertes, which she unpicked every night — so the wandering artist still felt his true ideal was Flaubert, the patient hermit of literature, alone in Normandy, scratching out his manuscript, and beginning again and again.

These lines express what many must have felt about Flaubert — the patron saint and doctor of the Novel.

'A good subject for a novel,' says Flaubert, 'is one that comes all in one piece, in one single jet. It is the mother-idea, whence all the rest flow. One is not at all free to write this or that. One does not choose one's subject. That is what the public and the critics do not understand. The secret of masterpieces lies in the concordance between the subject and the temperament of the author.'[8]

To say of a novel that it is good, or even beautiful, in parts, is ultimately a condemnation. In so many novels in which there are beautiful passages, this essential concordance between the subject and the author's temperament is lacking; worse, there is no single subject. Perhaps Henry James was the last English novelist to receive a subject all in one piece, in a single jet.

When this miracle has taken place, then we have a novel conceived with the sort of radiance that happiness can shed round a human being. Such a novel is like Emma Bovary herself, at the height of her passion for Rodolphe: 'She had that indefinable beauty which comes from joy, from enthusiasm, from success, and which is simply the harmony of the temperament with outward circumstances.' This is the harmony we feel in perfect novels, in *Emma*, in *Madame Bovary*, in *The Spoils of Poynton*.

Any novel conceived without this harmony inevitably must fall short of classical perfection. It may be a romantic, lopsided structure, with certain beauties of its own which would not be possible in a classically perfect novel. But there are limits beyond which tastes may not be allowed to differ, and yet still be called taste. It is not permissible to prefer Westminster Abbey to the Parthenon, if you have seen the Parthenon; though you may rightly love them both. Similarly one may and should admire such romantic structures as the novels of Hardy and George Eliot, which contain certain excellences inseparable from gravely imperfect plots, and in some cases from preposterous distortion of character. Of such novels it should be said that their beauties more than justify their existence, and that they (at any rate the best of them) are perhaps as good as they could be, allowing for the original fault in their conception. They are infinitely better than lifeless copies of classically perfect novels would be. To some eyes their very distortion has an appeal, like that of pots swollen to odd and fascinating shapes by faulty baking. But when all has been said and done for them, they cannot be placed with those lovely and harmonious works that are the highest achievement of the novelist's art.

§3 THE NOVELIST'S 'RANGE' DISTINGUISHED FROM HIS 'EXPERIENCE'

Lord David Cecil in his recent book on Hardy excellently defines and limits the novelist's range in his choice of a subject. 'A novel', he writes, 'is a work of art in so far as it introduces us into a living world; in some respects resembling the world we live in, but with an individuality of its own. Now this world owes its character to the fact that it is begotten by the artist's creative faculty on his experience. His imagination apprehends reality in such a way as to present us with a new vision of it. But in any one artist only some aspects of his experience fertilize his imagination, strike sufficiently deep down into the fundamentals of his personality to kindle his creative spark. His achievement, therefore, is limited to that part of his work which deals with these aspects of his experience.'[9]

The metaphors are mixed. Lord David Cecil appears uncertain which is the masculine, and which the feminine principle. But for all that, the distinction between the novelist's range and his experience is valuable.

The word *Experience*, like the word *Life*, is much abused in contemporary writing about artists. It appears to mean to most critics Doing or Suffering, but oddly enough only Doing or Suffering in the External world, not in the Mind, where the worst is done or suffered.

> . . . The mind, mind has mountains, cliffs of fall
> Frightful, sheer, no-man-fathomed, hold them cheap
> May who ne'er hung there . . .

And so they are held cheap by those who perhaps never hung there, and who call Experience that which is done or suffered in the world where men and women fight, and drink and make love. This Experience they speak of as a sort of stuff to which the artist is more or less passively exposed — and they hold that the more he is exposed to the better.

There are two capital errors here. In the first place, what is important to an artist is not his experience but his range. 'Only some aspects of his experience fertilize his imagination, strike sufficiently deep down into the fundamentals of his personality to kindle the creative spark': these aspects alone are within his range. Early life has probably so conditioned him that he cannot greatly extend his range; the intelligent course is to find out what his range is, and to keep within it. But everyone can, if he pleases, extend his experience. If, for instance, an artist has never gone up in a balloon, then he can go up in one. But if (as is most probable) ballooning turns out not to be one of those aspects of his experience that fertilize his imagination, it will profit him nothing.

In the second place, the artist never passively receives experience. If the novelist can be like a camera at times, then he can only be like one of those primitive, nineteenth-century, hand-made cameras, of which no two were alike. Mr. Isherwood may have thought he was 'a camera with its shutter open, quite passive, recording, not thinking', but, whether consciously or no, he was also selecting. Experience is not merely that which life places in front of us, it is that which the experiencing eye chooses to let through into the brain; and even before it is consciously worked on, it undergoes considerable transmutation.

§4 THE PARABLE OF THE NOVELISTS AND THE CRIPPLE

One would like to place several authors in front of the same experience; that is, to provide them with the same external data, and to test both their reactions at the time, and their subsequent final versions of them. We cannot do this; but we are in a position to look at the similar experiences of three different novelists in a half-digested state — much as a radiologist examines, half-way, our digestion of a cup of barium. We must see what we can learn from what we may call 'the parable of the novelist and the cripple'.

We have records of three novelists passing in front of a cripple. They have left not their immediate impressions, which of course they could not have recorded without some distortion, but they have left half-digested versions in intimate letters to friends. We are looking at their experience somewhere near half-way between the actual impression when it was given, and its fixed and developed and printed state, in which they might have offered it to the public.

Here is the first novelist: 'I was out this evening to call on a friend and, coming back through the wet, crowded, lamp-lit streets, was singing after my own fashion *Du hast Diamanten und Perlen*, when I heard a poor cripple man in the gutter wailing over a pitiful Scotch air, his club-foot supported on the other knee, and his whole woe-begone body propped sideways against a crutch. The nearest lamp threw a strong light on his worn, sordid face and the three boxes of lucifer matches he held for sale. My own false notes stuck in my chest. How well off I am! — is the burden of my songs all day long — *Drum ist so wohl mir in der Welt!* And the ugly reality of the cripple man was an intrusion on the beautiful world in which I was walking. He could no more sing than I could; and his voice was cracked and rusty, and altogether perished. To think that wreck may have walked the streets some night, years ago, as glad at heart as I was, and promising himself a future as golden and honourable!'[10]

Here is the second novelist: 'Strange the sea was, so strong, I saw a soldier on the pier, with only one leg. He was strong and handsome: and strangely self-conscious, and slightly ostentatious but confused. As yet he does not realize anything, he is still in the shock. And he is strangely roused by the women, who seem to have a craving for him. They look at him with eyes of longing, and they want to talk to him. So he is roused, like a roused male, yet there is more wistfulness and wonder than passion or desire. I could see him under chloroform having the leg amputated. It was still in his face. But he was brown, and strong, and handsome.'[11]

Here is the third novelist (if we may use the term for a writer of short stories): 'On Bank Holiday, mingling with the crowd I saw a magnificent sailor outside a public house. He was a cripple; his legs were crushed, but his head was beautiful — youthful and proud. On his bare chest two seagulls fighting were tattooed in red and blue. And he seemed to lift himself — above the tumbling wave of people, and he sang: *Heart of mine, summer is waning.* Oh! Heavens, I shall never forget how he looked and how he sang. I knew it at the time, "this is one of the things one will always remember". It clutched my heart. It flies on the wind to-day — one of those voices, you know, crying above the talk and the laughter and the dust and the toys to sell: "Life is wonderful — wonderful — bitter-sweet, an anguish and a joy" — and "Oh! I do not want to be resigned — I want to drink deeply — deeply. Shall I ever be able to express it." '[12]

The three pictures are different enough, though the three

writers are all romantic in their treatment of the subject. Yet had they not been speaking of three cripples, but of one and the same, the differences might have been as great. He might have appeared to the first writer (Stevenson, in Edinburgh) as remembering former joys, and to the second (Lawrence, at Bognor) as a magnificent, maimed, male animal — as symbolic as the stallion in one of his stories, whom his owner (very sensibly) wanted to geld, because he was too wild. He might have appeared to the third writer (Katherine Mansfield, in London) as symbolic of the diversity of life — of the bewildering fact round which she wrote her story, *The Garden-Party*, that Love and Death and Pain and Happiness all go on at the same time, and in the same place.

Beside these three cripples, recorded in writers' correspondence, it may be of interest to set a finished portrait — that of the 'poor devil' who limped about the inn yard at Rouen, where Emma Bovary took the diligence home to Yonville every Thursday, after her visit to her lover.

'A mass of rags covered his shoulders, and an old staved-in beaver, rounded like a basin, hid his face; but when he took it off he discovered in the place of eyelids empty and bloody orbits. The flesh hung in red shreds, and there flowed from it liquids that congealed into green scales down to the nose, whose black nostrils sniffed convulsively. To speak to you he threw back his head with an idiotic laugh; then his bluish eyeballs, rolling constantly, beat at the temples against the edge of the open wound. He sang a little song as he followed the carriages:

Maids in the warmth of a summer day
Dream of love, and of love alway.

And all the rest was about birds and sunshine and green leaves.'[13]

§5 THE NOVELIST'S RANGE CANNOT, VOLUNTARILY, BE EXTENDED

The range of the novelist, that is those parts of his experience which he is able to use creatively, is probably a matter over which he possesses little control. It has generally been dictated to him by his nature or his early environment. The importance of early environment in determining a writer's range could be proved over and over again. Two direct statements may here suffice.

'At present my mind works with the most freedom and the keenest sense of poetry in my remotest past,' wrote George Eliot. 'And there are many strata to be worked through before I can begin to use artistically any material I may gather in the present.'[14] It may be doubted if she ever managed to use artistically any material gathered after her early middle life.

Katherine Mansfield, after the shock of her brother's death, returned to her early New Zealand memories, the source of most of her best stories. 'The people who lived, or whom I wished to bring into my stories don't interest me any more. The plots of my stories leave me perfectly cold. Granted that the people exist and all the differences, complexities and resolutions are true to them — why should I write about them. They are not near me . . . Now — now I want to write recollections of my own country. Yes, I want to write about my own country till I simply exhaust my store.'[15]

The novelist generally wants to write about his own country, mental, social or geographical, and no other is equally interesting to him.

Of those forces which can extend the writer's range, the most powerful is grief — Flaubert and Proust are agreed that the chief value to him of love is that it makes suffering possible. However if a writer were to make a voluntary pursuit of suffering in order to improve his work, it would hardly answer that end; it is sufficient to take the less heroic course of waiting for it.[16]

§ 6 A NOVELIST MAY USE HIS RANGE TO ITS LIMITS: FORSTER, ISHERWOOD, MAUGHAM

Though a novelist generally cannot extend his range, there are two things he can do. He can accept his limitations, and not court certain disaster by going outside his range; and sometimes by ingenious choosing of a position he can get far more within his range than might be expected. The first, the negative acceptance of limitations, is far the more important; it has been the principle behind the production of great works of art. The second, the ingenious choosing of a position in order to get the greatest amount possible within the novelist's range, is sometimes felicitous, sometimes results merely in clever virtuosity, and always makes the novelist's final limitations, beyond which he cannot go, all the more obvious.

We shall look first at some novelists who try to squeeze as much as possible into their limited picture. All novelists have not the wide-angled lens, the panoramic range of Tolstoy. Mr. Forster, for instance, stands patiently waiting while Man, ever restless and irregular, about this earth doth run and ride; in the end the creature will be tired, and will want his tea; then is Mr. Forster's hour. The creature will come within his view-finder, and his shutter will click.

Mr. Isherwood, writing of Mr. Forster, speaks of his talent for 'tea-tabling' incidents.[17] What he means is this; in any series of events, however dreadful, the worst tragedies can always be regarded as taking place between meals. People may go mad, elope, be accidentally killed — but it is certain that those who are left will sooner or later want something to eat.[18] Mr. Forster has chosen, and wisely, for it is his range, to represent events very much as they appear to people at their meals — his characters see them and speak of them in the kind of frame of mind in which they drink their tea. This is a legitimate and useful viewpoint, but it is strictly limited.

For example, a novelist may require violence to take place — it shakes up the plot and the characters, and they settle down after it in new and interesting positions. Mr. Forster writes in *Aspects of the Novel*,[19] that in the domain of violent physical action, Jane Austen is feeble and ladylike. She was a novelist of character, and now and then needed to shake up her people. He is a novelist of situation, and uses violence from time to time to achieve it. But a rattle of spoons, and a storm in a teacup is what ensues. Violence is out of place at a tea-table; and in the domain of violent physical action Mr. Forster is no more at home than Miss Austen. Whether he goes too far into the domain of violence and passion, which is not his, and looks lost and unhappy, or whether he goes as far as he safely can, and halts rather wistfully at the boundary, Mr. Forster equally strongly stresses his limitations.

Two other contemporary novelists illustrate the virtuosity of an artist who, by shifting his position, or by choosing a particularly artful stand-point, can bring a puzzling variety of objects within a limited range. One is not used to seeing them compared, and yet the comparison might be expected to be a commonplace of criticism. They have both given careful study to technique, and have even published histories of their several formations as novelists. They have both learned something from writing for the stage. Their style, in each case the fruit of years of study, is singularly clear and apparently artless — they excel at speaking impersonally in the first person singular. They have had, they have deliberately courted, a varied experience. At first sight they seem to have a lot to write about. But if we look carefully at their work, we find a foreshortening of many aspects of life, in order to get them in. We may find, perhaps, the background falling away, because they have been obliged to tilt their narrow-angled lenses upwards in an attempt to get everything into the picture. We may find bodies with their heads cut off, and heads lacking bodies and legs. They both have very limited ranges, are both extremely ingenious in their manipulation, both constantly overreach themselves. Their failures make us suspect their successes of being no more than technical triumphs.

It must have been obvious that these two novelists are Mr. Somerset Maugham and Mr. Christopher Isherwood.

§7 A NOVELIST MAY WORK WELL WITHIN HIS RANGE: JANE AUSTEN

A novelist writing absolutely in the middle of his true range will be writing his best, like a singer singing in the best part of his register. It is a temptation to stretch and strain; critics will praise a writer for a wide range, for it is an easy and obvious thing for them to distinguish.[20] Moreover, every artist must take some pleasure in mere technical accomplishment, and ought to have exercised himself in it; when he is practised in the gymnastic of his art, it is very natural for him to yield to the temptation to give his public a gymnastic display.

Of the artist who really knows his range, and sticks to it, the supreme example is Jane Austen. Everyone knows the story of the Prince Regent's librarian, who tried to tempt her into writing 'an historical romance illustrative of the august house of Coburg'. Everyone knows her admirable reply that such a book might well be more popular than such pictures of domestic life in country villages as she dealt in, but that she could no more write a romance than an epic poem. 'No,' she wrote, 'I must keep to my own style, and go on in my own way; and though I may never succeed again in that, I am convinced that I should totally fail in any other.' She went on, and she wrote *Persuasion*.

Of the wisdom of knowing how to work within a limited range, Jane Austen's works are the triumphant proof—she gives us no blurred, formless panorama, but a neat, perfectly composed, sharply focused picture. And she shows that it is not width of vision but depth that is important. In the small section of humanity that she has chosen to depict, she has given us the greatest of English comic characters. And in the marriages of her ladylike young women with her eligible young men, she has combined a great variety of incident with a corresponding variety and delicacy of feeling. No attentive reader of *Mansfield Park* or *Persuasion* can deny her power to depict physical passion.

That she had temptations towards a larger world one can hardly doubt. Her hard, eighteenth-century humour, the exuberance of her early writings such as *Love and Freindship*, and an occasional passage in the serious novels where a touch of Fielding's racy, knock-me-down violence proves her his heiress, all suggest that she may at times have wanted the big world of *Tom Jones*. The daughter of an eighteenth-century parsonage did not know many aspects of that world, and knew that she did not know them. A modern lady-novelist (one fears) might in her position have complained that women did not have their rights. Miss Austen was not a person to complain. Within her small world — and it was not so small as it is often made out — she had known affection, boredom, anxiety, love and loss, hatred and impatience. That is quite enough experience on which to set up as a novelist, if one has the mind.

§ 8 A NOVELIST WILL ERR IN GOING OUTSIDE HIS RANGE: HARDY AND OTHERS

In contrast with Miss Austen's spirit of self-sacrifice, and of resignation to her lot, we must look at novelists who have strained to extend their range.

There is the melancholy case of Hardy, who deliberately tried to move in higher society for the sake of learning its speech and manners. We know how unsuccessful he was at painting it; he might just as well have stayed at home, instead of going to those dinner-parties at which he was so shy and unhappy. And there are the brothers Goncourt, who spent so much time and energy researching into the lives of people in different walks of life, in order to write realistic novels about them. Yet so slight was their grasp on reality that they never even noticed that their own servant was robbing them right and left, was continually drunk, and had had two children by the milkman. When these facts were drawn to their attention, after her death, they investigated them with the utmost conscientiousness, and wrote a novel about her.

In our own time we have seen authors making as melancholy researches as those of Hardy, but (like the Goncourts) at the lower end of the social scale. Their parents (like those of Mr. Stephen Spender) have 'kept them from children who were rough', in their early impressionable years. Now that 'proletarian' writing is fashionable, they vainly try to mix with and to understand the viewpoint of industrial workers — but it will never be real enough to them for them to be able to write well about it.

It cannot be doubted that many writers have chosen to concern themselves with 'proletarian' themes, not merely to be in the fashion, but also out of a genuine concern for the lot of people less fortunate than themselves. We may, to a certain extent admire them for this altruism. But there are some things which writers are not entitled to sacrifice for the good of people less fortunate than themselves, or indeed for any cause whatever. They may not sacrifice their artistic integrity. If they do so under the impression that they are obeying the dictates of their social consciences, then their social consciences are diseased — for the duty of a writer to the community, as a writer, is simply this: to write as well as he can. If he goes outside his range, he will fail to fulfil this duty.

§9 THE NOVELIST SHOULD RESIST ALL TEMPTATIONS OR EXHORTATIONS TO GO BEYOND HIS RANGE

Lord David Cecil has well summed up this part of the novelist's duty. 'The artist's first obligation is to his vision rather than to his moral point of view . . . The artist must stick to his range, whatever is fidgeting his conscience. And even when writing within his range, he must be careful not to point his moral so ostentatiously that it diverts our attention from the imaginary world he has created. Indeed his moral views are best left to reveal themselves involuntarily. The artist's only conscious duty should be to the truth of his creative vision. Every other consideration must be sacrificed to it.'[21]

This is not to posit any sort of unnatural isolation for the novelist. He may live much the same sort of life as other people; he must have some links with the world, which provides his material, and while he is in actual contact with it, he probably looks at it in very much the same way as other people do. His life is swayed by political and economic forces, and by the weather; he is subject to hatred and love, hope, fear and desire.

But when he comes to write, then there is real isolation, as real as that of a man who has shut out the world in order to pray. 'Do not live in an ivory tower,' Salvador de Madáriaga has advised, 'but always write in one.' Flaubert, the priest of the ivory tower, had no other meaning, 'Let us shut our door,' he says, 'let us climb to the top of our ivory tower, to the last step, the nearest to heaven. It is cold there, sometimes, isn't it? But who cares! One sees the stars shine clear, and one no longer hears the turkey-cocks.'[22] A writer may gather experience in the world, but it is in the 'ivory tower' that he learns what part of his experience falls within his range.

Never, since it first became a respectable art-form, has so much nonsense been talked about the Novel as in our own day. We are told, even by people who should know better, that it is a function of the novelist to interpret the present age to us, or to prepare us for the world of the future — whereas, as likely as not, the slow, digestive process of art is now only just enabling him to use his experience of many years past. A creative writer cannot keep pace with the world;[23] he is, as we have seen, an old-fashioned camera, needing to be carefully focused, and capable of giving an exquisite and original picture of a subject within his range — he is not a cine-camera, and it is not he who will present current events to the eyes and ears of the world. There are others to do that office, and if they do it well or ill is no concern of his.

For the novelist, as it was affirmed at the beginning of this book, is a creative artist. It is his business not to teach or to reform, but to convey to the world in the best chosen language the most thorough knowledge of human nature, the happiest delineation of its varieties, and the liveliest effusions of wit and humour.

It may be objected that the novelist's range has been severely limited. Yes, each individual novelist has a limited range, if he have not the wide, panoramic lens of Tolstoy — and it is not to be desired that he should have, for Tolstoy lost as much in form and precision as he gained in content and movement.

But in limiting the range of each novelist, we are not limiting the range of the novel in general. Though each writer can only illuminate certain facets of the truth, yet there is no facet of the truth which there may not one day be found a novelist to illuminate. 'The proper stuff of fiction,' said Virginia Woolf, 'does not exist, everything is the proper stuff of fiction.'[24] Everything may be the proper stuff of fiction, though only some things are the proper stuff for the novel of this or that writer. For instance, for Mrs. Woolf as a writer the lower classes hardly exist; and we have seen that for Hardy as a writer it would have been better if the upper classes had not existed. The novelist must find his own range; if he sees good things impossibly outside it, then he must hope that they may be of use to some other writer. If a good situation or character seem to go to waste, he must remember that there are more situations and characters in life than ever came out of it. He must have faith in two things — the prodigality of life, and the diversity of talent of his brother-artists.

Caveat. While the novelist's 'range' has here been maintained to be more limited than what is ordinarily called his 'experience' nothing has been said of that creative power which transcends what is ordinarily called 'experience'. This does not mean that this power is denied, not even that it is considered ineffable—something might well be said about it at another place and time. But other terminology would probably be required.

NOTES

1. *A Berlin Diary.*
2. *Correspondance,* II, p. 102.
3. cit. Lord David Cecil: *Hardy the Novelist* (1943), pp. 39-40.
4. ibid.
5. Preface to *The Spoils of Poynton.*
6. *Correspondance,* June 1853.
7. ibid.
8. ibid., III, p. 220.
9. loc. cit., p. 13.
10. *Letters of R. L. Stevenson,* September 6th, 1873.
11. *The Letters of D. H. Lawrence* (1934), p. 222: March 1916.
12. *Letters of Katherine Mansfield,* I, p. 233: June 1919.
13. A fine example of the different way in which two writers can react to the same external data is provided by Proust. In a pastiche of the *Journal des Goncourts* he shows Edmond de Goncourt dining with Madame Verdurin: a very different picture from his own of the Salon Verdurin and its 'faithful'. (*Le Temps Retrouvé,* I, pp. 24 ff.)
14. *George Eliot's Life,* by J. W. Cross (1885), II, p. 128.
15. *Journals,* p. 41: January 22nd, 1916.
16. 'Un écrivain peut se mettre sans crainte à un long travail. Que l'intelligence commence son ouvrage, en cours de route surviendront bien assez de chagrins qui se chargeront de le finir. Quant au bonheur, il n'a presqu'une seule utilité, rendre le malheur possible. Il faut que dans le bonheur nous formions de liens bien doux et bien forts de confiance et d'attachement pour que leur rupture nous cause le déchirement si précieux qui s'appelle le malheur. Si l'on n'avait été heureux, ne fût-ce par l'espérance, les malheurs seraient sans cruauté et par conséquent sans fruit.' Proust, *Le Temps Retrouvé,* II, p. 65.
17. *Lions and Shadows.*

18. A 'mystery' play, at one time performed by the players of St. Paul's Covent Garden, showed St. Martha preparing a meal for the disciples, who were likely to come back hungry from witnessing the Crucifixion. That is to go far in 'tea-tabling' events.
19. p. 103.
20. cf. 'In some ways *Between the Acts* is an advance upon *Mrs. Dalloway, To the Lighthouse* or *The Waves* because, without loss of depth, it has greater width of interest and greater variety of effect than they have.' Joan Bennett: *Virginia Woolf* (1945), p. 131.
21. loc. cit., p. 130. cf. '(Le livre intérieur) . . . pour sa lecture personne ne pouvait m'aider d'aucune règle, cette lecture consistant en une acte de création où nul ne peut nous suppléer, ni même collaborer avec nous. Aussi combien se détournent de l'écrire, que de tâches n'assume-t-on pas pour éviter celle-là. Chaque événement, que ce fût l'affaire Dreyfus, que ce fût la guerre, avait fourni d'autres excuses aux écrivains pour ne pas déchiffrer ce livre-là; ils voulaient assurer le triomphe du droit, refaire l'unité morale de la nation, n'avaient pas le temps de penser à la littérature . . .' Proust, *Le Temps Retrouvé*, II, pp. 25-6.
22. *Correspondance*, II, pp. 149-50 (1852).
23. cf. the admirable self-denying ordinance of Miss Compton-Burnett (loc. cit.): 'I do not feel that I have any real or organic knowledge of life later than about 1910. I should not write of later times with enough grasp or confidence. I think this is why many writers tend to write of the past. When an age is ended, you see it as it is.'
24. *The Common Reader*, I, 'Modern Fiction'.

CHAPTER III

THE NOVELIST'S VALUES

§ 1 WE ARE CONCERNED ONLY WITH THE VALUES OF THE 'WRITING SELF'

By 'the novelist' is here intended the writing self; that part of the whole man who is left in the Ivory Tower, with the door shut, writing books. How much of the whole man that will be, will vary from writer to writer. It will depend on how much of his total experience falls within his range as an artist. Our evidence for a writer's 'values', for what he thinks important, can then only validly be drawn from his writings. If we know, for example, from other sources that a writer was in the *maquis*, or that he was with Pétain, we should forget it as a piece of irrelevant gossip. If it was not a part of his experience that fell within his range, it has nothing to do with his work; if it fell within his range as a writer, he will himself tell us what we need to know about it — he cannot avoid it. Therefore any heresy-hunt that proceeds *ab extra*, and not from the examination of a man's works, is, no matter what principles are behind it, as objectionable as the insistence on an artist's 'racial purity'.

§ 2 THE NOVELIST SHOULD BE A HUMANIST: MR. ELIOT'S EIGHT POINTS OF HUMANISM

The novelist's function we have declared to be the conveying to the world in the best chosen language of the most thorough knowledge of human nature, and the happiest delineation of its varieties. If a novelist is to know human nature thoroughly, and to think its varieties worth delineating, then his values must be, fundamentally, humanist values.

Humanism is a vague word — Mr. Eliot says 'necessarily

vague . For we need vague as well as precise words. The word 'gentleman', for instance, is not philosophical or scientific, but the conception still has its uses. Though we may still dispute about the meaning of the term in detail, yet there is some common agreement about the general meaning. Such a proposition as 'the Prime Minister' ought to be a gentleman' would be generally understood, and could be seriously debated.

Of the same order is the statement: 'the novelist ought to be a humanist'. And since the novel itself is not a thing that has ever been very precisely defined, it is clearly improbable that any very precise terms can with propriety be applied to the novelist.

Mr. Eliot has set out eight marks of Humanism:[1] they are not meant to be definitions, they are not meant to be exhaustive. We shall apply them to the novelist and his art.

I. *The function of humanism is not to provide dogmas or philosophical theories . . . it is concerned less with 'reason' than with common sense.*

We have already found Mr. Huxley's egregious young man in *After Many a Summer* complain of the novel that it had 'no co-ordinating philosophy superior to common sense', and Miss Austen's Sir Edward Denham was like-minded with him.

> Sword of Common Sense . . .
> Thine is the service, thine the sport
> This shifty heart of ours to hunt . . .

this is Meredith's address to the Comic Spirit. The novel is certainly one of the time-honoured hunting-grounds of the Comic Spirit, the *Sword of Common Sense.*

And of a work of fiction that provides dogmas or philosophical theories, Proust says simply that it is 'like an object with the price ticket left on'.[2]

II. *Humanism makes for breadth, tolerance, equilibrium and sanity. It operates against fanaticism.*

III. *The world cannot get on without breadth, tolerance and sanity; any more than it can get on without narrowness, bigotry and fanaticism.*

There is undoubtedly a place in Literature, as in Life, for

narrowness, bigotry and fanaticism — bitterness and propaganda can have a place in poetry, as we are often reminded, and Dante was not invariably distinguished by breadth, tolerance, equilibrium and sanity. But it is one thing to do, as poetry and history can do, to pass judgment on a finished action, quite another to show an action taking place, as fiction has to do. The novelist has to get near to or inside his people, to understand not judge them. Satire and heavy irony are things he has to guard against — they are too unsubtle for the work he has to do. Recent research into Miss Austen's methods of work show her controlling her hatred of her characters, suppressing the kind of feeling that expresses itself in satire;[3] and if research into Proust's methods reveals that they were the opposite, some of his later touches were not an improvement.[4]

It would not be easy to find exceptions, great novelists distinguished for narrowness, bigotry and fanaticism. Lawrence might be mentioned, but it is precisely on account of these defects that he fails as a novelist — distorting plot and character in the interests of, and as a result of his anti-humanist values. If he remains a great writer, that is beside the point; for it is certainly not to be maintained that every great writer need be a humanist.

IV. *It is not the business of humanism to refute anything. Its business is to persuade, according to its unformulable axioms of culture and good sense. It does not, for instance, overthrow the arguments of fallacies like Behaviourism: it operates by taste, by sensibility trained by culture. It is critical rather than constructive. It is necessary for the criticism of social life and social theories, political life and political theories. . . .*

V. *Humanism can have no positive theories about philosophy or theology. All that it can ask, in the most tolerant spirit, is: Is this philosophy or religion civilized, or is it not?*

These marks are so obviously true of fiction, that it is hardly necessary to apply them. Novels are nearly always concerned with life as it is or has been lived, and only very exceptionally (and seldom satisfactorily) with life as it might be. And the novelist's only possible comment quâ novelist on a philosophy, a theology or a social theory, is to show its influence on the lives of people who profess it — that is, it can only be critical, not constructive. Thus Dickens in *Hard Times* shows Benthamite Utilitarianism to be uncivilized, thus the novels of Geoffrey Dennis show the religion of the Plymouth brethren to be uncivilized, and those of Jane Austen show early nineteenth-century Anglicanism (touched with Evangelicalism) to be supremely civilized. This is not to affirm that anything about the truth or falsehood of the opinions in question has been demonstrated in those novels.

VI. *There is a type of person whom we call the Humanist, for whom Humanism, is enough. This type is valuable.*

It is perhaps unlikely that the novelist will often belong to this type. 'The pitfall for such an author is obvious,' Mr. Forster has written. 'It is the Palace of Art, it is that bottomless chasm of dullness which pretends to be a palace, all glorious with corridors and domes, but which is really a dreadful hole into which the unwary aesthete may tumble, to be seen no more.'[5] There have, however, been novelists of this type, and Mr. Forster goes on to claim that Virginia Woolf was such a one, who have nevertheless escaped this pitfall.

VII. *Humanism is valuable* (a) *by itself, in the 'pure humanist', who will not set up humanism as a substitute for philosophy and religion, and* (b) *as a mediating and corrective ingredient in a positive civilization founded on definite belief.*

As an example of the humanist who accepts a definite system of belief, which he is able to reconcile with humanist standards, Mr. Eliot cites the great Catholic writer, Baron Friedrich von Hügel. Mr. Eliot himself is probably the most distinguished living humanist of this type.

The novelist, naturally, may belong to either type, but if he accepts a definite system of belief, then it must be a system or belief in itself not incompatible with humanist standards, and he must not accept it with an anti-humanist fanaticism — an attitude which can, unhappily, be applied to systems of belief which do not require it, and which are not in themselves opposed to humanism.

Thus a novelist may be Protestant, Catholic, agnostic or atheist; he may be imperialist, pacifist, conservative, liberal or socialist, independent or apolitical. He may be any of these things with complete conviction — a conviction firm enough for him to think all other points of view mistaken. But he may not have an angry conviction. He must be able to understand and to sympathize with views he does not share. He must not think that everyone who differs from him is ill-informed, unintelligent, or acting in bad faith.

Whether a Marxist or a Fascist can be a Humanist may be doubted, and therefore it may be doubted whether tolerable novels can be written by a Marxist or a Fascist. But it would be altogether a wrong and unhumane procedure to say that such a man was a Marxist or Fascist, and therefore *a priori* could not write tolerable novels. We must look at the books, not at the party labels. If we find that, after all, a Marxist or Fascist has managed to be a Humanist, we shall, if we are Humanists, be inclined to rejoice at the fact — rather than to lament that a Humanist could be a Marxist or a Fascist. Although the careful toeing of a party-line does not make for humanism, it is quite certain that 'near-Marxists' and 'near-Fascists' may be very good Humanists indeed.

In looking at a novelist's belief, then, we should not greatly trouble ourselves about what external system, if any, he accepts. We should trouble ourselves rather about the disposition with which he accepts it. We should inquire whether his private and personal values are humane or no. And, holding the eminently humanist view that there are good men in every camp, we should ask whether the novelist is one of those good men, in whatever camp he may be found. That is, of course, we should ask if his 'writing self' is a good and valuable self. And, we are to remember, the 'writing self' may differ in important respects from the self that votes or goes to church — only the evidence of the written word is valid here.

The understanding of these so simple principles would save a world of heresy-hunting and of pseudo-criticism. It would prevent the asking of such unreal questions as: 'Should the novelist concern himself with contemporary social problems?'

It may be laid down that to all such questions, if they begin *should*, the answer is *No*; if they begin *may*, the answer is *Yes*. Even when (which is rare) they are couched in the most rudimentary form which has any claim to be an intelligent question, e.g.: 'in what circumstances may the novelist concern himself with contemporary social problems?' — the answer is so simple that it can be stated in a few words: 'if they lie within his range, if he looks at them as a humanist, and if he treats them as a novelist — that is, in terms of character in action.'

Such questions ought not to trouble a creative writer, though their parrot-like reiteration is bound to sink into his consciousness, and there can be little doubt that harm has been done to literature in this way. For example, the absurd question: 'ought literature to have a social message?' may ring like an advertisement slogan in a writer's ears till he comes to think that it ought, and that when writing he ought to try to put such a message in — oblivious of the fact that a 'message' is something that the reader gets out of a book, not something that the writer puts into it.

VIII. *Humanism, finally, is valid for a very small minority of individuals. But it is culture, not any subscription to a common programme or platform which binds these individuals together. Such an 'intellectual aristocracy' has not the economic bonds which unite the individuals of an 'aristocracy of birth'.*

To this aristocracy we have a right to demand that any novelist or any critic who is to be taken seriously shall belong. A novelist who insists too much upon the external system of belief which he accepts, a critic who insists too much upon the external system of belief accepted by an author, are being vulgar; they are putting their aristocracy in doubt. It is on their common humanism that humanists meet.

Therefore, for example, a Catholic may delight in Samuel

Butler, and hold Belloc and Chesterton in abhorrence — and this does not mean that he is not in agreement with Belloc and Chesterton over things which he regards of infinitely more importance than the nausea with which their style affects him. For it is Humanism, rather than doctrine that will (if we are Humanists) decide what books we read. The same principles will to some extent determine who are our friends; and in certain circumstances our actions may be determined by them in a crisis. A 'pure humanist' will choose to die with his friends, rather than for this or that cause.

Catholic and Socialist critics have claimed that for a novelist it is a positive advantage to be, respectively, a Catholic or a Socialist. For, they say, our view of the world is the right one, and if you look at the world from the right point of view, then you will see everything in its proper place, including those things which are the subjects of fiction.

This looks reasonable upon the face of it. But if we ask ourselves if it would help a botanist, quâ botanist, if he were a Catholic or a Socialist, we shall see at once that that would be absurd. The novelist is concerned, like the botanist, with particular manifestations of life, for which he requires very sharp eyes, and not with life in general. The only advantage of a true belief about Life in general to a novelist would be negative: it would protect him from false belief. Thus a Catholic novelist is protected from Behaviourism — a belief which would make it difficult for him to regard the particular manifestations of life, which are his subject-matter, as a novelist should.

However, any general philosophy of life, true or false, applied deductively by a novelist to particular instances would be almost certain to have a fatal effect upon his art. Whether he saw Original Sin everywhere, or the Oedipus Complex, the results would be equally disastrous. This is not to affirm that they are not everywhere.

§3 A NINTH POINT: THE PROPER VIRTUES OF THE NOVELIST

To Mr. Eliot's eight marks of Humanism, we might add a ninth. If Humanism makes for breadth, tolerance, equilibrium and sanity, then the humanist virtues will be Justice, and its better part, Mercy.

To persons gifted or cursed with the abnormal Sensibility which is associated with the man of letters, the virtues of temperance, fortitude and prudence may well be difficult; they may have peculiarly strong temptations against them. There have been excellent writers who have not been prudent, temperate or brave. Fortitude, in particular, is so easy to practise on paper that it can hardly be attributed to the writing self at all. And it is with the writing self, not the whole man, that we are concerned. How good or bad the whole man is does not matter to the critic or the reader, if the vices have been kept out of the writing self; and there have been very bad men who have kept their writing selves clean.[6]

The virtues of Justice and Mercy, however, are as hard to practise on paper as anywhere else. They are the specific virtues of the critic, and without them he has no claim to that title; and they are of almost equal importance to the novelist.

The important thing to discover about the novelist is not chiefly what characters he thinks good, but rather what characters he thinks 'nice' — in spite of Henry Tilney, this vague word is yet the best for what is in part, but by no means entirely, a moral value. We are not satisfied with a nice character unless he embodies some degree of Mercy and Justice — Justice being understood to include honesty with oneself as well as with other people.

It might be thought that this is a modern prejudice. 'For about a hundred years,' writes Mr. C. S. Lewis, 'we have so concentrated on one of the virtues — "kindness" or mercy — that most of us do not feel anything except kindness to be really good or anything but cruelty to be really bad. Such lop-sided ethical developments are not uncommon, and other ages too have had their pet virtues and curious insensibilities.'[7]

Nevertheless, while we agree with Mr. Lewis that the possessors of other virtues have in other times been more esteemed for goodness than the just or the merciful, we may yet claim some degree of catholicity for the view that they are especially 'nice' — as something *quod semper, quod usque, quod ab omnibus receptum est*. There can be no attempt here to prove this point, but one might mention, for example, how *nice* some people are in the *Inferno* (e.g. Brunetto Latini), and how nice Dante evidently thought them; yet they could not be good, or they would not be there. They are never people who have sinned against Mercy.

No doubt it would be a grave fault in a novelist to belittle Prudence, Temperance or Fortitude in any way, or ever to represent them in themselves as less than good; though they well might form part of extremely unattractive characters — the same would be true of Justice dissociated from Mercy.[8] But, if one may say so without irreverence, the blessing pronounced upon the Merciful appears to have effect in the natural as well as in the supernatural order, and in Letters as well as Life — they shall obtain mercy. It would be hard to find a conspicuously merciful person, in Life or Letters, whom one could regard as a disagreeable character. One could not indeed make a similar judgment about any other virtue.

§4 THE DETACHMENT OF THE NOVELIST

There is an argument against the Humanism of the novelist (or indeed of any writer) which is often and noisily put forward. It should therefore be answered, though it is not in fact very intelligent.

It is objected that in 'these critical times' civilization is in danger, and that there is no time for tolerance or sanity. The novelist, like everyone else, must fight.

Now if people who said this meant that in a moment of crisis the whole man (of which the writing self is a part) may be required in the general interest to engage in some work of public importance, no one could well object. If Rome were burning, the novelist, like everyone else, might be needed to fill buckets of water. But his 'writing self' cannot fill buckets of water, and must resist all efforts at mobilization. One may be too busy filling buckets of water to have time to write, but if one manages to go on writing (as writers generally do) it will not be any part of one's duty to write against the fire.

This popular error is due to several causes. In the first place an exaggerated reaction against the doctrine of 'Art for Art's sake' has morbidly affected some writers, so that they are anxious at any moment to justify their work on practical grounds. Next, in wartime everyone becomes so anxious to do his 'bit', or to prove that he is doing it, and to see that his neighbour is doing the like, that the 'writing self' has not been exempted — has not been understood to be essentially non-belligerent.

Of course any dangers to civilization and to humanist values that may arise, are best combatted by the novelist if he continues to affirm those values in his quiet, unfanatical way. On a short time view, his worst danger is not the Enemy (whoever that may happen to be) but those worthy people who, on the highest grounds, and with the motive of preserving civilization, attack that little part of civilization which is the equilibrium and sanity of the writer. On a long time view, it would probably be hard to find any cultivated person who sincerely believed that civilization has at any time since the renaissance been in danger of more than a temporary eclipse or setback. Any historian is likely to have handled enough books that have at one time or another been condemned to be burnt, to laugh at any threatened burning of books. Anyone who has learnt Latin has learnt that 'captive Greece tamed her fierce victor', and knows that civilization is always an incomparably more dangerous enemy to barbarism than the barbarians can be to civilization.

The acceptance of these simple, even platitudinous, axioms

would put an end to the abuse of such words as 'Escapism' — which have had their day. And the 'contemporary subject' would not be allowed to exercise the same tyranny over the short story that the 'poetical subject' exercised over the lyric at the beginning of this century. Both tyrannies are death to creative writing, and *Folios of New Writing*, now not so new, have joined in the lumber-room *Poems of To-day*, whose day has become the day before yesterday.

It has to be remembered that a writer's is a contemplative, not an active vocation. 'A man who has set up as an artist', says Flaubert, 'has not the right to live as others.'[9] This does not mean indifference to the life of the world outside the Ivory Tower; it does mean detachment from it. 'I am prepared', says Conrad, 'to put up serenely with the insignificance which attaches to persons who are not meddlesome in some way or other. But resignation is not indifference. I would not like to be left standing as a mere spectator on the bank of the great stream carrying onward so many lives. I would fain claim for myself the faculty of so much insight as can be expressed in a voice of sympathy and compassion.'[10]

The contemplative writer serves the world in detachment from it, just as in his different and harder way the contemplative religious serves the world. And the writer also can offer his pains for the world, and they are no mean pains. Among minor pin-pricks, not worthy to be mentioned beside the pains of creation, are the pushes and nudges he receives from people who try to disturb his essential equilibrium and sanity, which they miscall complacency and indifference.

The writer is in no way severed from the world, nor is his art an abstract skill. Therefore when Mr. F. L. Lucas says: 'To ignore the values of real life in judging the values of literature, to talk as if art were a sublime bag of tricks, to care nothing whether a book is sordid, or whimpering, or cruel, is a new *trahison des clercs*',[11] we may agree with him — except that there is nothing new about it — little as we may agree with his applications of this point of view. He continues: 'This does not mean returning to the prejudices of 1850 and screaming at *Jane Eyre* as immoral; the trouble with such judges was not that they treated literature as bearing on life, but that their view of life happened to be stupid.' We should also add that their view of the way in which literature bore on life was also stupid; it was illiberal, not humane.

§5 THE FOREGOING PRINCIPLES APPLIED: A BRIEF EXAMEN OF MR. E. M. FORSTER'S NOVELS

It is not the purpose of this chapter to prove or to refute anything that moral philosophers or social theorists may have to say about the place of the novelist in the world, and the duties of his place. Its method is that of persuasion rather than proof. Its purpose is in part casuistical (in the good and proper use of that word), aiming to quiet consciences of general readers, critics, or writers, that have been inflamed by much contemporary journalism and conversation. And though it would be an intolerable impertinence to offer a writer advice about the choice of an outlook on life, it is not at all improper to suggest that a novelist may examine himself (and that his critics and readers may examine him), whether he holds his outlook on life (whatever it may be) with the tolerance and sanity proper to a humanist. If he is temperamentally a bigot, then his vocation as a novelist may be questioned.

Moreover a right understanding of what a novelist's values should be has a practical value in criticism. Let us illustrate this point by applying the foregoing principles to the work of a given writer. We will make a brief examen of some early works of Mr. E. M. Forster.

The values which Mr. Forster defends, when they are his main subject, are always those of culture and civilization. Monteriano, with its architectural and natural beauty, and the gay and natural life of its inhabitants, is defended against the drab, suburban conventionality of Sawston — *a land of lobelias and of tennis flannels.* Cambridge, with its sweetness and light, provides a standard for the condemnation of the minor public school at Sawston, and the sham Roman virtues that it inculcates. The wisdom of the Schlegels about personal relations, and their love of the Arts, shows up the 'outer world' of the Wilcoxes, behind all their 'telegrams and anger', as one of 'panic and emptiness'. Aziz, with his imaginative enthusiasm for the great Mogul past, Professor Godbole, with his Hindu mysticism, even Miss Quested, with her earnest attempts at intellectual honesty, all stand for something higher than the English Club at Chandrapore, with its purely conventional decencies and loyalties — which are valuable as far as they go, but which are shown not to stand the test of a real crisis.

Mr. Forster is a Humanist, we see clearly from his fiction, and he has made the fact abundantly clear in his other writing. If we apply the 'cabman's test' to his novels, opening them at random and examining a single page here or there, we are certain to discover an exquisite sensibility at work, and to hear a beautiful, gentle, wise, truthful and virtuous voice speaking.

It is a truthful, that is a sincere voice that is speaking; but though we never doubt the sincerity, we may at times have grave doubts about the truth of what is said. It is the maintenance of several minor heresies (from the humanist point of view) that detracts from the total value of some of the earlier of Mr. Forster's novels. The elucidation of these heresies — which critics appear to have neglected — may help us to see why these books, though in many ways so beautiful, are so unsatisfactory in their total effect.

The first false doctrine may be called the doctrine of the Great Refusal.

Rickie Elliot in *The Longest Journey* sins against truth, by entangling himself with his wife and his brother-in-law, and by becoming involved in their shiftiness and false standards; one sin leads to another, until his character is so warped that only a violent break could save him. This part of the moral tale is true and convincing.

But he also sins against kindness; he commits a small, though an extremely deliberate sin. He has learned that Stephen (a 'Rough Diamond' or 'Noble Savage') is his illegitimate half-brother, and he is disgusted. But Stephen seems in an odd way to be important to him, though he does not like him.

He says to Agnes, his wife: 'It seems to me that here and there in life we meet with a person or incident that is symbolical. It is nothing in itself, yet for the moment it stands for some eternal principle. We have accepted it, at whatever cost, and we have accepted life. But if we are frightened and reject it, the moment, so to speak, passes; the symbol is never offered again.'

Stephen calls under Rickie's window three times — Rickie hesitates, is held back by Agnes, and does not reply to his call. We are meant, no doubt, to think of another three-fold denial. This time, however, there is no saving cock-crow. It is the beginning of Rickie's spiritual death. Two years later he confesses it to Stephen, adding: 'Ever since then I have taken the world at second-hand. I have bothered less and less to look it in the face — until not only you, but everyone else has turned unreal.' Stephen says nothing to this, and one cannot imagine that he could have understood a word of it.

This is not to attack the psychology of the book. A rather feeble character like Rickie, and one for whom the imagination took the foremost place, and not the intellect, if he had made unto himself a symbol, and had then out of cowardice rejected it, might not improbably have a general physical and spiritual breakdown afterwards.

What is wrong is the morality of the book. Mr. Forster makes it clear that he is handing out to Rickie what be believes to be suitable punishment. Yet we cannot really think that Rickie has done anything so terrible as to deserve his spiritual hell. He has been rather weak, but unless (as it is to be feared Mr. Forster has) we also make a fetish of the Noble Savage, we cannot feel a turning-away from him, if slightly unkind, to be deeply wicked. The doctrine of the Noble Savage, the second heresy we shall speak of, must however be isolated, and reserved for a later attack.

The notion of a Great Refusal — of a life spiritually laid waste by a very small sin of omission — is, if we look at it, more stupid and vindictive than the crudest medieval or puritan view of Hell. It is contrary to traditional moral philosophy, in which virtue is a good habit, not destroyed, though possibly rendered more difficult, by the commission of a bad act. If it is true in any psychology, it can only be in the psychology of morbid states. A healthy, adult soul can digest a certain amount of evil, even of its own evil, without being permanently the worse. Though Christian theology teaches that grace can be destroyed in the soul by a single sin, yet it requires such a sin to be of much more moment than poor Rickie's, and provides means for the restoration of grace.

The notion of the Great Refusal is neither sensible nor civilized: it looks like a superstitious and sentimental perversion of a religious doctrine, of the kind one sometimes encounters in the work of writers who neither have a definite system of belief, nor find it easy to get on without one. A nineteenth-century tract-writer, who might have shown a small sin like this of Rickie's leading to lies, and on to worse sins, would be setting forth a more convincing morality than that of this part of *The Longest Journey* — and such has been Mr. Forster's own method with Rickie's decline from truth. But this one rejection of Stephen has been allowed to cut Rickie off from 'Life' — 'Life', presumably, being a vague and muddled secular equivalent of sanctifying grace.

But there is worse to come. In *A Room with a View* the heroine, Lucy, is aware that she is in love with George (like Stephen, he is something of a Noble Savage). She honestly breaks her engagement to another man, but she is determined (for many excellent reasons) to resist her love for George. This is how Mr. Forster puts it: 'Love felt and returned, Love which our bodies exact and our hearts have transfigured, Love which is the most real thing that we shall ever meet, reappeared now as the world's worst enemy, and she must stifle it.' As if this were not how Love often makes his appearance.

Lucy, in short, intends to make the Great Refusal, in which she is backed up by her cousin Charlotte. And Mr. Forster takes it very tragically.

'It did not do to think, nor, for the matter of that, to feel. She gave up trying to understand herself, and joined the vast armies of the benighted, who follow neither the heart nor the brain, and march to their destiny by catchwords. The armies are full of pleasant and pious folk. But they have yielded to the only enemy that matters — the enemy within. They have sinned against passion and truth, and vain will be their strife after virtue. As the years pass, they are censured. Their pleasantry and their piety show cracks, their wit becomes cynicism, their unselfishness hypocrisy; they feel and produce discomfort wherever they go. They have sinned against Eros and against Pallas Athene, and not by any heavenly intervention, but by the ordinary course of nature, those allied deities will be avenged.'

Whatever spiritual truth there may be behind the doctrine of the Great Refusal — for, like every other heresy it contains some truth — it is here a good deal overstated. Lucy has decided to reject the purely physical advances of a very ineligible young man — no friendship has had opportunity to spring up between them. Mr. Forster lets the reader know that George was in fact the right man for Lucy, but she herself had no way of knowing it. Their bodies might exact love, but their hearts had not yet transfigured it. And even if Love is the most real thing we shall ever meet — one wonders why it should be more 'real' than any other experience, but let that pass — Lucy, who was young and attractive, might well have met it again and again, if she had rejected it upon this occasion. Mr. Forster is being harder than God or Life would have been to Lucy — he wants to deny her another chance. The 'night' is to receive her, as it received Charlotte thirty years before. Even if Lucy must follow Charlotte's example, rejecting love, and retiring to Tunbridge Wells, there are many worse ways of managing one's life.

Mr. Forster is hard on Lucy, he is hard on Rickie, because of an inordinate value which he sets upon Stephen and George. He believes in the Noble Savage, and in Passion.

To some extent, of course, we all do. We have had the happiness to know 'Noble Savages' or 'Nature's Gentlemen' — people who by native goodness judge and act wisely and rightly and graciously, where less favoured people have to be guided by thought and training. We ought to love and respect their natural wisdom and goodness, as we ought to love and respect wisdom and goodness wherever they occur. And over-sophisticated persons who fail to appreciate the Noble Savage are to be pitied. Possibly Mr. Forster wanted to give the Noble Savage a fair deal in Letters; he may have thought that he had there been neglected. This is a piece of justice that does not at all cry out to be done. The 'Noble Savage' has a fine time in Life, for which he is admirably adapted — if Letters should do him less than justice, he has no right to complain.

Intellectual persons are often less beautiful than the Noble Savage — at all events while he is young, for in old age they sometimes get their own back on him. They tend to stoop, to be too thin or too fat, or both at once, and in the wrong places. They are bad at doing things which he does superbly — such as riding a horse or handling a boat. They are often full of jealousy and dislike for each other. They are apt to lack the noble virtue of Fortitude — particularly in its more dashing form.[12] Therefore it is a great temptation to intellectual persons to fall in love with the Noble Savage, and to exalt him and his passions over people of their own sort, and their thoughts and feelings.

If this is carried too far, and the Savage is exalted beyond his due, intuition and instinct are made of more account than the intellect — it is a very bad form of the *trahison des clercs*. It is, in subtle disguise, the very sin of Sawston, which Mr. Forster has in its place condemned, 'the contempt for the intellect'. Stephen as much as Agnes, cannot be infinitely over-estimated without 'the lie in the soul'.

Idolatrous worship of the Noble Savage is a sin that generally brings its own punishment with it. Mr. Forster has not escaped.

This heresy involves him, as it nearly always involves writers who hold it, in an artistic fault. The Noble Savage is extremely hard to portray convincingly, and generally comes into fiction with his nobility left behind. It is no good an author saying he is noble, as he might say that his heroine is beautiful; we withhold our respect from him, unless he is convincingly worthy of our respect. George in *A Room with a View*, and Stephen in *The Longest Journey*, do not really convince; therefore any emotional argument based on their nobility falls to the ground.

These two departures from Humanist values, these doctrines of the Great Refusal, and of the Noble Savage, heresies from the point of view of culture, sanity and common sense, mar some of Mr. Forster's early work, for all the wise Humanism of his considered attitude.

NOTES

1. *Second Thoughts on Humanism.*
2. *Le Temps Retrouvé*, II, p. 29.
3. Recent essays in *Scrutiny* by Q. D. Leavis, particularly '*Lady Susan*' *into* '*Mansfield Park*' (Oct. 1941).
4. Albert Feuillerat: *Comment Marcel Proust a-t-il composé son roman?* Esp. for the characters of Françoise and of Madame de Marsantes.
5. Rede lecture, *Virginia Woolf*, p. 9.
6. 'That writer's books you tell me about, the books the virtuous in England will not read because his private life was disgraceful, beautiful books, you say, into which went his best, in which his spirit showed how bright it was, how he had kept it apart and clean, I shall get them all and read them all. No sinner, cursed with a body at variance with his soul and able in spite of it to hear the music of heaven and give it exquisite expression, shall ever again be identified by me with what at such great pains he has kept white. I know at least three German writers to whom the same thing has happened, men who live badly and write nobly. My heart goes out to them. I think of them, lame and handicapped, leading their muse by the hand with anxious care so that her shining feet, set among the grass and daisies along the roadside, shall not be dimmed by the foulness through which

they themselves are splashing.' 'Elizabeth': *Fräulein Schmidt and Mr. Anstruther*, XLVII.

7. *The Problem of Pain*, pp. 43-4.
8. This is misunderstood by those persons who accuse Lytton Strachey e.g. of belittling the humanitarianism and courage of Florence Nightingale, to which he extends full admiration, because he shows them coexisting (as they did) with other less amiable traits of character.
9. *Correspondance*, August 28th, 1876.
10. *A Personal Record:* 'A Familiar Preface'.
11. *Critical thoughts in Critical Days* (P.E.N. Books), p. 53. Against this nasty, little pamphlet, whose author lacks the effrontery to blame inter-war literature for the losing of the Peace and for the defeat of France, but affirms that *tout se tient*, one should set the sanity of M. André Gide: '*Il me paraît aussi absurde d'incriminer notre littérature au sujet de notre défaite qu'il l'eût été de la féliciter en 1918, lorsque nous avions la victoire . . .*' But Mr. Lucas has received condign execution at the hands of Sir Osbert Sitwell in *A Letter to my Son*.
12. We are not to deny to any writer some measure of endurance: without it he could not finish writing a book. Whereas some people lack the endurance even to finish reading a book. This point might have been given more consideration by such writers as Mr. C. S. Lewis, who seek to put down the artist from his place and to exalt the 'little man' — a dreary object of worship. In some rare cases the writer's endurance attains the degree of heroism. See Appendix I: the examples of heroism there may even be a little frightening to those who are only called to be conscientious, minor writers. So those who are only called to be everyday Christians may sometimes be frightened when they read the lives of the Saints. Moreover, the novelist requires the fortitude to see life steadily, even if he is not obliged to see it whole: like the governess in *The Turn of the Screw* (see Appendix II) he needs the 'indispensable little note of courage, without which he wouldn't have had his data'.

CHAPTER IV

THE MAKING OF PLOT

§1 PLOT ONLY ARTIFICIALLY SEPARABLE FROM CHARACTER

ANY writer of fiction will tell you that he is commonly asked this question: 'Which do you think of first, the characters or the plot?' It is a very banal question, and it generally makes writers very angry. It is an ignorant question, and yet it has in it something of the malice of fools. It is ignorant, because with a little thought anyone could realize that characters and plot are only artificially separable. As Henry James says: 'Character, in any sense in which we can get at it, is action, and action is plot, and any plot which hangs together, even if it pretend to interest us only in the fashion of a Chinese puzzle, plays upon our emotion, our suspense, by means of personal references. We care for people only in proportion as we know what people are.'[1] In a perfect novel interesting characters are displayed in a coherent and well-shaped action, and probably they have grown together in the author's mind. But very often a situation or a character has been what the novelist started from; he has had to look for characters, or he has had to look for a story. Perhaps he is not quite satisfied with his final union of story and people, and the questioner has put a finger on a sore place.

§2 THE EXPANSION OF A SITUATION: 'THE SPOILS OF POYNTON'

Henry James himself nearly always began with plot, and the germ or seed of the plot he picked up in some way from life, by observation or hearsay. 'Such is the interesting truth', he writes, 'about the stray suggestion, the wandering word, the vague echo, at touch of which the novelist's imagination winces as at the prick of some sharp point; its virtue is all in its needle-like quality, the power to penetrate as finely as possible . . . one's subject is in the merest grain, the speck of truth, of beauty, of reality, scarce visible to the common eye.'[2] Life, so to speak gave Henry James a pin-prick, and injected a germ, and this germ was nearly always the germ of a story. Heine said that out of his great sorrows he made his little songs: *Aus meinen grossen Schmerzen mach' ich die kleinen Lieder*. Henry James made his great novels out of little scraps of other people's talk.

Changing his metaphor, he tells us: 'Most of the stories straining to shape under my hand have sprung from a single small seed, a seed as minute and windblown as that casual hint for *The Spoils of Poynton* dropped unwitting by my neighbour, a mere floating particle in the stream of talk.'[3]

His neighbour at a dinner-party, in the course of conversation, gave him the subject of that wonderful novel. This is how he narrates it, and it is no doubt almost an exact reproduction of the written or mental note which he made after the dinner-party. 'A good lady in the north, always well looked on, was at daggers drawn with her only son, ever hitherto exemplary, over the ownership of the valuable furniture of a fine old house just accruing to the young man by his father's death.'[4]

This little anecdote gave Henry James what in another place he speaks of as 'a jog of fond Fancy's elbow'.[5]

Creation is a mysterious process, perhaps, as Mrs. Wharton suggested, ineffable like the mystic's experience, and only vaguely to be conveyed, by analogy. Therefore it is necessary to be patient with all the metaphors which are used about it. The fact that Henry James uses so many is due to his closer approach than that of any other man to the description of the indescribable.

He tells us that he wished to stop the lady's story then and there; he had received enough. She went on telling it, and it was full of details that were no use to him. In the sequel he saw 'clumsy life again at her stupid work'. For life 'has no direct sense whatever for the subject and is capable, luckily for us, of nothing but splendid waste . . .'[6] Life, that is, is full of subjects, but with no idea how to treat them.

Man is always ready to recreate God in his own image: the novelist is no exception. He is apt to see the Almighty as a novelist, author of a grandiose *Comédie Humaine* — an enormously vital and creative novelist, but clumsy, and with no idea of construction. Some few characters show an observable pattern in their lives, but most do not. He is like Balzac, or Dickens, or Proust — an immense genius, but careless. The only carelessness, almost, that He does not commit is that of Thackeray in *The Newcomes* — He does not forget when characters have died. When we have died we are dead, and not liable to appear again a few chapters ahead. As Flaubert said, He mixes His genres: tragedy and comedy are inextricably muddled up in life.

A novelist like Henry James, with a love of architecture, will be inclined to extract passages from this vast *Comédie Humaine*, and to treat them in his own way, with more artistry. And because he sees life itself as a huge work of fiction, and his own fiction as a form of life, he can feel that an historical fact is not 'what really happened'. What really happened was what Art demanded should have happened.

Therefore to Henry James the beautiful implications evolved in his own mind were of a higher reality than the vulgar quarrel between mother and son that his neighbour at dinner told him about. *The Spoils of Poynton* tells us what really occurred: it is the perfect expansion of a situation.

Starting as he did, with a single situation, Henry James had to discover what characters could have brought such a situation about, and were best fitted to bring out its beautiful implications. Two characters were given in the situation: 'the good lady in the north, always well looked on', had presumably some special claim to the furniture, therefore (he decided) she had originally collected it, therefore she must be extremely clever, and must have a passion for beautiful things. The only son, 'ever hitherto exemplary' must be a right-feeling gentleman;

otherwise the quarrel over possessions with his mother would be merely sordid and uninteresting. And because Henry James intended developments of extreme subtlety, he needed a character to appreciate the finer points, which would be lost on the mother, who stood mainly for cleverness, and on the son, who stood for average good behaviour. Therefore the mother was given as a confidant an exquisite being, rather cruelly named by her creator Fleda Vetch, who stood for the most refined intelligence, and the most sensitive honour. Acting as go-between for mother and son, Fleda transfigures their ugly disputes by the beauty of her personality. Moreover she and the son fall in love, which very much contributes to the distress of the story.

But unfortunately cleverness, right-feeling, sensitiveness and honour are on the whole static qualities; a dynamic character was needed to precipitate Action. Will initiates Action, therefore the son was given a fiancée embodying brute will-power, and she made the story go.

Thus the functions of the four chief characters were dictated by the story — but they are four living people, not dressed-up abstractions, and in their turn they have taken over the working out of the story into their own hands and have (incidentally) brought it to the saddest ending in English fiction.

It all looks so simple, the architecturally built plot, the interesting characters, that for a moment we may be tempted to believe that we ourselves could have done what Henry James did with his material. We could not. Probably we should not even have thought twice about the little anecdote, if it had been told to us.

'The power that recognizes the fruitful idea and seizes it, is a thing apart,' wrote Percy Lubbock. 'For this reason we judge the novelist's eye for a subject to be his cardinal gift.'[7] Henry James had this gift eminently, and it is the singleness of subject in his most successful plots that gives them a simplicity underlying all their subtlety; and that is why they look as if they had been easy to think of. On the other hand a really ungainly plot, like that of *The Return of the Native*, looks as if it had been very difficult to think of. Would, as Dr. Johnson might have said, it had been impossible!

§3 THE NOVELIST'S PERVERSITY

Using Henry James's own word, we have spoken of the implications in the story of *The Spoils of Poynton* as 'beautiful' — a story full of intrigue, jealousy and acquisitiveness. Clearly this is not what ordinary people mean when they speak of situations or characters as beautiful; there is no connection here with moral beauty. However, as to a portrait painter a merely pretty face may present no interest, but an old woman such as Rembrandt painted may serve him as a model for the beauty he wishes to express — so moral ugliness, baseness of character, or a thoroughly unrighteous state of affairs may make a novelist exclaim: 'how beautiful!' This sometimes annoys other people very much, and they think him perverse because he is not so much shocked as they are. It is not, however, that he is blind to moral turpitude or social injustice — it is that if he looks at a situation, as a novelist, he is most concerned with the complications lurking in it, and he is fascinated by the side-lights that it gives him upon human life. The broad, full-face meaning of the situation may matter less to him. And there is no reason why he should be condemned for looking at life aesthetically, not ethically or politically. No sane person would expect a landscape artist to be thinking of the crops or the farmers every time he looked at the weather.

And to some extent, of course, the novelist really is perverse: it may be doubted if anyone would trouble to write if there were nothing at all wrong with him.

A perfect world would provide no copy, and it is much to be doubted whether a perfect man could write readable novels even about this world we live in. Literature is one of the happier consequences of the Fall of Man, and those of us who do not believe in human progress may find this thought a consolation when, like Camilla in *Great Expectations*, we wake up in the night.

The perversity of the novelist will generally be found to contain a streak of cruelty, and it will need all his humanistic reverence for mercy and justice to keep it from over-development — it would be difficult to name a good novelist who is not in some way cruel. Henry James, gloating over the kind of evil situation which inspired *The Spoils of Poynton* is such an instance. And as the novelist, like anyone else, does not take in experience passively, but transmutes it from the first moment into something that he can assimilate, very odd things may happen to the germs or seeds of plot that observation or hearsay give him.

§4 THE GENESIS OF AN EPISODE: 'DU CÔTÉ DE MONTJOUVAIN'

The best example of the genesis of an episode, due to the perversity of a novelist, is one that is both famous and extremely unpleasant. It is that story which, if we extract it out of the immense novel of Proust, we may find it convenient to label with a name of its own. Let us call it 'Du Côté de Montjouvain'.

Montjouvain was situated *du côté de chez Swann*; to reach it, one turned off the road somewhere between Combray and Méséglise. It had been the residence of M. Vinteuil, the music teacher, and after his death it belonged to his daughter. One evening the narrator, hidden in the shrubbery, witnessed the loves of Mademoiselle Vinteuil and her friend. Mademoiselle Vinteuil, as a preliminary preparation, had put her father's photograph in a prominent position; then by repeated remarks such as: 'what would he say if he could see us now?' she incited her friend to insult him, and to spit upon his photograph. This was apparently part of the ritual of their love-making. To the reader, who remembers M. Vinteuil's former pride in his daughter, and the pain her conduct subsequently gave him, and his broken life and ambitions, and great musical genius, the scene is one of almost diabolic cruelty. It is the more unbearable because we know that all the time Mademoiselle Vinteuil profoundly loved her father; we shall see later the proof she gave of it.

By great good fortune we know how Proust came to conceive this incident. The Duchesse de Clermont-Tonnerre has told us, in her recollections of Marcel Proust, the innocent little story which was the origin of this tale of horror.

A man, though devoted to his wife and child, had a mistress. Such was his devotion to his wife and child that he never stopped talking about them when he visited her. She got tired of this, and said she never wanted to hear again about 'my wife' and 'my child'. 'What am I to call them, then?' asked her lover. She answered pettishly: 'The monster, and the little monster.'

In Proust's memory this story became deformed into one where a man perversely delighted to call his wife and child, whom he really loved, by abusive names, when he was making love with his mistress. By easy transitions from this state, and rendered into terms of Lesbianism, it ended up in the horrible incident *du Côté de Montjouvain*.

Here we see raw material passing through a novelist's mind, and perhaps not a very nice mind. However it was the mind of the greatest man of this century, and therefore a little more ought to be said. If Proust degraded Mademoiselle Vinteuil to the depths, yet he also raised her. She and her friend later, in penitence for what they had made Vinteuil suffer in his lifetime, gave him an immortality after death by the most devoted puzzling out from scraps of manuscript, and the most careful editing of his great septet, in comparison with which, we are told, even his great sonata, whose unheard melodies haunt us all through Proust's novel, was merely banal.[8]

This is only one of the many stories in *A la Recherche du Temps Perdu* which show that it is more a Divine than a Human Comedy. This is often lost sight of because there is so much and such fearful Inferno, and because so many readers lose their way and never get to the end, or are tired when they get there. And it is a great seer who is our guide.

§5 A PLOT FORMED BY LINKING EPISODES: 'LES FAUX-MONNAYEURS'

The novelist is not one who delights to see the best in everybody. He is, on the contrary, particularly fond of Crime. In Murder, for instance, human passions are laid extraordinarily bare, and the principal character, at least, acts with a decision and a violence that the novelist seldom ventures to give to one of his own creatures. Moreover, there is often a very good story. Turn the pages of *Who's Who* and you will find that, of those novelists who have the bad taste to give personal details about themselves, many name Criminology as one of their hobbies. Henry James himself (though indeed in a private letter) wrote almost lyrically about the great poisoner, Madeleine Smith. Dickens took the greatest interest in Wainwright (whom he had been privileged to meet), and also in Professor Webster. Although out of a sense of duty a novelist may read the front pages of his newspaper, his natural inclination is to the *faits divers*.

M. André Gide for years collected reports of crimes from the newspapers: two cases haunted him, stirred in his mind, and gave him no rest until he had made a plot that linked them together. We have seen in the incident at Montjouvain how the genesis of an episode has occurred in a novelist's mind; in *The Spoils of Poynton* we have seen a single situation expanding into a plot — in M. Gide's novel *Les Faux-Monnayeurs*, we see a plot built out of disparate incidents.

There is first the group of young students and artists who were concerned with a traffic in counterfeit money in 1906 — the mixture of false coin, and literary discussion appeals to the imagination, and the obvious symbolism will leap to the eye of anyone who has ever frequented any sort of literary or artistic circle; for such circles have (figuratively speaking) generally much more false coin than true in circulation.

The second principal theme is taken from the very curious suicide of a boy of fifteen in the class-room of a Lycée at Clermont-Ferraud in 1909. The boy belonged to an association in which his fellow-pupils appear to have mutually urged each other towards suicide.[9]

The two incidents seem to have been linked together in M. Gide's mind by his interest in 'motiveless crimes', and it is significant that at first he intended the chief character of this novel to be Lafcadio. Lafcadio dropped out of *Les Faux-Monnayeurs*: he is the hero of *Les Caves du Vatican*, in which he commits a motiveless murder. His temporary juxtaposition with the story of the counterfeit coin and the suicide story must have helped M. Gide to bring them together: motiveless, or nearly motiveless criminality is the link between them. His students make very little profit out of their false money.

Incidents and characters out of the author's past, which we have met in a more nearly raw state in *Si le Grain ne Meurt*, were adapted, and used to fill in the gaps. Moreover the daily life of an artist engaged upon a serious work may sometimes seem to take on the pattern of that work, and may throw out scraps which can be incorporated in it — such scraps, offerings of life, are recorded together with his own mental work on the novel by M. Gide in that extremely interesting document, the *Journal des Faux-Monnayeurs*.

§6 A PLOT UNSUCCESSFULLY DEDUCED FROM ONE EPISODE: 'ADAM BEDE'

Sometimes an author has been fascinated by a single incident, not in itself the whole subject of the novel, and has discovered his subject after following up the clues given in that incident. An example of a not-very-good plot deduced from one striking incident is *Adam Bede*.

The story was suggested to George Eliot by an incident in the life of her aunt, Mrs. Samuel Evans, a Methodist preacher. Mrs. Samuel Evans had once spent a night in prison with a girl convicted of child-murder, had prevailed on her to make a confession of her guilt, and had next day attended her to the gallows. G. H. Lewes, with whom George Eliot was living, remarked that the night in prison would make a good scene in a novel — and *Adam Bede* was constructed to lead up to and down from that scene.[10]

This scene started George Eliot off with two indispensable characters — Dinah Morris, the Methodist preacher, and Hetty Sorrel, the seduced village maiden. She had the good idea to make them antecedently connected, to add poignancy to the prison scene, and to make it arise more naturally out of the action. She therefore gave them an uncle and aunt in common, a farmer and his wife, the latter one of the comic, rustic characters in which she excelled.

At the farm, of course, Hetty met her seducer; the plot evidently requires a seducer, and who more fit for the role, by all traditions, than the young officer, heir to the village squire?

To get the full pathos out of the story, the girl is given a true lover of her own class, with honourable intentions: this is Adam Bede. Lewes suggested that the novel ought to end with Adam's marriage to the woman preacher, and this certainly makes a neat, rounded conclusion. He also wished for a clash of some sort between the true lover and the seducer — and while she was listening to *Wilhelm Tell* at the Munich opera, it occurred, we are told, to George Eliot to make the rivals fight. Tell's adventures must have been her inspiration, and it is amusing to follow a great novelist's mind so closely.[11]

George Eliot softened the story given in her data in two respects. Hetty is not really guilty of murder, but only of temporary desertion of her baby; and she is not hanged. At the last minute, thanks to her lover's energy, the sentence is commuted to transportation, and she goes to Botany Bay. Probably it was right to make these changes. Hetty is naturally more sympathetic for not being a murderess, and the book is less melodramatic because she is not hanged — Hardy did not do well to hang Tess. The changes, however, add to the faults of construction.

It is a fatal weakness in *Adam Bede* that the great prison scene, which more than any other scene remains in the memory, the scene round which the book was written, does not advance the plot at all. Hetty's confession does not tell us anything that we did not already know, and has no influence upon her fate. If she had indeed been hanged, it might have given us a melancholy satisfaction to know that she had confessed her crime, and died penitent; but she was only transported. Sir Leslie Stephen well points out how ineffective in fact Dinah Morris is, and how much more Jeanie Deans, with whom her situation may in some ways be compared, contributes to the plot of *The Heart of Midlothian*.

Lewes was quite right in thinking the prison scene would be impressive in a novel — it is. As he was not a novelist it is not surprising if he never thought about the constructional difficulties which such a scene implies. However, it is a peevish sort of criticism that harps upon the imperfections that inevitably go with certain excellences. One cannot see — and George Eliot evidently could not see — how this scene could occur in a perfect novel. Yet it is one of the great scenes in nineteenth-century fiction, and it is much better to have it in an imperfectly constructed book, than not to have it at all.

§7 A PLOT SUCCESSFULLY DEDUCED FROM ONE EPISODE: 'THE AMBASSADORS'

Adam Bede, then, is a plot unsuccessfully deduced from one striking incident. To find a plot successfully deduced from one incident, we naturally turn back to Henry James. Unlike *The Spoils of Poynton*, the expansion of a situation, *The Ambassadors* springs from one single incident. The incident is not so dramatic as the night which Mrs. Samuel Evans spent with the infanticide; it is again 'the merest grain, the speck of truth', that Henry James loved.

This is the 'little germ'. A young friend of his, in Whistler's garden in Paris, had spoken with a distinguished American author, also a friend of Henry James's. The older man had vigorously exhorted his young friend to live, not to miss life.

This incident, and its background, were etched into his mind. He began to ask himself: 'What would be the story to which it would most inevitably form the centre?'[12]

'It is part', he goes on to say, 'of the charm attendant on such questions that the "story" . . . puts on from this stage the authenticity of concrete existence. It then *is*, essentially — it begins to be, though it may more or less obscurely lurk; so that the point is not in the least what to make of it, but only, very delightfully and very damnably, where to put one's hand on it.'

Henry James began by putting his hand on the character who should pronounce the exhortation in the Paris garden. He saw him as a man who felt that he had missed life, who was beginning to be dissatisfied with himself, who had come in a frame of mind that was undergoing change, who was in a mental false position. 'The false position for him was obviously to have presented himself at the gate of that boundless menagerie' (that is, Paris) 'primed with a moral scheme of the most approved pattern which was yet framed to break down on any approach to vivid facts; that is to any at all liberal appreciation of them.'

There was one obvious difficulty — in the Anglo-Saxon world, and particularly in Puritan America, Paris is vulgarly associated with the most banal naughtiness, and with the coarsest and most commonplace breakdowns of the moral schemes of Anglo-Saxon visitors. Henry James was very anxious to have no association of this sort about his book, and indeed there is nothing common or mean to be found in *The Ambassadors*. The theme is a serious one — of a missionary sent to convert the inhabitants of a country who, through no mental or moral collapse, but rather through the breakdown of his illiberal, fixed opinions, learns to admire their standpoint more than his own, and is converted to it.

Strether, the chief of the ambassadors, is sent to Europe by an American lady, whom he much admires, to reclaim her son who is staying in Paris, where he is believed to be retained by a woman who has some hold upon him. He is wanted at home to take his part in the family business — the 'manufacture of a small, trivial, rather ridiculous object of the commonest domestic use'. We are never told what this object is, it is left to our guess. However, when Strether gets to Paris he is so charmed by European artistic life that business life in America seems less and less the obviously better way of living that he had first thought it. So far from wanting to reclaim the young man to his status as a good American, and as manufacturer of the 'small, trivial, rather ridiculous object', he wants to turn himself into a good European, and regrets that he is starting so late.

§8 THE PLOT AS A PRE-EXISTING PATTERN, TO WHICH NOVELISTS WORK

After considering Henry James, and the evolution of his plots, it is a shock to remember how haphazardly some authors (and the greatest are among them), have chosen the outline for their books. It will help us here if we borrow Mr. Forster's distinction between the 'plot' and the 'story'.[18] Writers of this sort are generally most interested in character, and their characters turn their stories into plots by the little twists they give to them.

The outline of the story may be lifted from elsewhere; it may even be a stock plot that many have used before. Shakespeare followed this method, so does Jane Austen in her early novels. A young woman goes for the first time into the world, a young man helps her out of an embarrassment, she falls in love with him, and after delays and difficulties they are eventually married. Two sisters are separated by misunderstandings from the men with whom they are in love, until a series of events brings them together again, and all is well. It is the detailed working up of these stories into plots that is fascinating to us, and it is the characters who do that working up. The story remains as a form of discipline, preventing the characters from straggling about aimlessly, narrowing but deepening the channels along which they may develop.

Some novelists will even look outside literature for a pattern. Mr. Aldous Huxley advises would-be writers to look at the relations between a couple of cats, for instance, and to translate them into human terms. Had he done so, he might indeed have found more interesting plots there than those of his later novels; and he would at least have presented a psychology so far agreeable to Masson as to hold good 'in a world of imaginary cats'.[14]

Some novelists have been inspired by the moves on a chess-board, or by the rules of other games. Meredith in *The Egoist* certainly had in mind (for both in the name of his chief character, Sir Willoughby Patterne, and in incidental symbolism he insists on it) the pairings and separations and reshufflings of couples which take place on a willow-pattern plate.

Other novelists have taken the patterns of some well-known classic for their own pattern; and the perception of this pattern working itself out in their novels is no doubt supposed to add to the reader's pleasure. The use of the Odyssey in this way by Fielding and by Joyce is the most obvious example: the *Oedipus Rex* and the book of Tobit have also been used by contemporary writers — no doubt the list could be added to extensively.

It is hard, however, to regard this kind of applied pattern as more than a curiosity of literature, a monstrosity like those seventeenth-century poems that were written in the shape of an altar or of a pair of wings. And if the work made on this pattern happens to be a work of genius, we tend to ignore the pattern.

§9 THE PLOT SHOULD RESULT FROM GROWTH, NOT MANIPULATION

When the plot of the novel has been conceived, by whatever means, it demands faithfulness from the writer. 'One must do as one has conceived', says Flaubert. The process of working out one's conception in fiction is not at all like arranging flowers, putting this here, that there, and giving a pull or a twist to a leaf or a spray in order to make it stand out. It is very much more like giving birth to a baby. Miss Rebecca West has compared it to the growth of a tree.

'For the non-sentimental artist,' she says, 'has an intention of writing a book on a theme which is as determined and exclusive as the tree's intention of becoming a tree, and by passing all his material through his imagination and there experiencing it, he achieves the same identity with what he makes as the growing tree does. Now neither tree nor artist has eyes, neither has ears, neither is intelligent; simply they are becoming what they make. The writer puts out his force and it becomes a phase of his story, as the tree puts out its force and makes a branch. Both know how much force to put out, and where to reassert it, because having achieved this identification with their creation they would feel a faulty distribution of balance as one would a withered limb . . . But the sentimental artist is becoming nothing . . . He is playing a game, he is moving certain objects according to certain rules in front of spectators . . . He sees that one of these objects occupies a certain position on the ground, and knows that he will score a point if he can move it to another position; he therefore sends another of these objects rolling along to displace it. *Shock* . . . one hears the ugly sound.'[15]

If we look back for a moment we can compare and contrast the methods of George Eliot and Henry James. George Eliot manipulates her people to get action and contrast, and listens to Lewes when he says: 'don't you think, Marian, you could put in this, or that?' Whereas Henry James does not play that sort of game; he sits still, watching for the story that 'more or less obscurely lurks', not in the least worrying about what to make of it, but 'only, very delightfully and damnably' where to put his hand on it.

On an altogether lower level of seriousness are such toyings with the novelist's art of those writers who, in Miss Austen's words, stretch out their books with 'solemn specious nonsense, about something unconnected with the story; an essay on writing, a critique on Walter Scott, or the history of Bonaparte. . . .'

Yet whether the plot results from the expansion of a situation, like *The Spoils of Poynton*, the linking together of incidents, like *Les Faux-Monnayeurs*, or the deductions drawn from one incident, like *Adam Bede* or *The Ambassadors*, the process which goes on in the novelist's mind, all the ways in which he works on his material, are more analogous to discovery than to invention. The story has early put on 'the authenticity of concrete existence'; the author asks himself 'what really happened?' not 'what shall I make happen next, to amuse my readers?'

And here we are up against the impenetrable residuum that is left, no matter how many external aspects of the novelist's creative activity we look at. Mrs. Wharton is right — we cannot put into words 'exactly what happens at that "fine point of the soul" where the creative act, like the mystic's union with the unknowable, really seems to take place'.

§ 10 THE NOVELIST AS MYSTIC: 'THE SONG OF HENRY JAMES'

Here is no place for the discussion of the nature of mysticism. Let us take the definition given by William James. He enumerates four 'marks' of mystical experience: ineffability — it cannot adequately be put into words, it can only be hinted at, or described by analogy; noetic quality — some knowledge is always conveyed; transiency and passivity — it can neither be summoned nor retained at will.[16]

With this in mind — unless we restrict the word 'mystical' to a religious sense — if we turn to Henry James's astonishing colloquy with his genius, we are unable to deny it the title of mystical writing. Though it does not tell us 'exactly what happens', it throws some light on the mystical nature of the creative act.

'I needn't expatiate on this — on the sharp consciousness of this hour of the dimly-dawning New Year, I mean; I simply make an appeal to all the powers and forces and divinities to whom I've ever been loyal and who haven't failed me yet — after all: never, never yet! Infinitely interesting — and yet somehow with a beautiful sharp poignancy in it that makes it strange and rather exquisitely formidable, as with an unspeakable deep agitation, the whole artistic question that comes up for me in the train of this idea . . . of the *donnée* for a situation that I began here the other day to fumble out. I mean I come back, I come back yet again and again, to my only seeing it in the dramatic way — as I can only see everything and anything now . . . Momentary side-winds — things of no real authority — break in every now and then to put their inferior little questions to me; but I come back, I come back, as I say, I all throbbingly and yearningly and passionately, oh mon bon, come back to this way that is clearly the only one in which I can do anything now, and that will open out to me more and more, and that has overwhelming reasons pleading all beautifully in its breast. What really happens is that the closer I get to the problem, to the application of it in any particular case, the more I get *into* the application, so that the more doubts and torments fall away from me, and the more I know where I am, the more everything spreads and shines and draws me on and I'm justified of my logic and my passion . . . Causons, causons, mon bon — oh celestial, soothing, sanctifying process, with all the high sane forces of the sacred time fighting through it, on my side. Let me fumble it gently and patiently out — with fever and fidget laid to rest — as in the old enchanted months. It only looms, it only shines and shimmers, *too* beautiful and too interesting; it only hangs there too rich and too full and with too much to give and to pay; it only presents itself too admirably and too vividly, too straight and square and vivid, as a little organic and effective Action. . . .

Thus just these first little wavings of the oh so tremulously passionate little old wand (now!) make for me, I feel, a sort of promise of richness and beauty and variety; a sort of portent of the happy presence of the elements . . . I seem to emerge from these recent bad days — the fruit of blind accident — and the prospect clears and flushes, and my poor blest old Genius pats me so admirably and lovingly on the back that I turn, I screw round, and bend my lips to passionately, in my gratitude, kiss its hands.'[17]

NOTES

1. *Partial Portraits* (Essay on Maupassant).
2. *The Art of the Novel: critical prefaces*, ed. Richard P. Blackmur (1935), p. 119. *The Portrait of a Lady*, however, began in 'the sense of a single character', ibid. p. 42.
3. ibid.
4. loc. cit., p. 121.
5. loc. cit., p. 221.
6. loc. cit., p. 120.
7. *The Craft of Fiction*.
8. See especially *Du Côté de chez Swann*, I, pp. 229-37, and *La Prisonnière*, II, pp. 79-85. In fact it was the friend who performed the act of atonement to Vinteuil, but she was inspired by his daughter's veneration for him. (Mr. Raymond Mortimer has pointed out to me a more probable origin for the Montjouvian story, cf. *Le Sabbat* by Maurice Sachs (1946), p. 285.)
9. *Journal des Faux-Monnayeurs*.
10. *George Eliot* by Leslie Stephen (English Men of Letters Series), pp. 64-5.
11. ibid., p. 66.
12. loc. cit., p. 311.
13. *Aspects of the Novel, passim.*
14. v, p. 27.
15. *The Strange Necessity* (1928), pp. 16 ff.
16. *Varieties of Religious Experience*, p. 380.
17. *The Letters of Henry James*, ed. Percy Lubbock (1920), vol. I, pp. xx-xxi.

CHAPTER V

THE MAKING OF CHARACTER

§1 CHARACTERS IN SOME WAY, ALWAYS, TAKEN FROM LIFE

HENRY JAMES, for whom the starting-point in the creation of his novels was generally a fragment of plot, gives an interesting account of the completely opposite method used by his friend Turgenieff. 'The germ of a story, with him, was never an affair of plot — that was the last thing he thought of: it was the representation of certain persons. The first form in which a tale appeared to him was as the figure of an individual, or a collection of individuals, whom he wished to see in action, being sure that such people must do something very special and interesting. They stood before him, definite, vivid, and he wished to know, and to show as much as possible of their nature. The first thing was to make clear to himself what he did know to begin with; and to this end he wrote out a sort of biography of each of his characters, and everything they had done and that had happened to them up to the opening of the story. He had their *dossier*, as the French say, and as the police has that of every conspicuous criminal.'[1]

It was in life that Turgenieff found the first suggestions for his people. He stated that he could not create character at all, unless he fixed his imagination upon a living person: without a definite person in mind he could not give vitality and idiosyncracy to his creation.[2] It is probable that this practice is almost universal. The note which is frequently placed at the beginning of a novel, and which announces: 'Every character in this book is entirely fictitious' is nearly always a lie. It is difficult to see what it is there for, since it deceives nobody, and would be no protection in a libel action. One must suppose that the common explanation is the true one: it is inserted by publishers so that illiterate booksellers' assistants may more easily be able to distinguish fiction from biography, memoirs and the like.

If a character is 'wholly fictitious', then we can be quite sure it is drawn largely from other characters in fiction, themselves in some way first drawn from life.

This is not to say that the novelist often puts people just as they are into his books, a thing which his acquaintance seem to fear and hope. For life and art are very different things, and existence in one is very different from existence in the other. For one thing, life enforces on us a continuous existence, whereas a character in fiction does not exist except at such times as he appears on the scene. And the fictional character must not appear too often on the scene without doing something very special and interesting — while all of us live days or years without doing anything very special and interesting.

Many of us, very likely, have little or nothing to give to the novelist, who has not the reasons that the Almighty appears to have for creating people who are not interesting. He should accept this difference, and not falsely reason that he *ought* to be able to interest himself in any person God has made. It is necessary for him to free himself from the tyranny of old tags like *quidquid agunt homines* or *homo sum, nihil humani â me alienum* — which seem to have a peculiarly binding force on those who know no other Latin, and which lead to such artistic idiocies as the cult of the 'little man' as hero.

§2 ATTEMPTS TO RENDER THE WHOLE MAN IN FICTION: JOYCE, VIRGINIA WOOLF

Mr. Forster has drawn an illuminating distinction between *homo sapiens* and *homo fictus*: among other things, he points out how free *homo fictus* is from work, and what a disproportionate amount of time he devotes to love.

Probably the only serious attempt to make *homo fictus* coextensive with *homo sapiens* is that of James Joyce. Though the characters of other authors are often seen eating, Joyce's Bloom is almost unique in fiction because he also digests his meals. But the experiment fails for three reasons — firstly, Bloom's acts and thoughts are as much a selection from his total twenty-four hours' experience as those of any other fictional character: a book many times longer even than *Ulysses* would be required to contain all a man's acts and thoughts in that space of time. Secondly, the absence of selection is, however, carried so far that much of what Bloom does and thinks is neither special nor interesting. Thirdly, it is impossible to develop any other character in the book on the same scale. You can only have one such close approximation to a *homo sapiens* in a book; the rest must be *homines ficti*. Therefore we have a solipsistic world in which one man is real and the rest fictitious. This is not so convincing a picture of the real world as even those fictions in which none but *homines ficti* appear. There are many of them on the same level of reality, and they can have their approximations to human loves and hates.

Not only does man in fiction commonly omit such external acts as washing his teeth, but his interior or mental life is correspondingly simplified. He proceeds from thought to thought, or from feeling to feeling, either in accordance with reason or with an easily understood process of association of ideas. He will not suddenly burst out singing, nor will he suddenly be overwhelmed by misery — he will be better-controlled than real people often are.

Virginia Woolf's characters, however, show all the passing moods of real people — the moods pass so quickly and are so varied that it is difficult to sum up any one of them in a few words. She has done one thing that Joyce has not, she has evolved a technique for showing more than one character, who is an approximation to *homo sapiens*, in action at the same time — but whereas Bloom is a solid person, with fine vitality and idiosyncracy, Mrs. Woolf's characters are all alike. The nearest she gets to showing real processes of thought and feeling — in *The Waves* — the most completely identical are her characters.

The book is a sextet of disembodied voices, beautiful and sometimes wise voices, but very hard to tell apart. Though Mrs. Woolf certainly conveys to the world 'the most thorough knowledge of human nature', and conveys it in 'the best chosen language', yet there is next to no 'delineation of its varieties'.

The truth is perhaps this: while we know the characters of Miss Austen as we know our friends (if we are abnormally observant), we know Mrs. Woolf's characters as we know ourselves. We know more and less about ourselves than about anyone else: we are all like the man in the scriptures who beholdeth himself in a glass, and straightway he goeth away and forgetteth what manner of man he is. We know so many changes in our expressions, that we hardly know what our faces are like. We know all our thoughts and actions, and they are so inconsistent that it is hard for any one of us to sum up his character in a few words, or even to be sure that he has a character at all. We are all alike, made of the same elements, but in different proportions: it is hard for us to stand back from ourselves, and to see what the proportions are in our own case — and it is hard to stand back in this way from the characters of Mrs. Woolf.

§ 3 'FLAT CHARACTERS': DICKENS

The opposite to the character which tries to reproduce the whole man, is what Mr. Forster has called the 'flat character'. He is summed up in a single phrase, such as: 'I will never desert Mr. Micawber', which sums up all Mrs. Micawber's nature and actions. The creation of the flat character is best studied not in fiction, but in drama, in Ben Jonson's theory of 'humours', and the best statement on the subject is that made by his most recent editors in the introduction to their monumental edition.

'He seizes character under one aspect, because he sees it so; neglecting, because he does not see them, the cross-play of impulses, the inconsistencies and conflicts, mingled strength and weakness, of which they are normally composed. His observation was prodigiously active and acute; but its energy was spent in accumulating observations of a single dominant trait, not in distinguishing fine shades. The nuances fell together for him, and the vast complexes of detail which his voracious eye collected, and his unsurpassed memory retained, grouped themselves round a few nuclei of ludicrous character . . . his personages are real men seen from a particular angle, not moral qualities translated into their human embodiments.'[8]

This is an extremely acute analysis of the way in which Jonson's mind must have worked when he was creating character, and it will stand for much of Dickens's character-creation as well. Not for nothing was Dickens an admirer of Jonson, and fond of impersonating his soldier-braggart Bobadil. Many of Dickens's most memorable characters, while 'flat' are yet 'real men seen from a particular angle, not moral qualities translated into their human embodiments'. We even know some of the real men exposed to this angular vision — for instance that Mr. Micawber and Old Dorrit are portraits of Dickens's father, seen from different angles, and Mr. Skimpole is a portrait of Leigh Hunt — they are not just embodiments of different types of fecklessness and irresponsibility.

In drama, where there is little time for subtlety, for more than a few characters to exhibit inconsistencies and conflicts and developments, it would be even harder than in fiction to get on without 'flat' characters. And in fiction their value is inestimable: almost every successful comic character is 'flat'. For when a comic character begins to put on three-dimensionality, to abandon his stock phrase, and to say something else — most of all when he appears tired of entertaining us, and seems to want our sympathy — we are generally displeased. He is apt to become sentimental. And as a corollary, those who in life have chosen to present a 'flat' picture of themselves to the world, a thing which it is often convenient to do, show better taste if they keep it up to the end: 'the clown with the breaking heart' is an abomination.

§4 'MIXED CHARACTERS'

Leaving on one side the experiments of Joyce and of Virginia Woolf, and on the other the 'flat' character, who is found in his most impressive form in the works of Dickens, the 'round' character of fiction is generally a compromise between Everyman in and Everyman out of his Humour. There are enough stable elements in his character for him to be seen as a character, and yet he still retains the power to surprise us — if he is successful he will surprise us in such a way, that, though his action was unexpected, yet we do not think it improbable — it is rather a revelation to us that he could act in such a way. And the subtler his drawing is, the more it should be possible for readers to disagree about whether he is a good character or no. That is, there should be no doubt that he is well drawn, but there may be very different opinions whether he is virtuous or agreeable. So wicked is the human heart that even the best of men, if fully known, would have much in them to disgust us — and there is no reason to disbelieve the Saints who, in their autobiographical writings, insist on their own depravity.

The successfully drawn character in fiction will certainly be no better than the Saints. Jane Austen, in her mock synopsis of a novel on a theme suggested by the Prince Regent's librarian, came to this climax of delightful absurdity: 'the scene will be for ever shifting from one set of people to another, but there will be no mixture: all the good will be unexceptionable in every respect. There will be no foibles or weaknesses but with the wicked, who will be completely depraved and infamous, hardly a resemblance of humanity left in them.' She might almost have been describing *Eyeless in Gaza*.

The unfortunate thing about the characters in that novel is that they are all quite inhuman. Either they indulge in promiscuous love on a sub-human level, and if any of them in the course of his amours experiences any genuine feeling, he is made to look foolish; or on the other hand they dabble in mysticism, and cease to look for any happiness in earthly things. They are more or less than human, angels or apes.

The answer to Disraeli's question, whether Man is an angel or an ape, is of course that he is neither — he is Man, perhaps a poor thing to be, though some people have made quite a good thing of it. And in Man Mr. Huxley is not much interested. He has written somewhere that Man can, as Man, expect no happiness — there is only happiness on the animal or spiritual level.

This is pernicious nonsense. Though some people are able to live on an entirely spiritual level, it is a matter of vocation — no religion has ever supposed that everyone was called to this plane. Is only animality left for everyone except a chosen few? On the contrary, although there are only too good reasons to suppose that Man can as Man expect no lasting happiness — we have here no abiding city — yet there is an enormous range of happiness that is specifically human, and that would make no appeal to an animal or a pure spirit.

If it is bad ethically to dismiss Man in this way, it is worse aesthetically. On an anti-human philosophy no good fiction can be built. The novel is about human beings. Physiology, Psychology, Biography, Hagiography may deal with the brute or the saint, with Heliogabalus or St. Theresa: they are outside the field of the novelist. Though one would be unwilling so to limit the novelist's range that holiness and brutality are excluded altogether from his picture, it is safe to say that a fictional character who was utterly holy or utterly brutal would not be a success except in a very minor role.

The characters in a novel, then, are neither to be 'unexceptionable' nor 'completely depraved', but a mixture of good and bad, like the characters we know in real life, from self-knowledge or from observation. No doubt each character does best on the whole if he keeps an even tenor, and acts from what one might call the centre of his character. It is not at all the duty of the novelist to show us how much good there is in the worst of us, or how much bad in the best of us.

Nevertheless, he has this power in reserve, and some extremely striking and moving scenes in fiction do depend on the use of the final resources of a character for good or evil. Such a scene as that in *A High Wind in Jamaica*, where a small girl is shown (fairly convincingly) as capable of committing a very cruel murder, may be called a mere *tour de force*. But there are few things more admirable in Proust than the delicate and inspired generosity, the self-sacrifice of Monsieur and Madame Verdurin on behalf of the impoverished Saniette, on the very evening of their atrocious and final act of treacherous cruelty to Monsieur de Charlus.[4] And the novels of Miss Compton-Burnett afford many instances of acts of beautiful and intelligent sympathy performed by terribly tyrannical and possessive people.

§ 5 THE RELATION OF FICTIONAL CHARACTERS TO THEIR 'ORIGINALS'

Yet for all their likeness to real people, fictional characters are not real people: they do not have to function in life, but in the novel, which is an art form. They function in plots, which are abstractions, patterns, conventions — and they themselves are, like the plots they function in, abstractions, patterns, conventions. It is quite common to find critics, and even novelists themselves, dismiss Plot with some impatience, but discuss Character with much more seriousness — and yet they are of the same order of creation.

The fictional character is therefore seldom the portrait of a living person, and more often a pattern or sketch suggested by a living person. It is on this account not surprising that character is often invented on a slender basis of observation, and is not often the result of the prolonged study by a writer of any particular individual. 'The writer', says Somerset Maugham, 'does not copy his originals; he takes what he wants from them, a few traits that have caught his attention, a turn of mind that has fired his imagination, and therefrom constructs his character. He is not concerned whether it is a truthful likeness; he is concerned only to create a plausible harmony convenient for his own purposes.'[5]

The biographer's method of research into further details, that he may know all that can be known of his original, and his purpose to draw a truthful likeness, even if the truth be neither plausible nor harmonious, is the exact opposite of the method and purpose of the novelist, who only requires enough knowledge of his original to fire his imagination. Both methods of character-creation are used by us in everyday life, when we are trying to get to know other people, or when we are making conversation about them. In the case of people who really matter to us, we are like biographers — anything about them is interesting and important to us. But more often we find it amusing to give free rein to the imagination, and to fill up gaps in our knowledge by guess-work — perhaps a more innocent pastime than research into other people's private affairs.

It is with such limitations that we can ask the question where novelists have drawn their characters from, and what relation characters bear to their 'originals'. Novelists have fixed their imaginations on particular persons, certainly, but they have seldom reproduced them realistically. 'Of course there must be a beginning to every conception', writes Miss Compton-Burnett, 'but so much change seems to take place in it at once, that almost anything comes to serve the purpose — a face of a stranger, a face in a portrait, almost a face in the fire.'[6] We should not be much advanced in our study of a writer's art if we knew what faces had served his purpose. Letters and Diaries of authors, where they exist, of course can only be regarded as early sketches of the people mentioned in them; the change has begun — and we never see mere raw material that a writer has worked up later. A writer is a writer, even if he is only writing his diary, or a private letter.

Of Emily Brontë, for example, we know that her imagination was fed on country gossip and legend in a country rich in eccentrics, solitary houses, and terrible stories — where it was a traditional saying: 'keep a stone in thy pocket seven years; turn it, and keep it seven years longer, that it may be ever ready to thine hand when thine enemy draws near.' And her sister Charlotte wrote of her: 'I am bound to avow that she had scarcely more practical knowledge of the peasantry amongst whom she lived, than a nun has of the country-people that pass her convent gates . . . intercourse with them she never sought, nor, with a few exceptions, ever experienced; and yet she knew them, knew their ways, their language, their family histories; she could hear of them with interest, and talk of them with detail, minute, graphic and accurate; but with them she rarely exchanged a word.'[7] This is all we know, or need to know, of the genesis of Heathcliff — a 'germ', picked up in this way, developed on solitary moorland walks, or in the fire-light of a home where life was both dramatic and intellectual.

Other novelists have begun from a face seen in the street or in a train, from a chance word overheard. It is enough to have seen or heard something significant, and the novelist is haunted — and 'haunted' is the right word for it — until the character has been given life. The process of character-procreation is like that in the procreation-myth in Samuel Butler's *Erewhon*; the unborn are determined to be born, and haunt and plague their future parents, and give them no rest until they have brought them into the world. And like the 'story' for Henry James, at an early stage embryonic characters put on 'the authenticity of concrete existence'.

It will depend on the mind of the writer whether the first hint of a character is more often audible or visible.

Oscar Wilde found two characters and a famous short story in the Louvre. He told the story to the two ladies who composed the single personality of the poet, 'Michael Field'. He had been fascinated by the Infanta of Velasquez, with the rose in her hand. 'He was bent', says Michael Field, 'on learning the history of that rose, and found it in a portrait near at hand of a dwarf. Now the princess — let history go off with her rags

— had given the dwarf that rose — the dwarf was dancing before the court, and she took it from her hair and flung it to him. He went away in rapture at the consciousness of her love . . . then the doctrine of doubles, and inattention on my part — ultimately the dwarf discovers from a mirror his own hideousness, and when they come in and try to raise him to dance, lies stretched responseless. He is dead — dead, they tell the princess, of a broken heart. She replies going away — "Let those who love me have no hearts" . . . "Fiction, not truth — I could never have any dealings with truth — if truth were to come unto me, to my room, he would say to me, 'you are too wilful'. And I should say to him, 'you are too obvious'. And I should throw him out of the window." Michael: "you would say to *him*. Is not truth a woman?" "Then I could not throw her out of the window; I should bow her to the door." '[8]

Jane Austen, on the other hand, went round picture galleries, after the completion of *Pride and Prejudice*, hoping to find portraits of Elizabeth and Jane. We must not take this little joke of hers, in a family letter, too seriously; but it does suggest that she had not completely visualized them, but would have known them if she saw them.

Since characters are generally built up on a slender basis, it is a common experience for an author to be accused of having drawn a malicious portrait of a living person in some character for which that person has provided no suggestion. And in cases where the same person has provided suggestions for more than one fictional character, those characters may very well bear little or no resemblance to each other. Compare the pedant, Casaubon in *Middlemarch* with the miser, Professor Forth in *Belinda*: George Eliot and Rhoda Broughton drew these two very dissimilar characters, as we know, from Mark Pattison — and there are plenty of materials for a biography of Mark Pattison, with which they could be contrasted. Compare the mean-spirited young man drawn by Lawrence from Peter Warlock in *Women in Love*, with the Rabelaisian figure whom Aldous Huxley drew from the same original in *Antic Hay*.

Or compare Dickens's two portraits of his own father, as Mr. Micawber or as Old Dorrit. They are not much alike; nor are Flora Finching and Dora Copperfield, who had the same original.

§6 AUTOBIOGRAPHICAL FICTION

There are of course novels, and great novels, that are almost purely autobiographical, and in these, as in some other novels there are characters drawn from assignable persons, and intended as portraits. We know from what personal experience parts of *Les Faux-Monnayeurs*, and almost all *The Way of All Flesh* derive. Butler says that writing his novel was 'a kind of picking up of sovereigns', for 'the novel contains records of things I saw happening, rather than imaginary incidents'.[9] M. Gide makes Edouard, his novelist within the novel, say: 'I always have the greatest difficulty in "making-up" the truth. Even to change the colour of the hair seems to me a fraud, which for me makes the truth less lifelike.'[10]

But even in such novels the character has to be shown in scenes, which must be invented and manipulated by an art entirely different from the biographer's. The author must pass his material through his imagination, and there re-experience it — he must become one with his characters in a way in which he was not one with them in real life. And since people in life, as Miss Compton-Burnett says, 'hardly seem to be definite enough to appear in print',[11] their definition has to be increased. To take a metaphor from the kitchen, they must be 'reduced', as soup is 'reduced' to a sufficient strength by boiling away superfluous water. This 'reduction' of a character is one of the processes it goes through in the imagination: observably some characters in fiction have not been sufficiently 'reduced'.

A novelist would not (or should not) feel that he had done less creative work in thus recreating a person whom he had known in real life, than in drawing a character from 'a face in the fire'.

§7 'CONFLATION'

Characters so directly drawn from life are probably rare, at least among novels that are important works of art. It is rare for fictional characters to have their origin each in only one real person. Conflation is probably the most common mode of character-creation, whether the character is round or flat. It is unlikely that, after the event, an author could give a list of all to whom he owed small suggestions for his characters, even if he kept such careful journals as the Goncourts or M. Gide, or even if he were as fanatically interested in his own work as Proust. Curiosity has seized on the characters of Proust with the enthusiasm of scholars seeking to identify an historical site, and there are (or recently were) people alive who claim to 'be' Albertine, Jupien, etc. But of the 'keys' to his novel Proust himself wrote to Lucien Daudet: 'there are so many to each door, that in fact there is none.'[12] And in his novel he wrote: 'there is no name of a fictitious character under which the writer could not put sixty names of people seen: one has posed for the grimace, another for the eyeglass, another for the anger, another for the becoming movement of the arm etc.'[13] Again: 'a book is a vast cemetery, and on most of the graves one can no longer read the obliterated names.'[14]

It is the act of conflation that is *par excellence* the creative act of the novelist: something new arises out of the conflated bits. If the word 'creator' is ever applicable to anyone but God, it may here be used. An analogy may be found in other creative acts of the intelligence, in Inference, or even better, in the making of Metaphors, which Aristotle saw as the act of creative genius: 'for to make good metaphors implies an eye for resemblance.'[15] This 'eye for resemblance' is as important in the creation of character as we saw the 'eye for a subject' to be important in the creation of plot.

§8 THE ELEMENT OF SELF-PORTRAITURE

The great source of character-creation is of course the novelist's own self. Some form of self-projection must always take place, of reincarnation in the fictional character. The writer, living for the time in his characters, divests himself of those parts of his own nature which are irrelevant, and develops the relevant parts of his nature to more than their normal size — his more successful characters are portraits of potential selves.

This is not to say that he often indulges in self-portraiture: it would not be a good thing to produce in a novel the startling effect which Corvo produced in a painting of the translation of St. William of Norwich, in which more than forty faces were given identical features — his own.

The novelist may have mentally to change his age, sex, social position, and other accidents, and also to develop to the full every suggestion of every vice or virtue he may possess. Here again the creation of character seems not unlike the process whereby we understand other people — since our knowledge of other people is derived from our knowledge of ourselves. 'The material for any picture of personal states', says Henry James, 'will have been drawn preponderantly from the depths of the designer's own mind.'[16] *Know thyself*, is the novelist's first maxim: and the novelist with the widest range as a creator of character is he who contains within himself the greatest variety of potential selves.

There is a perpetual strain between the mould of the character and the novelist's mind that is poured into it — the novelist's mind is always trying to distort the mould, and to make the character more like the author. If writers speak of impersonality in their work, we must not take them quite literally — they mean that they respect the mould. For instance, they will have tried indeed to give a jealous character something of the jealousy which they know in their own hearts, but purified from the idiosyncracies which it may there have acquired—it has to be not *their* jealousy, but the jealousy of the character.

'I have always forbidden myself to put anything of myself into my work', wrote Flaubert, 'and yet I have put in a great deal . . . I have written most tender pages without love, and boiling pages with no fire in my veins. I have imagined, remembered, combined.'[17]

However, he complained: 'It is difficult to express well what one has never felt.'[18] And again he wrote, of *Madame Bovary*: 'The reason I go so slowly is that nothing in this book is drawn from myself, never can my personality be less useful to me . . . Imagine, I must all the time enter into skins that are antipathetic to me. For six months I have been making platonic love, and at the moment I am going into Catholic ecstasies at the sound of church bells, and I want to go to confession.'[19] And yet it was indeed Flaubert himself who was entering into these skins, so antipathetic to him, so much so that he could exclaim: 'I am Madame Bovary!' — so much so that he suffered the physical symptoms of arsenical poisoning, when he was writing about her suicide.[20]

'One must', he said, 'by a mental effort transport oneself into the characters, and not draw them towards oneself.'[21] And he advised a friend, also a writer, to attempt this kind of impersonality: 'you will see how well your characters talk, the moment you stop talking through their mouths.'[22]

It will no doubt depend on the make-up of the author whether, like Flaubert, he loses his own personality in one of the characters he has set in action, or whether, like M. Gide, he has rather the sensation of sitting and listening and looking on, while his characters act and talk.[23] Probably most authors experience a confused mixture of the two experiences, as in our dreams we commonly are at the same time both actors in, and external witnesses of an action.

Even the most unexceptionable writer can, in imagination, enter the skins of very bad characters. Those holy women, 'Michael Field', were seriously troubled in conscience about this necessity, and consulted a priest as to the duties of a Christian dramatic poet who 'must needs deal with sinners and become, as Matthew Arnold says, "what we sing".' Fortunately they consulted a priest as imaginative as he was saintly, who put before them the Incarnation of Christ as an example, and told them that it was the poet's duty to bear sin.[24] And at the other end of the scale there are writers whose lives are infinitely less noble than their work.

But though a writer can make characters very much better or worse than himself, in one way his own nature definitely limits his range: he cannot make them much more witty and intelligent than he is. He can make them more nimble-witted, certainly; he can also endow them with memories much better than his own. They can indulge in long, abstruse and apposite quotations — even in prose. They say things impromptu which he has carefully worked out for them — brilliant writers of dialogue are not always brilliant conversationalists — Dryden was not, for all the sparkling wit of his comedies and satires. Writers often do not use the spoken word very well — a defect which may have helped to make them writers. But a character can only say what his creator puts into his mouth to say. It is very unbecoming, therefore, for a writer to laugh too loudly at the wit of one of his characters, for he is laughing at his own jokes, and he must not applaud their cleverness, which is his own cleverness. Probably no worse example of this sort of bad taste is to be found than the passage in *Evelyn Innes*, where George Moore comments on the very commonplace reflections of one of his characters: 'never had he thought more brilliantly.' Seldom can an author have made a worse gaffe. Much more commendable is M. Gide's sarcasm about two of his people in *Les Faux-Monnayeurs*: 'as their conversation continued to be very witty, there is no need for me to report it here.'

§ 9 THE 'RIGHTS' OF CHARACTERS

Since we call the making of characters Creation, and since it is in many ways analogous to the way in which human beings are themselves made out of bits and pieces of their ancestors, the novelist, who has breathed life into them, stands towards them in the position of God. They might sing to him in the hundredth psalm:

> Without our aid he did us make,
> We are his flock, he doth us feed,
> And for his sheep he doth us take.

Moreover, himself unmoved, he stands in the midst of them, like the Goddess of Love (whom otherwise he little resembles), rousing their passions and murmuring:

Cras amet qui nunquam amavit, quique amavit cras amet.

A God has a debt to his creatures: Providence. By analogy, it seems that the novelist owes his characters something.

It would be perverse or whimsical to maintain that fictional characters had duties or rights; yet it is hard to find other words for the conviction that a novelist has certain obligations towards them. Perhaps as they are *simulacra* of human beings, we are shocked if they are not treated as we ought to treat other human beings, as ends in themselves, and not as means to ends of our own.

Certainly we ought not to tell lies about them for the sake of the story, as Thackeray tells a lie about Becky — she could not and would not have murdered Josh, and we feel that he is merely trying to blacken her character by this calumny. And he tells a lie about Major Pendennis in order to advance his plot — certainly he was too honourable to have indulged in blackmail. He was a worldly old gentleman, but incapable of real wickedness — incapable, for instance, of the obstinate resentfulness of Colonel Newcome. If characters ever come to a judgment, it may very well be more tolerable in that day for Arthur's uncle than for Clive's father.

Wanton cruelty on the part of an author towards his characters is also shocking. This does not mean that fictional characters need always have things their own way, nor that fiction should conform to Miss Prism's definition, and end well for the good and ill for the bad. But the unhappy ending, when it comes, must be justifiable and necessary. We do not object to dreadful things happening to Hardy's characters, we know that it is a law of their being that everything must go wrong with them — they live in a world of disastrous coincidences, and are as sure to come to a bad end as the people in *The Beggar's Opera* are to be hanged or transported. But if the calamities which sometimes threaten Miss Austen's characters really took place — if Marianne Dashwood had died of her putrid fever at Cleveland; if Mr. Bennet had fought a duel with Wickham, and had been killed; if Louisa Musgrove had never recovered consciousness after her fall on the Cobb — we should be indignant, and rightly. Yet all these things would be perfectly possible, and indeed far more probable than almost anything that happens in *The Return of the Native* or in *Tess of the d'Urbervilles*.

Stevenson, in a letter to Barrie, makes as good a comment as one could wish on this point, and cites the classic instance of an author's cruelty to his people.

'If you are going to make a book end badly, it must end badly from the beginning. You let yourself fall in love with, and fondle, and smile at your puppets. Once you had done that, your honour was committed — at the cost of truth to life you were bound to save them. It is the blot on *Richard Feverel*, for instance, that it begins to end well, and then tricks you and ends ill. But in that case there is worse behind, for the ill-ending does not inherently issue from the plot — the story had, in fact, *ended well* after the great last interview between Richard and Lucy — and the blind, illogical bullet which smashes all has no more to do between the boards than a fly has to do with the room into whose open windows it comes buzzing.'

A contemporary instance is possibly worth taking because of

the high reputation that the novel in question enjoys. It may be that herein lies the reason for the great dissatisfaction that some readers feel with it. In *The Death of the Heart* Miss Elizabeth Bowen draws a painful picture of a small girl, cruelly betrayed by her elders, who read her private diary, lay bare her secrets, and play with her affections — we are filled with pity at her heart-rending situation. 'Ah, the exposure indeed, the helpless plasticity of childhood that isn't dear or sacred to *some*body!' wrote Henry James — but his helpless young people, Morgan Moreen, Maisie, Miles and Flora are always dear and sacred to at least one person — to Henry James. Portia Quayne may be dear, but she is not sacred to Miss Bowen who, one cannot help feeling, has betrayed her more cruelly than anyone else — who invites us, as one of her treacherous elders might have done, to look over her shoulder and smile at the child's pathetic diary. Her honour was committed to respect Portia's secrets.

An author, then, must deal honourably with his characters. But for all that we must never forget that characters, if *simulacra* of human beings, are not human beings. We should not, one hopes, had we been living at the time, have been among those who wrote to Richardson, begging him to spare Clarissa's virtue, or among those who wrote to Dickens begging him to spare the life of little Paul Dombey, or little Nell. We are sorry that he abandoned his original, unhappy ending to *Great Expectations*.

A final illustration may help to establish the status of characters in fiction. Monsignor Ronald Knox has written an entertaining sequel to Trollope's Barsetshire novels: in it he has made a number of Barsetshire people embrace Catholicism. Had he been a mission priest in Barchester in real life, this might well have been a part of his duty. But Barsetshire people exist only in fiction, and aesthetically it is far more suitable that they should remain in the Church of England — as Monsignor Knox would probably agree. We have Cardinal Newman's word for the fact that Birmingham people have souls — some of us might have been tempted to doubt this without his authority: 'one has not great hopes from Birmingham', said Mrs. Elton in *Emma*. But Barchester people, though possibly more attractive, have no souls to save — that is the difference between them.

NOTES

1. *Partial Portraits* (1888), p. 314. Turgenieff, unfortunately, is so attached to his dossiers that he frequently prints them in full.
2. Somerset Maugham: *The Summing Up*, § 57.
3. Herford and Simpson: *Introduction to Every Man in his Humour*.
4. *La Prisonnière*, II, pp. 163 ff.
5. loc. cit.
6. loc. cit., p. 25.
7. Mrs. Gaskell: *Life of Charlotte Brontë*.
8. *Works and Days from the Journal of Michael Field*, ed. by T. and D. C. Sturge Moore (1933), pp. 135-6.
9. *Notebooks*, s.v. 'The Choice of Subjects'.
10. *Les Faux-Monnayeurs*, I, xi.
11. loc. cit., p. 25. And see Appendix I, p. 135 — a most important passage by Henry James.
12. cit. Léon Guichard: *Sept études sur Marcel Proust* (Le Caire, 1942); p. 95.
13. *Le Temps Retrouvé*, II, pp. 54-5.
14. ibid., p. 59.
15. *Poetics*, xxii. 9.
16. *The Art of the Novel*, p. 221.
17. Flaubert: *Correspondance*, I, p. 128.
18. ibid., II, p. 149.
19. ibid., II, pp. 198-9.
20. ibid., III, p. 349.
21. ibid., III, p. 331.
22. ibid., III, p. 157.
23. *Journal des Faux-Monnayeurs*, *passim*.
24. loc. cit., p. 313.

CHAPTER VI

BACKGROUND

§ I DESCRIPTIVE WRITING IS GENERALLY TOO MUCH ESTEEMED

THE aesthetics of descriptive writing have not yet received sufficient attention — it is commonly held in too great esteem, particularly when it occurs in works of fiction. Painting or music that has a strong literary element is now severely criticized. It is time for an attack to be made upon the pictorial element in literature. Mr. Richards, in *Practical Criticism*, has done much to teach us not to look for 'pictures' in Poetry — nevertheless, the Novel is still in need of a purge.

Like many errors in the criticism of fiction, a love of 'descriptions' comes from not taking fiction seriously enough as an art, from not valuing highly enough work in which 'the most thorough knowledge of human nature, the happiest delineation of its varieties, the liveliest effusions of wit and humour are conveyed to the world in the best chosen language'. 'It is only a novel', Miss Austen reproaches young ladies for saying, when they are asked what they are reading — and though Stendhal, Balzac, Flaubert, Dickens, Henry James and Conrad, Tolstoy and Dostoievsky, not to speak of Miss Austen herself, have written since then, a young woman in a novel by Miss Elizabeth Bowen is still ashamed of reading a novel before luncheon: one cannot doubt this shame is true to life.

If the delineation of character in action is not considered serious, the critic will easily be brought to take the delineation of Nature seriously. Since the time of Dr. Arnold there has been a premium on Nature-study in English education, while a 'thorough knowledge of human nature' has, on the contrary, been rather discouraged — understandably, for it is obviously a more desirable hobby for a boy, from a schoolmaster's point of view, to study the habits of sticklebacks or water-voles, rather than those of the Senior Common-room.

Another cause for the prejudices of critics in favour of descriptive writing lies in the vicious distinction between 'style' and 'subject-matter' in which so many of us have been educated. In a descriptive passage in which a novelist is not getting on with his story, it is thought his 'style' has freer play, and can better be displayed — unhappily many novelists have thought this too. False criticism of this sort has exalted Conrad as a painter of sunsets and tropical landscapes, and has obscured his dramatic powers; this great novelist has so often been praised for anything but those qualities which make him great as a novelist, that his reputation has suffered, and his better work has been neglected, particularly by those who might get the most intense pleasure from it.

§2 ITS SUBORDINATE PLACE IN THE NOVEL

Fiction is the delineation of character in action, and the landscape in the background is merely incidental. In travel-books the situation is generally reversed, and it is the landscape that predominates in importance. There is no reason why 'landscape-writing' (if admitted to be a valid form of writing) should not have figures in the foreground, and why these figures should not be fictitious characters, if the author wishes. But such fictionized or moralized travel or guide-books will depend for their chief interest on qualities that have nothing to do with the art of the novelist; and it is in their own interests that we shall refuse to consider such books as *The Plumed Serpent* or the so-called 'novels' of Mr. Prokosch as novels. They are landscapes with figures, and require to be judged by standards of their own, with which we are not at all here concerned.

In fiction that is a representation of characters in action, the background will probably serve a negative rather than a positive purpose. It will be there less for the sake of being what it is, for example, an English country village, as for the sake of not being anywhere else. Its function is limitative, to keep the characters still, and to allow us to concentrate upon them, and upon the happenings. When we can see the characters and the action clearly, then the background may fade out of focus. Similarly St. Ignatius bids us make a 'composition of place' at the beginning of each of the spiritual exercises — to place ourselves, for example, in Hell or Purgatory, or in the place where some scene in the Scriptures was enacted — but the place is presently allowed to fade out of our meditations. A writer returning to his manuscript will often have to make a 'composition of place', also when he shifts his scene; the reader need not so often perform this exercise.

By background is intended primarily that which in a theatre we see on the stage: the sea-coast of Illyria, the palace of Theseus at Troezen, or the like. It is sometimes alleged that fiction, since it does not dispose of the visual effects of drama, ought in some way to supply their place by description. To this argument the best reply is that in the best days of drama there was a good deal of austerity about visual effects: the Greek stage does not appear to have made much difference between the primeval rocks of the *Prometheus Vinctus* and the palace at Troezen of the *Hippolytus*; nor did the Elizabethan stage make much difference between 'a street in London', and the coast of Illyria or the forest of Arden. And it is more imaginatively effective to present drama with simple means than with the distracting pomp of the Edwardian theatre.

Too many stage-directions are boring and confusing if we read a play; if we see them carried out on the stage, the result is a fussy and undignified ritualism. They are worst of all in a novel.

§3 BACKGROUND IN JANE AUSTEN: UTILITARIAN

One would hesitate to recommend to a novelist the classic rule of the Théâtre Français that no chair is to appear on the scene unless someone is presently going to sit on it. Interpreted in its full simplicity, this rule has two inconvenient consequences. Firstly, the scene is unnaturally stark and bare — it is common to have in a room more chairs than are in use. Secondly, every chair would thus receive an undue significance — we should look at it, and wonder who was going to sit on it, just as we look at the revolver on the table, and wonder nervously when it is going to go off. It would be a safer rule to keep as near this starkness as we can, without making it too remarkable. This approximates to Miss Austen's practice.

'You describe a sweet place', she wrote to Anna Lefroy, 'but your descriptions are often more minute than will be liked. You give too many particulars of right hand and left.' She herself had parodied this sort of detailed description in *Love and Freindship*: 'A grove of full-grown Elms sheltered us from the East—. A Bed of full-grown Nettles from the West—. Before us ran the murmuring brook and behind us ran the turnpike road. We were in the mood for contemplation and in a Disposition to enjoy so beautiful a spot.'

In reaction from the ancient and gothic of the horror novels, Miss Austen's houses were generally neat, modern edifices, with not much to be said about them. Northanger and Pemberley are to some extent characterized, because they have a function in the plot. Northanger's gothic temptations are too much for Catherine's good sense; and Pemberley makes Mr. Darcy more valued, not for the great possessions, which we always knew he had, but because it stands for cultured and elegant wealth, and for conscientious stewardship of property. The description of Sotherton, on the other hand, was meant to be boring.

Mrs. Rushworth began her relation: 'This chapel was fitted

up as you see it, in James the Second's time. Before that period, as I understand, the pews were only wainscot; and there is reason to think that the linings and cushions of the pulpit and family-seat were only purple cloth; but this is not quite certain . . .' This scrupulous and boring accuracy about points of no importance is intended to show Jane Austen's contempt for detailed description, as well as the dullness of the Rushworth family.

A very fine example of her simple, low-toned, descriptive writing, intended to throw the human drama into relief, is the scene of Harriet and the Gipsies in *Emma*.

'Miss Smith and Miss Bickerton, another parlour boarder at Mrs. Goddard's, who had been also at the ball, had walked out together, and taken a road, the Richmond road, which, though apparently public enough for safety, had led them into alarm. About half a mile beyond Highbury, making a sudden turn, and deeply shaded by elms on each side, it became for a considerable stretch very retired; and when the young ladies had advanced some way into it, they had suddenly perceived at a small distance before them, on a broader patch of greensward by the side, a party of gipsies. A child on the watch, came towards them to beg; and Miss Bickerton, excessively frightened, gave a great scream, and calling on Harriet to follow her, ran up a steep bank, cleared a slight hedge at the top, and made the best of her way by a short cut back to Highbury. But poor Harriet could not follow. She had suffered very much from cramp after dancing, and her first attempt to mount the bank brought on such a return of it as made her absolutely powerless.'

There could be no quieter description of natural scenery. We are shown, however, precisely what is necessary to the drama of the young ladies' fright — the distance of the spot from the village, the turn of the road which put it out of view, and the shady and therefore sinister stretch of the road in front. The broader patch of greensward was there to accommodate the gipsies — one may think they had pitched their camp on it.

The bank was steep enough to separate Harriet from her more active companion — and, as it was the Richmond road, presently Mr. Frank Churchill came along and rescued her.

Mr. Herbert Read complains that Miss Austen's descriptive prose is not written 'in any mood of compulsion', he complains of 'the lack of internal necessity', and damns her style with the word 'quaintness'.[1] But we ought rather to recollect the purely functional nature of her descriptions, in which we may not properly look for any 'necessity' but that to provide the barely necessary background and props for the action.

Miss Austen is like an early Italian artist, providing an exquisite, neat, clear, little background to her scenes of human action — the background itself untouched by emotion. Other novelists will make more of the background, developing its symbolism in relation to the characters, or even developing it as an end in itself, so that they become the landscape painters of fiction. Others will develop it photographically, with the enormous fidelity to detail of an English nineteenth-century painter.

§4 BACKGROUND IN DICKENS: SYMBOLIC

Of the symbolists, Dickens is supreme: he provides vast, Wagnerian settings for his dramas. The Thames in *Our Mutual Friend*, the marshes in *Great Expectations* are symbolic and exciting. They prepare us to see extraordinary things and people — and Dickens's people are big enough to set against their background, while Hardy's are apt to get lost on Egdon Heath. Dickens does not forget that it is for the sake of the human drama that the background is provided. If, in *Bleak House*, it rains in Lincolnshire, it is because it rains in the heart of Lady Dedlock.

'The Waters are out in Lincolnshire. An arch of the bridge in the park has been sapped and sopped away. The adjacent low-lying ground, for half a mile in breadth, is a stagnant river, with melancholy trees for islands in it, and a surface punctured all over, all day long, with falling rain . . . The weather, for many a day and night, has been so wet that the trees seem wet through, and the soft loppings and prunings of the workman's axe can make no crash or crackle as they fall. The deer, looking soaked, leave quagmires, where they pass. The shot of a rifle loses its sharpness in the moist air, and its smoke moves in a tardy little cloud towards the green rise, coppice-topped, that makes a background for the falling rain.'

The feeling of damp chill is the physical counterpart to Lady Dedlock's fears, and the remorseless rain a fit background to her approaching ruin. Unfortunately the actual drama in this case, as so often in Dickens, is strained and impossible. A truer pity and terror at Lady Dedlock's plight is produced by the echoing terrace at Chesnay Wold and the Lincolnshire floods, than by the preposterous schemes of Mr. Tulkinghorn. Dickens is a great artist, nevertheless it must be said that it is more creditable to cause pity and terror by the happenings in a story, rather than by the atmosphere.

§5 BACKGROUND IN HARDY

Hardy is more difficult to comment on. In one thing he is superb, in giving to his characters that immediate background, which one can better describe by a change of metaphor, saying that he digs them up by the roots, with the earth on them. No writer is better than he at showing people at their jobs. His countrymen are real countrymen, and we feel the same satisfaction at watching their work, and the same respect for them when they do it as it should be done, that intelligent people generally feel when they see a craft worthily exercised.

Giles Winterborne, in *The Woodlanders*, planting trees with Marty South, is particularly satisfying.

'He had a marvellous power of making trees grow. Although he would seem to shovel in the earth quite carelessly there was a sort of sympathy between himself and the fir, oak or beech that he was operating on; so that the roots took hold of the soil in a few days. When, on the other hand, any of the journeymen planted, although they seemed to go through an identically similar process, one quarter of the trees would die away during the ensuing August.

Hence Winterborne found delight in the work . . . Marty, who turned her hand to anything, was usually the one who performed the part of keeping the trees in a perpendicular position whilst he threw in the mould. . . .

The holes were already dug, and they set to work. Winterborne's fingers were endowed with a gentle conjuror's touch in spreading the roots of each little tree, resulting in a sort of caress under which the delicate fibres all laid themselves out in their proper direction for growth. He put most of these roots towards the south-west; for, he said, in forty years' time, when some great gale is blowing from that quarter, the trees will require the strongest holdfast on that side to stand against it and not fall.

"How they sigh directly we put 'em upright, though while they are lying down they don't sigh at all," said Marty. . . .

She erected one of the young pines into its hold, and held up her finger; the soft musical breathing instantly set in, which was not to cease night or day till the grown tree should be felled — probably long after the two planters should be felled themselves.'

We respect Giles, we respect Gabriel Oak in *Far From the Madding Crowd* for his presence of mind and skill in saving sheep that are blown up with wind after getting in the clover, and in saving hayricks from fire and from a storm. We rather despise people in Hardy's novels who do not really belong to country life, and are not efficient at it — Troy, the soldier, who endangers the hay-harvest by his stupid arrogance, and Jude, the scholar, who cannot kill a pig properly — just as in real life we are apt to despise people who forget to shut gates, or who are afraid of cows or dogs.

Hardy's great excellence in depicting a natural background lies in the fact that he really knows what he is writing about, and that he offers no artificially pretty view of nature — nature is more likely to impress his characters by her unkindness, than in any other way. But he has the defects of these qualities; his close observation of nature may tempt him to a pre-raphaelite accuracy in depicting her, and when he chooses some of her more uncomfortable features to depict like this, the result may be unintentionally comic. For example, there are the various country messes with which Tess covered herself.

'The outskirt of the garden in which Tess found herself had been left uncultivated for some years, and was now damp and rank with juicy grass which sent up mists of pollen at a touch; and with tall blooming weeds emitting offensive smells — weeds whose red and yellow and purple hues formed a polychrome as dazzling as that of cultivated flowers. She went stealthily as a cat through this profusion of growth, gathering cuckoo-spittle on her skirts, cracking snails that were underfoot, staining her hands with thistle-milk and slug-slime, and rubbing off upon her naked arms sticky blights which, though snow-white on the apple-tree trunks, made madder stains on her skin; thus she drew quite near to Clare, still unobserved of him.'

Such a chapter of accidents, such a series of booby tricks played upon Tess by Nature, well enough parallel the booby tricks which Destiny plays on her, as on so many of Hardy's characters. But he never saw that such an accumulation of disasters was farcical, not tragic — part of the technique of the comic pantomime, rather than of the serious novel.

When Nature does not intervene to make Hardy's characters uncomfortable, they are often rather indifferent to her. Egdon Heath is there, vast and brooding, but never of the importance to Eustacia that the Yorkshire moors are to Catherine Earnshaw. Eustacia is urban in her tastes; she would like to go to Paris, or even to Budmouth, which has at least an Esplanade. Neither she nor Wildeve are real creatures of the moors, which look on at their love-making, and dwarf it into philandering.

Though we may begin a story, like Turgenieff, with a group of people, and decide that such people are sure to do something special or interesting, or we may begin, like Henry James, with a happening, and decide that the people who were agents or patients in that happening must have been worth looking at, one way in which we cannot begin is to take an impressive, natural scene, and decide that the people and happenings there must be worth telling about. For people are not so very much influenced by natural beauties, particularly by those that they live amongst — there is no reason at all why the inhabitants of a striking place should in themselves be interesting, or do interesting things. Too grand a scene in the background may overpower the people in the foreground, so that the author will lose more than he gains by his scenic effects. Highbury is really a more satisfactory background for a work of fiction than Egdon, apart from the fact that the people of Highbury are of incomparably greater interest.

§6 CHARACTERS AND BACKGROUND: BALZAC AND FLAUBERT

Hardy has been much praised for his rendering of the sounds on Egdon, in a way possible only to a countryman born and bred. 'Who else', asks Lord David Cecil, 'would realize that the wind made a different noise when it was blowing through hollow or heather or over bare stones, let alone be able to distinguish them?'[1] Yet though Eustacia no doubt heard these noises, and may subconsciously have distinguished them, she was not listening to them, and they do not contribute to her tragedy.

Such irrelevance, and lack of fusion, is common to novelists who excel at and are therefore tempted to overdo natural description. 'All around were the famous hills,' says a good contemporary writer . . . 'magnificent, chameleon hills, shaped like molars and eye-teeth — but in the mist they might as well not be there.' As they were invisible, they might as well not be mentioned — nor, if they had been visible should they have been mentioned unless they had in some way mattered to the people who were present.

Characters are often too much the prey of violent emotions to pay much attention to their surroundings. It is when he begins to take his eye off his characters that the novelist is most apt, in idleness, to focus it upon their background; it is easy and restful for him. Novelists, says Montherlant, have always made phrases about the setting in which their lovers meet, but it is only the novelists who see the details of this setting. The lovers see nothing, '*engloutis qu'ils sont dans la bouillie pour les chats*'.[3] The reader, who likes concentrating on the people and the happenings, is not refreshed, but annoyed, to have to focus on the herbaceous border in the background.

Yet in some circumstances the background may be so lit up by an emotion as to become particularly significant in a moment of stress. There is a very fine example of this in *Eugénie Grandet*, when Eugénie's young cousin learns of his father's ruin and suicide.

'In the great moments of life, our soul strongly attaches itself to the places where joy or grief rushes upon us. So Charles examined with special attention the box-hedges of this little garden, the pale leaves that were falling, the crumbling of the walls, the irregularity of the fruit-trees, picturesque details that were to remain engraved on his memory, for ever mixed with this supreme hour by a mnemotechnic peculiar to the passions.'

In the same way lightning is said to imprint on a man's body the picture of the tree under which he has been struck.

Parallels can be found in Hardy's poetry, for example in the poem *Neutral Tones*, of which Mr. Middleton Murry writes: 'he declares that he concentrates a whole world of bitterness in a simple vision: the feeling of bitterness of love shapes into its symbol: *Your face*, *and the God-curst sun*, *and a tree*, *and a pond edged with grayish leaves*. A mental process of this kind is familiar to most people. At an emotional crisis in their lives some part of their material surroundings seems to be involved in their emotion; some material circumstance suddenly appears to be strangely appropriate, appropriate even by its very incongruousness, to their stress of soul; their emotion seems to flow out and crystallize about this circumstance, so that for ever after the circumstance has the power of summoning up and recreating the emotion by which it was once touched. It gives to that emotion a preciseness which is never possessed by emotions which did not find their symbol.'[4]

It is the absence of this fusion that makes the wind on the heath irrelevant to Eustacia Vye, while its presence gives relevance and emotional force to a sound that she *was* listening for — the plop of a stone into the water, that told of Wildeve's coming. It is the constant presence of this fusion that enabled Flaubert, as exquisite a descriptive artist as Hardy, and an infinitely greater novelist, to provide a beautiful and significant background to Emma Bovary, a person who was really not much unlike Eustacia, and whose loves were just as ignoble. Flaubert, concentrating his thought and feeling on his character, was able to give in his background that beauty which her sordid story would otherwise lack, without ever for a minute diminishing our interest in that story, but on the contrary, heightening its intensity with every sight and sound.

'The soft night was about them, masses of shadow filled the branches. Emma, her eyes half-closed, breathed in with deep sighs the fresh wind that was blowing. They did not speak, lost as they were in the rush of their reverie. The tenderness of the old days came back to their hearts, full and silent as the flowing river, with the softness and perfume of the syringas, and threw across their memories shadows more immense and more sombre than those of the still willows that lengthened out over the grass. Often some night animal, hedgehog or weasel, setting out on the hunt, disturbed the lovers, or sometimes they heard a ripe peach falling all alone from the espalier.

"Ah! what a lovely night!" said Rodolphe.

"We shall have others," replied Emma.'

Or this passage:

'Once, during a thaw, the bark of the trees in the yard was oozing, the snow on the roofs of the outbuildings was melting; she stood on the threshold, and went to fetch her sunshade and opened it. The sunshade, of silk of the colour of pigeons' breasts, through which the sun shone, lighted up with shifting hues the white skin of her face. She smiled under the tender warmth, and drops of water could be heard falling one by one on the stretched silk.'

Or this:

'They returned to Yonville by the water-side. In the warm season the bank, wider than at other times, showed to its base the garden walls, whence a few steps led to the river. It flowed noiselessly, swift and cold to the eye; long, thin grasses huddled together in it as the current drove them, and spread themselves upon the limpid water like streaming hair; sometimes at the top of the reeds or on the leaf of a water-lily an insect with fine legs crawled or rested. The sun pierced with a ray the small blue bubbles of the waves that, breaking, followed each other; branchless old willows mirrored their grey backs in the water; beyond, all around, the meadows seemed empty. It was the dinner-hour at the farms, and the young woman and her companion heard nothing as they walked but the fall of their steps on the earth of the path, the words they spoke, and the sound of Emma's dress rustling round her.

The walls of the gardens with pieces of bottle on their coping were hot as the glass windows of a conservatory. Wallflowers had sprung up between the bricks, and with the tip of her open sunshade Madame Bovary, as she passed, made some of their faded flowers crumble into a yellow dust, or a spray of overhanging honeysuckle and clematis caught in its fringe and dangled for a moment over the silk.

They were talking of a troupe of Spanish dancers who were expected shortly at the Rouen theatre.

"Are you going?" she asked.

"If I can," he answered.

Had they nothing else to say to one another? Yet their eyes were full of more serious speech, and while they forced themselves to find trivial phrases, they felt the same languor stealing over them both.'

These passages, incomparably beautiful in the original, defy but survive translation, and show up Hardy's clod-hopping effects in comparison. One is temped to think only two kinds of background tolerable: Yonville or Highbury.

§7 'COUNTRIES OF THE MIND': JANE AUSTEN'S SATIRE

As well as the setting in which characters physically live and act, there are countries of the mind, places where their hearts and minds are present, in memory, fear, hope or desire – they carry about with them this second background, an effect too subtle for the stage, though the novelist may wish to avail himself of it.

Jane Austen, with her common-sense attitude to life, made a satirical use of the world of fantasy. Two of her descriptive scenes stand out by reason of their 'internal compulsion', but they are both scenes where a character is being mocked for not living in the actual but in a fantastic world. They have the flavour of her juvenile parodies, and one is inclined to think that they date from the earlier recensions of the novels in which they occur. If that is so, their vivacity no doubt earned their preservation, and we may be glad of it.

'My stupid sister has mistaken all your clearest expressions,' says Henry Tilney to Catherine Morland. 'You talked of expected horrors in London; and instead of instantly conceiving as any rational creature would have done, that such words could relate only to a circulating library, she immediately pictured to herself a mob of three thousand men assembling in St. George's Fields; the Bank attacked, the Tower threatened, the streets of London flowing with blood, a detachment of the 12th Light Dragoons (the hopes of the nation) called up from Northampton to quell the insurgents, and the gallant Captain Frederick Tilney, in the moment of charging at the head of his troop, knocked off his horse by a brick-bat from an upper window. Forgive her stupidity. The fears of the sister have added to the weakness of the woman; but she is by no means a simpleton in general.'

We may compare this with a mental picture from *Pride and Prejudice.*

'In Lydia's imagination, a visit to Brighton comprised every possibility of earthly happiness. She saw, with the creative eye of fancy, the streets of that gay bathing-place covered with officers. She saw herself the object of attention to tens and scores of them at present unknown. She saw all the glories of the camp — its tents stretched forth in beauteous uniformity of lines, crowded with the young and the gay, and dazzling with scarlet; and, to complete the view, she saw herself seated beneath a tent tenderly flirting with at least six officers at once.'

§8 BACKGROUND IN VIRGINIA WOOLF: KALEIDOSCOPIC

We do not live wholly either in the physical world, or in some country of the mind, evoked by memory, fear, hope, or desire. Mrs. Woolf, and other writers, who have followed the 'association of ideas' or the 'stream of consciousness', have provided a kaleidoscopic background for their characters: they live in several worlds at once.

Here is Septimus Warren Smith, in *Mrs. Dalloway*: 'lying on the sofa in the sitting-room; watching the watery gold glow and fade with the astonishing sensibility of some live creature on the roses, on the wall-paper. Outside the trees dragged their leaves like nets through the depths of the air; the sound of water was in the room, and through the waves came the voices of birds singing. Every power poured its treasures on his head, and his hand lay there on the back of the sofa, as he had seen his hand lie when he was bathing, floating, on the top of the waves, while far away on shore he heard dogs barking and barking far away. Fear no more, says the heart in the body, fear no more.'

And it is not only in the moment of drowning that our past life swims before our eyes, not only in moments of great emotional tension that we say: 'I shall never forget this.' In a trivial, boring moment the mind may suddenly decide to focus in this way, and an indelible picture is printed on the memory. It is in the reproduction of such moments that Virginia Woolf is a unique artist. Since they are rare, one may choose one of her humorous pictures to look at: an academic luncheon-party from *Jacob's Room.*

'Mr. Plumer got up and stood in front of the fireplace, Mrs. Plumer laughed like a straightforward friendly fellow. In short, anything more horrible than the scene, the setting, the prospect, even the May garden being afflicted with chill sterility and a cloud choosing that moment to cross the sun, cannot be imagined.'

It is humorous, certainly, but the horror is real — any reader who has had experience of such a scene will feel his blood run cold.

§9 THE UPHOLSTERY OF GALSWORTHY, CONTRASTED WITH HENRY JAMES

How crude in comparison is the descriptive writing of those novelists who tackle the problem of character presentation in the reverse way, not looking, as Mrs. Woolf does, at the external world through the eyes of the soul, with its complicated double and treble vision, but describing the town, then the street, then the house, then the room, then the clothes, and then the body that enclose the soul. They hope they have got their net so tightly round the soul itself that it cannot escape them, but it always does.

Mrs. Woolf herself attacked Bennett, Galsworthy and H. G. Wells for this practice. It can hardly be better illustrated than from *The Forsyte Saga.* Each Forsyte, or group of Forsytes, is built up from the background; we learn to know them apart by their furniture or their food. Old Jolyon has a study 'full of dark-green velvet and heavily carved mahogany', and when he gives a family dinner the saddle of mutton, the Forsyte *pièce de resistance*, is from Dartmoor. Swithin has an 'elaborate group of statuary in Italian marble, which placed upon a lofty stand (also of marble), diffused an atmosphere of culture throughout the room'. His mutton is Southdown. Soames 'inhabited a house which did what it could. It owned a copper door-knocker of individual design, windows which had been altered to open outwards, . . . and at the back (a great feature) a little court tiled with jade-green tiles, and surrounded by pink hydrangeas in peacock-blue tubs.' Soames belonged to the younger generation of Forsytes, who were tired of saddle of mutton, and had something else for dinner.

This is not at all a clear way of distinguishing character. We are expressly told that Soames's house had no real originality, but was like a great many others. If you collected and multiplied traits of the kind Galsworthy has here given, you might in the end arrive at some slight discrimination of character. But it is obvious that this is an extremely laborious way of doing things. One ought rather to deduce from the character of any Forsyte, if he had been well drawn, what sort of furniture he would be likely to have, and what he would be likely to offer one if one dined with him — if it is really a matter of interest to know. But conjecture of this sort has more to do with pencil-and-paper games, and 'literary' competitions than with literature.

The careful upholstery of Galsworthy is in striking contrast with the methods of Henry James, who, if ever a novelist had an excuse for detailed furnishing of a fictitious house, had such an excuse provided by the plot of *The Spoils of Poynton*. Yet we are told very little about the beautiful Poynton, we know only that there were double doors throughout, that there were precious tapestries, that there was a crucifix from Malta which was one of the best 'pieces'. However, Mrs. Gereth and Fleda are built up in our minds as persons of exquisite taste: they worship Poynton, so of course it must be exquisite.[5]

Waterbath, the Hell of vulgarity and ugliness, whence Mona Brigstock issues to threaten the Paradise of Poynton, is made real to us, guaranteed in exactly the same way — a week-end there made both Mrs. Gereth and Fleda cry. Otherwise its atrocities are left mercifully vague: 'The house was perversely full of souvenirs of places even more ugly than itself, and of things it would have been a pious duty to forget. The worst horror was the acres of varnish, something advertised and smelly with which everything was smeared: it was Fleda Vetch's conviction that the application of it, by their own hands and hilariously shoving each other, was the amusement of the Brigstocks on rainy days.'

§ 10 BACKGROUND: SEEN OBJECTIVELY AND SUBJECTIVELY

When all is said and done, there are only two ways of looking at the background in a novel. If it is looked at objectively, it must be seen only in so far as it explains the action, like scenery in a play. The piling up of details for their own sake is tedious and irrelevant.

The subjective view of the background is only legitimate when it is the view of one of the characters; there is no excuse for the author's subjective view, except perhaps when he enters into the story as Chorus, in the capacity of Time and Fate. Dickens is present in such a capacity when he evokes the rain in Lincolnshire, the fog of the Law Courts, or other of his symbolic atmospheres.

It would be said, no doubt, in justification of Hardy, that he is likewise present on the scene as the representative of Destiny. The artistic objections to Egdon Heath are, firstly, that Hardy the countryman forgets his function as representative of Destiny when he loads his picture with details of observation — for example about the different sounds made by the wind. Next, that when Hardy remembers he is the representative of Destiny, the Destiny he represents is so vast and crushing that his characters become trivial pygmies in comparison — they cannot stand up to Egdon Heath.

BACKGROUND

The backgrounds that are satisfying in fiction are the unemotional backgrounds of Miss Austen's novels — (though she can, when she pleases, paint landscape subjectively: Elinor looks at it with Sense, Marianne with Sensibility); the grand symbolic backgrounds of Dickens; Yonville, penetrated with the emotions of Emma Bovary. The sounds we continue to hear in the memory are the splash of Wildeve's stone into the water, the thud of the ripe peach in *Madame Bovary*, the dog in *Mrs. Dalloway*, 'far away barking and barking'.

NOTES

1. *English Prose Style* (1937), p. 118.
2. loc. cit., p. 71.
3. *Les Jeunes Filles*, p. 110. cf. Proust: 'Le cadre social, le cadre de la nature, qui entoure nos amours, nous n'y pensons presque pas. La tempête fait rage sur la mer, le bateau tangue de tous côtés, du ciel se précipitent des avalanches tordues par le vent et tout au plus accordons-nous une seconde d'attention pour parer à la gêne qu'elle nous cause, à ce décor immense où nous sommes si peu de chose, et nous et le corps que nous essayons d'approcher.' *Le Temps Retrouvé*, I, pp. 192-3.
4. cit. Denys Thompson: *Reading and Discrimination*, pp. 50-1.
5. Henry James has been rewarded, and Poynton is timelessly beautiful — changes of taste leave it unaffected. If he had described it, it might have been a disaster. I am informed by Miss Margaret Jourdain, than whom there can be no greater authority, that the illustrations he permitted to appear for *The Spoils of Poynton* suggest that, as he visualized it, it was perfectly hideous.

APPENDICES

I

'CLASSICAL PLACES'

It seems convenient to append here certain passages that may be called '*loci classici*' for the novelist's art, statements of experience or principle that have found no suitable place elsewhere in this treatise. They are not offered as a coherent body of doctrine, but for what they are: 'places'. It will not therefore at all matter if there should happen to be contradictions between them.

The Novelist's Pains

PROUST

On peut presque dire que les œuvres comme dans les puits artésiens, montent d'autant plus haut que là souffrance a plus profondement creusé le cœur.

Le Temps Retrouvé, II, 66.

Les années heureuses sont les années perdues, on attend une souffrance pour travailler. L'idée de la souffrance préalable s'associe à l'idée du travail, on a peur de chaque nouvelle œuvre en pensant aux douleurs qu'il faudra supporter d'abord pour l'imaginer. Et comme on comprend que la souffrance est la meilleure chose que l'on puisse rencontrer dans la vie, on pense sans effroi, presque comme à une délivrance à la mort.

ibid., p. 68.

Certes, nous sommes obligés de revivre notre souffrance particulière avec le courage du médecin qui recommence sur lui-même la dangereuse piqûre.

ibid., p. 62.

C'est souvent seulement par manque d'esprit créateur qu'on ne va pas assez loin dans la souffrance.

Sodome et Gomorrhe, III, p. 216.

FLAUBERT

(Writing to another novelist, whose wife was fatally ill): Tu as et tu vas avoir de *bons* tableaux et tu pourras faire de *bonnes* études! C'est chèrement les payer. Les bourgeois ne se doutent guère que nous leur serrons notre cœur. La race des gladiateurs n'est pas morte, tout artiste en est un. Il amuse le public avec ses agonies.

Correspondance, III, p. 170.

The Novelist's Vocation

PROUST

Que celui qui pourrait écrire un tel livre serait heureux, pensais-je; quel labeur devant lui. Pour en donner une idée, c'est aux arts les plus élevés et les plus différents qu'il faudrait emprunter des comparaisons; car cet écrivain qui d'ailleurs pour chaque caractère aurait à en faire apparaître les faces les plus opposées, pour faire sentir son volume comme celui d'un solide, devrait préparer son livre, minutieusement, avec de perpétuels regroupements de forces, comme pour une offensive, le supporter comme une fatigue, l'accepter comme une règle, le construire comme une église, le suivre comme un régime, le vaincre comme un obstacle, le conquérir comme une amitié, le suralimenter comme un enfant, le créer comme un monde, sans laisser de côté ces mystères qui n'ont probablement leur explication que dans d'autres mondes et dont le pressentiment est ce qui nous émeut le plus dans la vie et dans l'art.

Le Temps Retrouvé, II, 239-40.

CONRAD

You must give yourself up to emotions (no easy task). You must squeeze out of yourself every sensation, every thought, every image, — mercilessly, without reserve and without remorse: you must search the darkest corners of your heart, the most remote recesses of your brain, — you must search them for the image, for the glamour, for the right expression. And you must do it sincerely, at any cost: you must do it so that at the end of your day's work you should feel exhausted, emptied of every sensation and every thought, with a blank mind and an aching heart, with the notion that there is nothing, — nothing left in you. To me it seems that it is the only way to achieve true distinction — even to go some way towards it.

loc. cit., I, p. 183.

Forethought

TROLLOPE

When we were young we used to be told, in our house at home, that 'elbow-grease' was the one essential necessary to getting a tough piece of work well done . . . Forethought is the elbow-grease which a novelist, — or a poet, or dramatist, — requires. It is not only his plot that has to be turned and re-turned in his mind, not his plot chiefly, but he has to make himself sure of his situations, of his characters, of his effects, so that when the time comes for hitting the nail he may know where to hit it on the head . . . It is from want of this special labour more frequently than from intellectual deficiency, that the tellers of stories fail so often to hit their nails on the head. To think of a story is much harder work than to write it. The author can sit down with the pen in his hand for a given time, and produce a certain number of words. That is comparatively easy, and if he have a conscience in regard to his task, work will be done regularly. But to think it over as you lie in bed, or walk about, or sit cosily over your fire, to turn it all in your thoughts, and make the things fit, — that requires elbow-grease of the mind. The arrangement of the words is as though you were walking simply along a road. The arrangement of your story is as though you were carrying a sack of flour while you walked.

Thackeray (English Men of Letters), ch. v.

Dryness

GIDE

Il arrive toujours un moment, et qui précède d'assez près celui de l'exécution, où le sujet semble se dépouiller de tout attrait, de tout charme, de toute atmosphère, même il se vide de toute signification, au point que, désépris de lui, l'on maudit cette sorte de pacte secret par quoi l'on a partie liée, et qui fait que l'on ne peut plus sans reniement s'en dédire. N'importe! on voudrait lâcher la partie. . . .

Je dis: 'on' mais après tout, je ne sais si d'autres éprouvent cela. Etat comparable sans doute à celui du catéchumène, qui, les derniers jours, et sur le point d'approcher de la table sainte, sent tout à coup sa foi défaillir et s'épouvante du vide et de la sécheresse de son cœur.

Journal des Faux-Monnayeurs.

CONRAD

And yet perhaps those days without a line, nay, without a word, the hard, atrocious, agonizing days are simply part of my *method* of work, a decreed necessity of my production.

loc. cit., II, p. 33.

Inspiration

CONRAD

One felt like walking out of a forest on to a plain — there was not much to see but one had plenty of light . . . All of a sudden I felt myself stimulated. And then ensued in my mind what a student of chemistry would best understand from the analogy of the addition of the tiniest little drop of the right kind, precipitating the process of crystallization in a test-tube containing some colourless solution.

Preface to *The Secret Agent.*

KATHERINE MANSFIELD

It was a little café and hideous, with a black marble top to the counter, *garni* with lozenges of white and orange. Chauffeurs and their wives and fat men with immense photographic apparatus sat in it. And a white fox-terrier bitch, thin and eager, ran among the tables. Against the window beat a dirty French flag, fraying out on the wind and then flapping on the glass. Does black coffee make you drunk, do you think? I felt quite enivrée . . . and could have sat three years, smoking and sipping and thinking and watching the flakes of snow. And then you know the strange silence that falls upon your heart — the same silence that comes one minute before the curtain rises. I felt that and knew that I should write here. . . .

Letters of Katherine Mansfield, I, p. 9.

FLAUBERT

Il faut se méfier de tout ce qui ressemble à l'inspiration et qui n'est souvent que du parti pris et une exaltation factice que l'on s'est donnée volontairement et qui n'est pas venue d'elle-même; d'ailleurs on ne vit pas dans l'inspiration; Pégase marche plus souvent qu'il ne galope, tout le talent est de savoir lui faire prendre des allures qu'on veut, mais pour cela ne forçons point ses moyens, comme on dit en équitation, il faut lire, méditer beaucoup, toujours penser au style et faire le moins qu'on peut, uniquement pour calmer l'irritation de l'idée qui demande à prendre une forme et qui se retourne en nous jusqu'à ce que nous lui en ayons trouvé une, exacte, précise. . . .

Correspondance, I, pp. 186-7.

MEREDITH

. . . The best fiction is the fruit of a well-trained mind. If hard study should kill your creative effort, it will be no loss to the world or you.

Letters of George Meredith, I, p. 163.

Agonizing

SAMUEL BUTLER

Never consciously agonize; the race is not to the swift, nor the battle to the strong. Moments of extreme issue are unconscious and must be left to take care of themselves. During conscious moments take reasonable pains but no more and, above all, work so slowly as never to get out of breath. Take it easy, in fact, until forced not to do so.

There is no mystery about art. Do the things that you can see, they will show you those that you cannot see. By doing what you can you will gradually get to know what it is that you want to do and cannot do, and so be able to do it.

Note-Books.

Creation of Character

PROUST

Les gens du monde se représentent volontiers les livres comme une espèce de cube, dont une face est enlevée, si bien que l'auteur se dépêche de 'faire entrer' dedans les personnes qu'il rencontre.

Sodome et Gomorrhe, I, p. 53.

Ce sont nos passions qui esquissent nos livres, le repos d'intervalle qui les écrit. Quand l'inspiration renaît, quand nous pouvons reprendre le travail, la femme qui posait devant nous pour un sentiment ne nous le fait déjà plus éprouver. Il faut continuer à la peindre d'après une autre et si c'est une trahison pour l'autre, littérairement, grâce à la similitude de nos sentiments qui fait qu'une œuvre est à la fois le souvenir de nos amours passées et la péripetie de nos amours nouvelles, il n'y a pas grand inconvénient à ces substitutions. C'est une des causes de la vanité des études où on essaye de deviner de qui parle un auteur.

Le Temps Retrouvé, II, pp. 65-6.

CONRAD

Conviction is found for others, — not for the author, only in certain contradictions and irrelevancies to the general conception of character (or characters) and of the subject. Say what you like, man lives in his eccentricities (so called) alone. They give a vigour to his personality which mere consistency can never do. One must explore deep and believe the incredible to find the few particles of truth floating in an ocean of insignificance. And before all one must divest oneself of every particle of respect for one's character.

Life and Letters, I, p. 301.

In a book you should love the idea and be scrupulously faithful to your conception of life. There lies the honour of the writer, not in fidelity to his personages. You must never allow them to decoy you out of yourself. As against your people you must preserve an attitude of perfect indifference, the part of creative power. A creator must be indifferent; because directly the 'Fiat!' has issued from his lips, there are the creatures made in his image that'll try to drag him down from his eminence, — and belittle him by their worship.

ibid., pp. 301-2.

GIDE

Il m'est certainement plus aisé de faire parler un personnage, que de m'exprimer de mon nom propre; et ceci d'autant que le personnage créé diffère de moi davantage. Je n'ai rien écrit de meilleur ni avec plus de facilité que les monologues de Lafcadio, ou que le journal d'Alissa. Ce faisant, j'oublie qui je suis, si tant est que je l'aie jamais su. Je deviens l'autre . . . Pousser l'abnégation jusqu'a l'oubli de soi total.

Journal des Faux-Monnayeurs.

Le mauvais romancier construit ses personnages; il les dirige et les fait parler. Le vrai romancier les écoute et les regarde agir; il les entend parler dès avant de les connaître.

ibid.

Observation

PROUST

La tendance centrifuge, objective des hommes qui les pousse à abdiquer, quand ils goûtent l'esprit des autres, les sévérités qu'ils auraient pour le leur, et à observer, à noter précieusement, ce qu'ils dédaigneraient de créer.

La Prisonnière, II, p. 123.

C'est que dans l'état d'esprit où l'on 'observe' on est très audessous du niveau où l'on se trouve quand on crée.

A l'Ombre des Jeunes Filles en Fleurs, III, p. 8.

Recreation of Experience in the Imagination

HENRY JAMES

No such process is *effectively* possible, we must hold, as the imputed act of transplanting . . . We can surely account for nothing in the novelist's work that hasn't passed through the crucible of his imagination, hasn't, in that perpetually simmering cauldron his intellectual *pot-au-feu*, been reduced to savoury fusion. We here figure the morsel, of course, not as boiled to nothing, but as exposed, in return for the taste it gives out, to a new and richer saturation . . . Its final savour has been constituted, but its prime identity destroyed . . . Thus it has become a different, and, thanks to a rare alchemy, a better thing. Therefore let us have here as little as possible about its 'being' Mr. This or Mrs. That. If it adjusts itself with the least truth to its new life it can't possibly be either.

The Art of the Novel, p. 230.

'Width of Range'

PROUST

Les niais s'imaginent que les grosses dimensions des phénomènes sociaux sont une excellente occasion de pénétrer plus avant dans l'âme humaine; ils devraient au contraire comprendre que c'est en descendant en profondeur dans une individualité qu'ils auraient chance de comprendre ces phenomènes.

Du Côté de Guermantes, II, p. 22.

Life and Fiction

JULIEN GREEN

Quel bizarre romancier que la vie! Comme elle repète ses effets, comme elle appuie de sa lourde main, comme elle écrit mal! Ou bien, elle revient sur ce qu'elle a dit, elle oublie le plan qu'elle avait en tête, elle se trompe de destinée et donne à l'un ce qui devait échoir a l'autre, elle rate le livre qu'elle tire à des millions d'exemplaires. Et tout à coup, de magnifiques éclairs de génie, des revirements, comme Balzac n'en rêva jamais, une audace de fou inspiré qui justifie toutes les erreurs et tous les tâtonnements.

Journal, Nov. 27th, 1932.

APPENDICES

Choice of Subjects

SAMUEL BUTLER

Do not hunt for subjects, let them choose you, not you them. Only do that which insists upon being done and runs right up against you, hitting you in the eye until you do it. This calls you and you had better attend to it, and do it as well as you can. But till called in this way do nothing.

Note-Books.

PROUST

(The narrator is here speaking to Albertine) Il est possible que les créateurs soient tentés par certaines formes de vie qu'il n'ont pas personellement éprouvées. Si je viens avec vous â Versailles . . . je vous montrerai le portrait de l'honnête homme par excellence, du meilleur des maris, Choderlos de Laclos, qui a écrit le plus effroyablement pervers des livres, et juste en face celui de Madame de Genlis qui écrivit des contes moraux et ne se contenta pas de tromper la duchesse d'Orléans, mais la supplicia en détournant d'elle ses enfants.

La Prisonnière, II, p. 240.

'*Representation*'

HENRY JAMES

The novelist who doesn't represent, and represent 'all the time' is lost, exactly as much lost as the painter who, at his work and given his intention, doesn't paint all the time.

loc. cit., p. 94.

Working out economically almost anything is the very life of the art of representation; just as the request to take on trust, tinged with the least extravagance, is the very death of the same.

ibid., p. 224.

The Pleasure of Writing

PROUST

Ecrire est pour un écrivain une fonction saine et nécessaire dont l'accomplissement rend heureux, comme pour les hommes physiques, l'exercice, la sueur et le bain.

Le Temps Retrouvé, II, p. 57.

The Writer's Duty

PROUST

Dès le début de la guerre, M. Barrès avait dit que l'artiste . . . doit avant tout servir la gloire de sa patrie. Mais il ne peut la servir qu'en étant artiste, c'est-à-dire qu'à condition au moment où il étudie les lois de l'Art . . . de ne pas penser à autre chose — fût-ce la patrie — qu'à la vérité qui est devant lui.

ibid., p. 38.

The Christian Novelist

Profero etiam Domine (si digneris propitius intueri), tribulationes plebium, pericula populorum, captivorum gemitus, miserias orphanorum, necessitates peregrinorum, inopiam debilium, desperationes languentium, defectus senum, suspiria iuvenum, vota virginum, lamenta viduarum.

Roman Missal.

II

THE 'HALLUCINATION' THEORY OF *THE TURN OF THE SCREW*

THE 'hallucination' theory of *The Turn of the Screw* is best known in the discussion of it by Mr. Edmund Wilson in *The Triple Thinkers*, though he disclaims having originated it. He states it as follows: 'according to this theory, the young governess who tells the story is a neurotic case of sex repression; and the ghosts are not real ghosts at all but merely the hallucinations of the governess.' This theory has been argued with such persuasiveness that it is time to refute it, and it can be refuted both by internal and external evidence.

Mr. Wilson analyses the story at length, in the interests of his theory, and it will be well to provide an analysis of the story on its face-value.

In the prologue one Douglas introduces the governess's manuscript. He makes it clear that he completely believes in her story, and regards her as a person of the greatest distinction of mind and character. She is the daughter of a clergyman; in answer to an advertisement she comes up to London, and is offered a post by a rich, young bachelor who wants a governess for his orphaned niece and nephew. The conditions attached to the post are that she is to take complete responsibility, and never bother the guardian about his wards. She accepts; it is admitted that she has fallen in love with her employer. She goes to Bly, his house in Essex, where Flora, the little girl, has been left with the housekeeper, Mrs. Grose, and some servants.

She learns that the boy, Miles, has been expelled from his school: no reason is given. She also learns from Mrs. Grose that the former governess, Miss Jessel, went away, and died: Mrs. Grose is obviously unwilling to pursue the subject.

In his analysis of this part of the story it is hard not to feel that Mr. Wilson has been slightly disingenuous, attempting to show the morbid mind of the governess. 'The boy, she finds, has been sent home from school for reasons into which she does not inquire but which she colours, on no evidence at all, with a significance somehow sinister . . . She learns that the former governess left, and that she has since died, under circumstances, which are not explained but which are made in the same way to seem ominous.'

After a period of halcyon days when the children are at their most charming, and when the governess thinks all that is needed to complete her felicity is the presence of their guardian, approving her endeavours for them, there comes a change 'actually like the spring of a beast'.

The figure of a man appears on one of the two towers of Bly, first taken by her for the master, and then seen obviously not to be he. Later he appears at the outside of a ground-floor window. She observes that he is wearing smart clothes, not his own. Mrs. Grose at once identifies the description: he is a valet of the master's, Peter Quint, who had once been in charge at Bly, and used to wear his master's clothes — Quint was dead. Mrs. Grose also reveals that he was a bad character, and that he was 'too free' with Miles, and 'too free' with everyone. The governess believes that he has come back to haunt the children, and that it is her duty to protect them.

Soon afterwards the governess is sitting by the side of the lake, and Flora is playing near her. She becomes aware of the presence of a third person on the other side of the lake. Flora has her back to the water: 'she had picked up a small flat piece of wood which happened to have in it a little hole that had evidently suggested to her the idea of sticking in another fragment that might figure as a mast and make the thing a boat. This second morsel, as I watched her, she was very markedly and intently attempting to tighten in its place.' She looks up and sees a handsome but evil woman in black, whom she concludes to be her predecessor. Mrs. Grose confirms that Miss Jessel was 'infamous', reveals that she had an affair with Quint, and implies that she went home to have a child by him, and died in consequence. The governess believes, encouraged in this belief by Mrs. Grose, that the children knew of and connived at the affair between Quint and Miss Jessel, and had been in some way corrupted by them; she further believes that they know that their dead friends haunt Bly.

At this point Mr. Wilson states, correctly, that there is no proof of anyone but the governess having seen the apparitions. He also calls attention to the Freudian imagery; the little girl's symbolic game with the pieces of wood, which so held the governess's gaze, and the first apparition of the male spectre on a tower, of the female behind a lake. These points will be considered later.

The only circumstance he admits as contradictory to his hypothesis that the ghosts are hallucinations, is the fact that the governess's description of the first ghost is identified by Mrs. Grose as Quint, of whom she has not yet heard. With great ingenuity he tries to show that she has built him up out of a chance hint from Mrs. Grose that there had been someone else in the place, other than the master, who 'liked every one young and pretty'. However, the description of Quint is so circumstantial that it cannot be so easily explained away. Furthermore, Miss Jessel is also seen distinctly before the governess has any details about her, and she is convinced of her 'infamy', although the worst Mrs. Grose had ever hinted was that she was not sufficiently 'careful' in some matters. Before her appearance behind the lake, nothing was known to her successor of Miss Jessel's affair with Quint: we are expressly told that there had been no servants' gossip. But the chief objection to the hallucination theory is the character of the governess herself, so carefully established in the prologue, and maintained throughout the story as that of a girl keeping her balance and courage in the most frightful circumstances.

After a second brief, halcyon period 'there suddenly came an hour' the narrator tells us, 'after which, as I look back, the affair seems to me to have been all pure suffering'. There is a third appearance of Quint, and the mysterious conduct of the children convinces the governess that they are in touch with the ghosts. 'They're his and hers . . . Quint's and that woman's', she tells Mrs. Grose. 'They want to get to them.' Quint and Miss Jessel are coming back to keep the children safe for Evil. Mrs. Grose wants the governess to write to their uncle, but she decides that she must keep to her pledge that he is not to be bothered.

The children keep up the fiction that their uncle is coming to see them. Miles asks the governess when he is going to school again, and says that he will get his uncle to come down to Bly. This plunges her into an agony of indecision, and she is tempted to run away from the situation, but decides that she ought not to desert her post. Mr. Wilson states at this point: 'she is now apparently in love with the boy' — but this is not apparent on a natural reading of the text.

There follows the second appearance of Miss Jessel, and a curious manifestation in Miles's room where Mr. Wilson admits that the supernatural element can only be explained away by throwing doubt not only on the governess's explanation of her sensations, but on her record of the sensations themselves. 'She has felt a "gust of frozen air" and yet sees that the window is "tight". Are we to suppose she merely fancied that she felt it?' We shall see later the value of this admission.

Flora, having been lost, is found by the side of the lake. The governess for the first time names the ghost: 'Where, my pet, is Miss Jessel?' she asks. The dead governess appears, dreadfully, across the lake: 'she was there, so I was justified, she was there, so I was neither cruel or mad.' (The first person to examine the 'hallucination' theory is the governess herself.) Mrs. Grose does not see the apparition, and Flora denies that she sees it, turning in a violent reaction of hatred against the living governess. She continues in this state, and is sent up to London with Mrs. Grose.

Miles and the governess are left alone together. She presses him to tell her why he was expelled from school, and he confesses. He 'said' things — to 'a few', to those he liked, and they must have repeated them 'to those they liked'. 'It all sounds very harmless', is Mr. Wilson's extraordinary comment. It is hard to imagine anything more harmful: the little boy of innocent, even angelic appearance, with a mind filled with the abominations of Quint and Miss Jessel, spreading his dirty secrets round the school. In a moment the governess has seen an even more dreadful possibility: 'there had come to me out of my very pity the appalling alarm of his being perhaps innocent.' He might have been the innocent carrier of the germs of corruption, punished unjustly for carrying them.

This is the moment of the governess's victory, when Miles's soul is purged by confession, and there is complete confidence between them. Quint makes a last attempt against him; the boy does not see the apparition at the window, but the governess cries: 'No more, no more, no more!' 'Is she here?' asks the boy, and names Miss Jessel. Mr. Wilson comments, in direct contradiction to the text: 'He has, in spite of the governess's efforts, succeeded in seeing his sister and has heard from her of the incident at the lake.' We have Mrs. Grose's word, as well as the governess's that the children have not met — but Mr. Wilson is bound to go to this length if he is to keep his theory.

The governess says that it is not Miss Jessel. 'It's *he*?' asks Miles — whom does he mean by 'he?' she inquires. 'Peter Quint — you devil!'

She holds him in her arms, shows him the figure has vanished, he gives a cry, and dies in her arms. On the 'hallucination' theory she has frightened him to death. On a natural reading he dies, worn out by the struggle between good and evil, in the moment of triumph, like Morgan Moreen in *The Pupil*.

The 'hallucination' theory can then only be held:

(1) If we disbelieve Douglas's estimate of the governess's character.

(2) If we give a very strained explanation of her description of Quint.

(3) If we believe she is deluded about the very sense-data experienced in Miles's room, not only about her interpretation of them.

(4) If we believe, on no evidence, that Miles had got into touch with Flora after the scene by the Lake.

But the chief objection is one of general impression: this is not what the story means, and only perverted ingenuity, of a kind which has little to do with literature, could have detected the 'clue'. This is the ultimate answer to all such theories, from the Shakespeare-Bacon controversy to Verrall's brilliant perversities about Greek tragedy. Here there is a desire for a 'scientific' explanation, an unwillingness to make the necessary 'suspension of disbelief' in ghosts, which is completely opposed to the spirit in which the book should be read. It is only because Mr. Wilson is such a distinguished critic that the theory is worth further examination, and final refutation.

Mr. Wilson cites the preface to *The Turn of the Screw* as external proof of his theory.

(1) 'Peter Quint and Miss Jessel are not "ghosts" at all, as we now know the ghost, but goblins, elves, imps, demons as loosely constructed as those of the old trials for witchcraft.'

(2) Henry James speaks of 'our young woman's keeping crystalline her record of so many intense anomalies and absurdities — *by which I don't of course mean her explanation of them, a different matter* . . .' (Mr. Wilson's italics). Mr. Wilson says of the words in italics: 'These words seem impossible to explain except on the hypothesis of hallucination.'

But if we believe 'our young woman's' record of the actual happenings to be 'crystalline' clear, it is on that alone extremely difficult to accept the hypothesis of hallucination, as I have already shown. Moreover the preface itself shows us how we can doubt her explanation of the happenings, without supposing her to be the victim of hallucination. She clearly believes that she sees the spirits that once animated the earthly bodies of Quint and Miss Jessel; we can believe that she did indeed see *ab extra* apparitions, that another person with the right vision could have seen, without accepting her view of their eschatological status. They are not spirits of the dead, matter for psychical research, but 'goblins damned' — devils that have assumed the form of Quint and Miss Jessel to tempt the children. And this is surely the clear meaning of what Henry James says in the preface.

If Henry James was trying to hint in his preface that the ghosts were hallucinations, then he went about this in a very tortuous way; it seems rather that he has there alone provided enough evidence to discredit this theory. Yet Mr. Wilson writes: 'When we look back in the light of these hints, we become convinced that the whole story has been primarily intended as a characterization of the governess.' If this is what he really intended, then we can only explain Henry James's references to *The Turn of the Screw* in his letters on the hypothesis that he was a pathological liar.

As he nearly always did, Henry James began to construct this story not from a character, but from a scrap of anecdote. This scrap of anecdote had been told him by Archbishop Benson at Addington: 'the vaguest essence only was there — some dead servants and some children. This essence *struck* me and I made a note of it (of a most scrappy kind) on going home.'

On the character of the governess his letter to H. G. Wells is quite final: 'Of course I had, about my young woman to take a very sharp line. The grotesque business I had to make her picture and the childish psychology I had to make her trace and present, were, for me at least a very difficult job, in which absolute lucidity and logic, and a singleness of effect, were imperative. Therefore I had to rule out subjective complications of her own — play of tone, etc., and keep her impersonal save for the most obvious and indispensable little note of courage — without which she wouldn't have had her data.'

In short, the governess is the Jamesian observer or narrator, deliberately left *flou*, and only characterized up to the point which will make her observation plausible. The point of the story lies in the original anecdote told by the Archbishop.

Mr. Wilson argues that it lacks 'serious point' unless sex-frustration is the point; and he links it with Henry James's studies of spinsters in *The Bostonians* or *The Marriages*. But the affinity is surely rather with *The Pupil* or *What Maisie Knew*, those other studies of children isolated in an evil world. With *Maisie*, published in 1896, a year previous to *The Turn of the Screw*, the affinity is particularly close: that book ends with the rescue of a small child by a faithful governess from possible corruption at the hands of two immoral step-parents. Of *The Turn of the Screw* Henry James wrote to F. W. Myers: 'the thing I most wanted not to fail of doing, under penalty of extreme platitude, was to give the impression of the communication to the children of the most infernal imaginable evil and danger — the condition, on their part, of being as *exposed* as we can humanly conceive children to be.' This is surely a sufficiently serious point, and the fact that the details of the Evil are left to our imagination, links *The Turn of the Screw* with other stories of Henry James's where a secret is never revealed to the reader, e.g. *The Figure in the Carpet* and *Owen Wingrave*.

The data given by the Archbishop to Henry James were an old

house, and two children haunted by dead servants with the design of 'getting hold' of them. He has added a governess, a rich and handsome guardian, and an old housekeeper. Whence do these three figures derive? Probably from *Jane Eyre*. Jane Eyre went as governess to the orphaned ward of a rich bachelor (as she thought him), and had a housekeeper for company; she also was in love with her employer. When the first apparition of Quint is seen, the governess of *The Turn of the Screw* asks herself: 'Was there a "secret" at Bly — a mystery of Udolpho or an insane, an unmentionable relative kept in unsuspected confinement?' It is much to say that she had read *Jane Eyre* as well as *Udolpho*; the events of *The Turn of the Screw* are dated about the time of the publication of Charlotte Brontë's novel. But Henry James must have read *Jane Eyre*, and it is hard to resist the conviction that he was here thinking of the mad Mrs. Rochester. It is from literature rather than from the abnormal psychology of himself or his governess that the relation between her and the ghosts arises.

All that is left of the hallucination theory after close examination is the fact, on which it is based, of the sexual imagery of *The Turn of the Screw*: the man appears for the first time on a tower, wearing the clothes of his master, with whom the governess is in love; Miss Jessel appears for the first time behind a lake; Flora plays a symbolic game with pieces of wood — even the name of the story might be added. This is an interesting discovery, but it is dangerous to draw too many conclusions from it.

Mr. Stephen Spender makes the following comment in *The Destructive Element*: 'The only difficulty is that if the imagery were worked out consciously, it is hardly likely that James would have anticipated Freud with such precision. The horrible solution suggests itself that the story is an unconscious sexual fantasy, or that James has entered into the repressed governess's situation with an intuition that imposed on it a deeper meaning than he had intended.'

This is not, as we have seen 'the only difficulty'. And fortunately a solution can be found less distasteful than to call (however indirectly) a great writer a 'repressed governess'.

The sexual imagery is of a surface nature, the decoration of the story and not the story itself — it is giving it quite a disproportionate importance to call the story a 'sexual fantasy' on the strength of it — one might as well, on the strength of Miss Spurgeon's discoveries, say that *Romeo and Juliet* was a sun myth, because the dominating image in that play is Light.

The imagery in *The Turn of the Screw* one need hardly doubt comes from the subconscious of an author, who was not aware of its sexual significance. Nor need that conclusion alarm us: let us consider what his conscious intelligence was at the moment triumphantly doing — it was making a great work of art out of a diabolically dirty story, treating the theme both with candour and with crystalline purity. If some unresolved elements lingering in the unconscious have found their resolution in the imagery, and have added to the total atmosphere of evil, it is only another illustration of the way that everything sometimes works together for good when a novelist is producing a great novel. If we are aware of the symbolism, and do not let it delude us, it adds to our appreciation of *The Turn of the Screw*.

Addendum. The recently published *Notebooks of Henry James* reveal that even the lake and the tower were implied in the Archbishop's story. The ghosts invite and solicit the children 'from across dangerous places ... so that the children may destroy themselves, lose themselves, by responding, by getting into their power'. Henry James adds: 'The story to be told—tolerably obviously—by an outside spectator, observer.' *The Notebooks of Henry James*, ed. F. O. Mathiessen and Kenneth B. Murdock (New York, 1947), pp. 178-9.

III

THE NOVELS OF I. COMPTON-BURNETT

A BRIEF BIBLIOGRAPHY

Dolores, 1911
Pastors and Masters, 1925
Brothers and Sisters, 1929
Men and Wives, 1931
More Women Than Men, 1933
A House and Its Head, 1935
Daughters and Sons, 1937
A Family and A Fortune, 1939
Parents and Children, 1941
Elders and Betters, 1944
A Conversation between I. Compton-Burnett and M. Jourdain (in *Orion: a miscellany*), 1945
Manservant and Maidservant, 1947

THE indebtedness of Miss Compton-Burnett to Jane Austen is generously acknowledged. It is the mark of one of her insincere or self-complacent characters that he does not much care for Jane Austen's novels.

'"What do you think of Miss Jane Austen's books, Jermyn," said Dominic, "if I may approach so great a man upon a comparatively flimsy subject?"

"Our row of green books with the pattern on the backs, Rachel?" said Sir Percy with a sense of adequacy in conversation. "Very old-fashioned, aren't they?"

"What do the ladies think of the author, the authoress, for she is of their own sex?" said Dominic.

"I have a higher standard for greatness," said Agatha, "but I don't deny she has great qualities. I give her the word great in that sense."

"You put that very well, Mrs. Calkin," said Dominic. "I feel I must become acquainted with the fair writer."'

The world that the two novelists depict is normally a limited one, the families at the big house, the rectory, and one or two other houses in an English village. Their social world ranges from a baronet to a respectable upper servant. In *Pastors and Masters* Miss Compton-Burnett has drawn a very vivid picture of a preparatory-school, but in her women's college in *Dolores* or her girl's school in *More Women than Men* little more education is shown taking place than in Mrs. Goddard's school in *Emma*; she has chosen the school simply as an example, like the family, of a group of people living too closely together. The men in her books are doctors or clergy, or are present for long week-ends — having work in London and outside the books — or else they have retired from their professions, or never had any. 'Their professions and occupations are indicated', she says in the *Conversation*, 'but I am concerned with their personal lives; and following them into their professional world would lead to the alternations between two spheres, that I think is a mistake in books. I always regret it in the great Victorian novelists, though it would be hard to avoid it in books on a large scale.'

Why has she chosen this world, and why has she dated the action of her books some time between 1888 and 1902?[1]

Not out of a desire to imitate — Jane Austen is inimitable, and Miss Compton-Burnett has a very original mind. Nor has she acted out of nostalgia for a quiet, old-fashioned world: there is nothing quaint about her work, any more than there is about Miss Austen's — no period properties and no local colour.

She herself claims that she is accepting her limitations: 'I do not feel that I have any real or organic knowledge of life later than about 1910. I should not write of later times with enough grasp or confidence. I think this is why many writers tend to write of the past. When an age is ended, you see it as it is. And I have a dislike, which I cannot explain, of dealing with modern machinery and inventions. When war casts its shadow, I find that I recoil.'

Such a recognition of her range is in itself admirable, but it is impossible not to see more than that in the limitations within which she works. She is writing the pure novel, as Jane Austen did, concentrating upon human beings and their mutual reactions. So rare is such concentration in the English novel that any writer who conscientiously practises it is almost sure to be accused of 'imitating Jane Austen' whether their minds are alike or not: and the minds of Miss Austen and Miss Compton-Burnett are in many ways alike.

[1] The events of *Pastors and Masters* take place after 1918: this is the one exception.

The isolation of her characters (and in all her novels except *Dolores* and *More Women Than Men* there is strict unity of place) brings them into clearer relief, and enables their creator to do her real business, the study and revelation of human nature, with greater freedom. This isolation of the characters, and their lack of interest in social conditions outside the family, or in economic problems apart from those of the family fortunes, is made more credible by isolating them in time as well as in place — situating them in a period when the impact of public events on private individuals was less immediate and crushing than at present. Therefore she has chosen the end of Queen Victoria's reign. A few years earlier, and she would have been obliged to weight down her books with the trappings of the historical novel: as it is, she has obtained a liberating absence of contemporaneity at the small cost of substituting carriages for cars.

As if to boast of her freedom, her references to Politics are deliberately and engagingly flat. 'So you see, Parliament thought that Bill a wrong one, and it was thrown out,' Mr. Burgess observes to one of his pupils in *Pastors and Masters*; and Duncan Edgeworth in *A House and its Head* asks: 'You don't think this election business will follow that course?'

Miss Compton-Burnett has freed herself from all irrelevances in order to write the pure novel. And like Miss Austen she has a dislike for merely descriptive writing, which she uses with even greater economy.[1] The village which is to be the scene of action is undescribed and, except for Moreton Edge in *Brothers and Sisters*, is not even named. Characters are often tersely but completely described, in terms which do not remain in the memory, and it is necessary to turn back if we wish to remind ourselves of their appearance.

'Duncan Edgeworth was a man of medium height and build, appearing both to others and himself to be tall. He had narrow, grey eyes, stiff, grey hair and beard, a solid, aquiline face, young for his sixty-six years, and a stiff, imperious bearing. His wife was a small, spare, sallow woman, a few years younger, with large, kind prominent eyes, a long, thin, questioning nose, and a harried, innocent, somehow fulfilled expression.'

One is inclined to wonder if much would be lost by the suppression of such passages. The author herself observes in the *Conversation*:

[1] She will introduce cushions, like an easily portable stage-property, as an emblem of prosperity. Peter (in *Brothers and Sisters*) spills his tea over Sophia's cushions. Sabine Ponsonby (in *Daughters and Sons*) puts out cushions only when visitors are expected. Hope Cranmer (in *Parents and Children*) has cushions, and the Marlowes haven't.

'I am sure that everyone forms his own conceptions, that are different from everyone else's, including the author's.'

Dialogue, to which in *Emma* Jane Austen had begun to give a far more important place, is the staple of this writer's work. It is a dialogue of a power and brilliance unmatched in English prose fiction. In her early and immature book, *Dolores*, the machine creaked audibly at times, but already functioned with precision. The style of that book is crude, bare and rather alarming. It is not like real English: it is like the language of translation. It reminds one of English translations of Russian novels and of Greek tragedy, and one may conjecture that both of them had formed an important part of her reading. Such a style is uneuphonious and harsh, but conscientiously renders a meaning — and that is what, like a translator, Miss Compton-Burnett already did, with a remarkable exactitude.

This ungainly, but precise language was later evolved into a dialogue, more dramatic than narrative, which, whether in longer speeches, or in the nearest equivalent in English to Greek tragic stichomythia, is an unrealistic but extraordinarily intense vehicle for the characters' thoughts and emotions, and enables their creator to differentiate them sharply, and, whenever she wishes, to condemn them out of their own mouths. Its nearness to or remoteness from ordinary spoken language will vary from place to place. There is no single formula that will cover it, and the author has indicated that no kind of 'figure in the carpet' is to be sought: 'it is simply the result of an effort to give the impression I want to give'.

'The key', says one critic, 'is the realization that her characters speak precisely as they are thinking.' This key will not unlock more than a part of her work: part of the utterances of her good characters, and the utterances of exceptionally simple or straightforward characters.

For she excels particularly at the revelation of insincerity on all its levels: from that of characters who tell flat lies, to that of characters who have deceived themselves into believing what they say. In between are characters such as Dominic Spong, who are more than half-aware and are wholly tolerant of their own smarminess and their own insincere ways of talking: 'if I may approach so great a man upon a comparatively flimsy subject.'

Her idiom sometimes approximates to what one might actually say if one were in the character's skin and situation, but also to what one might think and conceal; to what one might think of saying and bite back; to what one might afterwards wish one had said; to what one would like other people to think; and to what one would like to think oneself. It is unlikely that these alternatives are exclusive. A full analysis, with the necessary illustrations, would require the full-length book that should be written on Miss Compton-Burnett's work.

A resemblance to Jane Austen may be noted in the use of stilted or unmeaning language to indicate a bad or insincere character. The pretentious vulgarity of Mrs. Elton with her 'Caro Sposo' or 'Hymen's saffron robe', the frigid pomposity of Sir Edward Denham's thoughts on the Novel, or of General Tilney's compliments to Catherine Morland have frequent parallels — generally in the speech of characters who pride themselves on their superior sensitiveness, subtlety, public spirit, or culture.

A speech of Dulcia Bode in *A House and Its Head* contains many of the worst horrors pilloried by Fowler in *Modern English Usage*. Fowler shows that such faults are not merely faults of expression, but generally spring from real faults in feeling and character; they are not merely due to faulty taste, but to moral faults — insincerity, vanity, cowardice, and more.

' "Now, Mother dear, lift up your head and your heart. Mr. Edgeworth has not roused himself from his own shock and sorrow — yes, and shame; for it must be almost that — to point us in our direction, without looking for a touch of resilience and response. We can best repay him by throwing up our heads, facing the four winds squarely, and putting our best foot foremost out of the morass, and also out of his house." '

Here are BATTERED ORNAMENTS, HACKNEYED PHRASES, IRRELEVANT ALLUSION, MIXED METAPHOR and FACETIOUS ZEUGMA. Elsewhere in the utterances of this irrepressible character are POLYSYLLABIC HUMOUR ('I suspect I shall come by a good deal of refreshment in the course of my peregrinations'), SUPERIORITY ('if I may be Irish') and many other atrocities.

Dulcia, however, is not a mere Slipslop or Malaprop, but a very penetrating delineation of an unsubtle and insensitive nature given to uncontrolled self-dramatization, and to the dramatization of her environment. Many other characters betray themselves by their speech, and some in ways too subtle to be illustrated by a brief citation. This feature of her style, alone, would make Miss Compton-Burnett a most remarkable writer.

Besides the terse descriptions of characters there are a few short descriptions of action, or brief paragraphs of introduction or transition, such as the exquisitely phrased entrance of Miss Charity Marcon in *Daughters and Sons*.

'Miss Charity Marcon walked up her garden path, crossed her hall and entered her plain little drawing-room, her great height almost coinciding with the door, and her long neck bending, lest the experience of years should prove at fault and it should quite coincide with it.'

Since the short study *Pastors and Masters*, published in 1925 after a fourteen years' silence, Miss Compton-Burnett has been completely mistress of her unique style, which has she used in increasing perfection in the novels that have followed. The texture is so close and dramatic that quotation of isolated passages is almost impossible without leaving a misleading impression. The detachment by reviewers of some of her comic passages, which are the most easily quotable, has perhaps tended to give the impression that she is only a humorous writer, and to obscure the fact, intensely humorous though she often is, that her ironic view of family life is also serious, and even tragic.

Miss Austen drew family tyranny in two characters: General Tilney in *Northanger Abbey* and Mrs. Norris in *Mansfield Park*. After her time family life went into a darker period. Victorian parents (though there were charming people among them) sometimes identified themselves with God, and modelled their behaviour towards their children upon that of Jehovah towards the Children of Israel at their most recalcitrant — and they claimed divine authority for their worst excesses. Theobald and Christina in *The Way of All Flesh* are terrifying family tyrants: they are closely drawn from Samuel Butler's own parents. Novels of the period are full of fearful autocracy, approved by the Victorian authors. There are plenty of memoirs to substantiate the evidence with genuine atrocity stories. Even in our own century, when the bonds of family life have greatly relaxed, the domestic dictator still horribly flourishes. You would not believe what goes on behind the façade of many a comfortable family residence. Those whose own lives have been happy in this respect, are shocked and incredulous when they obtain an insight into the terrors of family life as it can be lived. As one of Miss Compton-Burnett's characters observes: 'people do not know about families.'

The subject-matter of all her books — tyranny in family life — is therefore neither unreal nor unimportant. On the contrary, it is one of the most important that a novelist could choose. The desire for domination, which in a dictator can plunge the world into misery, can here be studied in a limited sphere. The courage of those who resist dictation, and the different motives which cause people to range themselves on the side of the dictator can be minutely studied. In avoiding contemporary chatter about public events, Miss Burnett has gone instead to the heart of the matter:

her works provide one with more penetrating social criticism than all propagandist fiction put together. The moral is this — and it is both edifying and beautiful — if a novelist refuses to be seduced by the clamour of contemporary fashion into a dissertation upon economics, politics, the philosophy of history or the like, and if he is true to his calling, which is the study of human nature, then all these other things will be given to him. He will inevitably be a social critic, a philosopher of history.

In each of the novels there is a tyrant; family tyranny is always an important, usually the most important theme. In *Dolores* the selfish claims of Cleveland Hutton are always liable to break up the academic career which his daughter has made for herself — in this youthful book her self-sacrifice is regarded as noble: in the later books it would have been thought horrible. In *Pastors and Masters* Henry Bentley, another clergyman, makes his children the victims of his nervous depression. In *Brothers and Sisters* Sophia Stace, and in *Men and Wives* Harriet Haslam are tyrannical and devouring mothers, though they differ from each other in their aims and methods, and their mental make-up.

The following scene, between Sophia Stace, her children and their former nurse, on the evening after her husband's funeral, is one of the author's finest comic scenes, but it is merely comic only to those who are too insensitive to see that the family tyrant is as evil as the dictator, and ethically far less easily defensible.

'"I don't know whether you all like sitting there, having your dinner, with your mother eating nothing? On this day of all days! I don't know if you have thought of it."

"Oh, I understood that you wouldn't have anything," said Patty, rising and hurrying to her side with food. "I am sure I thought you said that."

"I may have said those words," said Sophia. "It is true that I do not want anything. I hardly could, could I? But I may need it. It may be all the more necessary for me, for that reason. I don't think I should be left without a little pressing to-day, sitting here, as I am, with my life emptied. I hardly feel you should let me depend quite on myself."

Her children's power of rising to such demand was spent. Patty pressed food with a simply remorseful face.

"No, I will not have anything," said Sophia, with her eyes on the things in a way that gave Dinah one of her glimpses of her mother as pathetic. "Nobody minds whether I do or not; and that would be the only thing that would persuade me, somebody's caring. I can't make the effort alone."

"Here, come, try some of this," said Dinah. "It is so light you can get it down without noticing."

"And this, and this," said Andrew, coming forward with a dish in each hand, and an air of jest.

"Darlings!" said Sophia, taking something from Dinah. "Dear ones! Yes, I will try to eat a little to please you. Let me have something from you, my Andrew. I will do my best." '

Josephine Napier, in *More Women Than Men*, is a more subtle type of tyrant, who is able to lead as well as drive her family and colleagues into obedience; she is the most attractive and the most dangerous of the tyrants, and the only one who combines that role with murder. Duncan Edgeworth, in *A House and Its Head*, has the superior honesty and directness of the male oppressor, but his oppression is the more open and ruthless. In *Daughters and Sons*, the matriarch, Sabine Ponsonby, and her unbalanced daughter, Hetta, both tyrannize over their household. In *A Family and A Fortune*, Matilda Seaton tries to tyrannize over her richer relations, and succeeds in making the life of her paid companion impossible. The tyranny of the grandfather, Sir Jesse Sullivan, in *Parents and Children*, and of the invalid aunt, Sukey Donne, in *Elders and Betters* come less in the middle of the picture of those two books, and yet are the cause of most of the happenings.

In most cases it is the economic dependence of other people upon them that enables the tyrants to exercise their shocking power — but this is not always the case. Some people who are not economically dependent submit to it, because they are bound in affection to others who are economically dependent, and therefore wish to live in the tyrant's house. And of course Miss Compton-Burnett is too subtle to accept the economic explanation as the only one. In some cases it has nothing to do with the question. Three of her tyrannical aunts hold no purse strings, and one of them is, on the contrary, a poor relation, a dependant — at any rate as far as extra comforts are concerned — on the family which she dominates by her will. Such was the position of Mrs. Norris in *Mansfield Park*.

Tyranny in the family generates a tense electric atmosphere in which anything might happen. Every thought, however outrageous, is given full and clear expression — for not only do the tyrants say exactly what they think, so, oddly, do their victims as well. The equivalent of the play-scenes in *Mansfield Park* are invested with the grimness of the play-scenes in *Hamlet*. A family conversation at the breakfast table is so pregnant with horror, that one feels things cannot go on like this for long; the storm must break some time. One is quite right, it does break. This may happen in one of two ways, but there will probably be violent happenings. It is the great distinction of Miss Compton-Burnett among highly civilized writers that her violence is always entirely credible.[1]

Violent action shakes up the characters in a novel, and it is foolish of writers to despise the strong situation: it may be most revealing about human behaviour. Mr. Forster says, with some justice, that in the domain of violent physical action Jane Austen is feeble and ladylike. Miss Compton-Burnett is neither: she comes serenely to violence like the great tragic artist that she is. She has so effectively prepared the way for it that when it inevitably comes, like war after a crisis, it is immediately felt to be a clearing of the air. The crime or adultery is seen to be less shocking than the daily cruelty at the breakfast table. After the violence has died down, the chief characters, completely revealed, and to some extent participating in the purge by pity and terror, which has been the lot of readers and minor characters alike, resume their old life rather more quietly, and everything is hushed up, though everyone knows.

The violent happenings are of two sorts, as in Greek tragedy: either there is a crime, or the discovery of something dreadful in the past. These respectable families, descendants it might be of Jane Austen's Bennets, Bertrams or Knightleys, have within them the same seeds of destruction as the houses of Oedipus or of Agamemnon. Those happenings in that setting produce the effect which Miss Elizabeth Bowen has well described as 'sinister cosiness'.

If we read the *faits divers* in the newspapers we are apt to find unexplained and mysterious happenings: sometimes we meet with them in our own circle of acquaintance. A devoted husband and wife suddenly separate; a brilliant boy is found hanging in his bedroom. We do not know why, but there are some people who know, and who will take care that we never know. How many more must be the happenings we know nothing of at all. 'I think there are signs that strange things happen, though they do not emerge', says Miss Compton-Burnett. 'I believe it would go ill with many of us, if we were faced by a strong temptation, and I suspect that with some of us it does go ill.'

She shows us how strange things happen — she really shows us how. She traces them from their roots in the characters of the people to whom they happen. Therefore there is no vulgar melodrama, no matter how sensational the happenings are.

In *Pastors and Masters*, a mainly humorous study, the crime is only

[1] The present writer must admit some difficulty in accepting the fraud in *Parents and Children*.

a fairly harmless literary forgery. In *Brothers and Sisters* it is found that Sophia Stace's husband was also her half-brother; and the secret of Christian Stace's parentage has caused other tangled relationships, which nearly become incestuous. The source of inspiration is again acknowledged. One of the characters remarks: 'We are beginning to leave off feeling branded, but all our friends seem shy of us. It is too like an ancient tragedy for them.'

In *Men and Wives*, Matthew Haslam poisons his domineering mother. In *More Women Than Men*, Josephine is morally, though not legally guilty of her nephew's wife's death. In *A House and Its Head*, Grant Edgeworth commits adultery with his uncle's second wife; their child is acknowledged as Duncan Edgeworth's son and heir, and is murdered by a servant at the instance of Sibyl, Grant's wife and Duncan's daughter, in order to remove the bar to Grant's inheritance of the family estate. In *Daughters and Sons* the crime is no more than a pretended (perhaps really attempted) suicide by Hetta Ponsonby. There is no crime or guilty secret in *A Family and A Fortune*, though two characters are driven to leave their homes sensationally in a snow-storm. Fraud of one sort or another is practised in *Parents and Children* and *Elders and Betters*: in the former it is dramatically unmasked, in the latter it remains triumphant — moreover the niece who has burnt one aunt's will drives another aunt to suicide.

The connection between tyranny and violence is generally causal. In *Men and Wives* the tyrant is the direct victim of the crime; in *More Women Than Men* and *Daughters and Sons* a tyrant, in the danger of losing power, commits the crime in an attempt to preserve her domination. In *A House and Its Head* the tense family atmosphere, caused by Duncan's tyranny, is itself the cause of Sibyl's lack of mental balance, and of her crime. In the last two books the causation is less immediate — but it is the tyranny of Sir Jesse Sullivan that encourages Ridley Cranmer to think that his daughter-in-law will do anything to get out of his house, even to the point of assenting to a bigamous marriage — and the tyranny of Sukey Donne makes possible Anna's fraudulent substitution of a will in which she disinherits those who have the first claim on her.

It is the mark of bad, stupid or insincere characters that they are wholly or partly on the tyrant's side, through weakness, cowardice, hope of personal profit, or through a conventional or sentimental veneration of the Family as an institution, and of the tyrant as the obvious head of a family. Harriet Haslam is toadied by her lawyer, Dominic Spong, and Sabine and Hetta Ponsonby by their clergyman, Dr. Chaucer. Most of the neighbours respect and over-indulge Duncan Edgeworth. It is only singularly acute people who avoid being taken in by Josephine Napier. The bad characters see virtues in the tyrants which have no objective existence; they do not dare to believe in the evil that is there, because they are too morally cowardly to take sides against it.

By contrast, and in themselves, the good characters are very good indeed. Where other novelists are often weak, Miss Compton-Burnett is strong, in the creation of likeable good characters. Her good people are intelligent and nice. They always have those qualities that we really most wish to find in our friends. Not that they are always conventionally irreproachable, though there is nothing to be said against Cassandra Jekyll in *A House and Its Head*, Helen Keats in *More Women Than Men*, or several others. 'I like good people,' says Maria Sloane in *A Family and A Fortune*. 'I never think people realize how well they compare with the others.'

The sex-life of Maria Rosetti, Felix Bacon and Grant Edgeworth has not been unblemished; Andrew, Dinah and Robin Stace, Evelyn Seymour, Terence Calderon and Dudley Gaveston are entirely idle; few of the good characters are particularly brave, most of them are irreligious, none of them are at all public-spirited — certainly they are not perfect. But they are serious, honest and sensitive, their human values are always right, and they will, if necessary, defend them. They never talk in slang or clichés; they never tell lies to others or to themselves about their feelings or motives — the bad characters think them unfeeling and selfish because they scorn pretence. They have virtues that are rare and unconventional: while many of the bad characters pride themselves on speaking good of everyone, the good characters know that it may be a higher form of charity to abuse tyrants to their victims, or to allow the victims the rare indulgence of speaking against their tyrants. The personal relations, whether of friendship or marriage or family affection, that subsist between the good characters, are as good as such relations can ever be, in life or in fiction. They are for Miss Compton-Burnett, as for Mr. Forster, the supreme value — and she vindicates them against worse dangers than anyone in his novels has to face. Her arms, however, are not mystical; it is by truth, affection and intelligence only that her good characters conquer — and the greatest of these is intelligence. No one in fact or fiction has, or deserves to have, more self-respect than they. 'He respects us,' says a woman in *Parents and Children* about the old tyrant Sir Jesse. 'Ah, how I respect us!' replies her brother.

In consequence of their character the utterances of the good people have a directness and ruthlessness with which no mere cynic could compete.

'Let us all speak with a lack of decent feeling,' says Dinah Stace. 'It is time we did something out of keeping with the dignity of bereavement. It is a bad kind of dignity.'

'Other people's troubles are what they deserve. Ah, how they deserve them!' says Oscar Jekyll.

'Are you of the stuff that martyrs are made of?' says Chilton Ponsonby to his sister France, who is in danger of submitting to parental tyranny. 'I hope not; it is useless stuff.'

'I suppose I shall subscribe to hospitals,' says Dudley Gaveston, on coming into his fortune. 'That is how people seem to give to the poor. I suppose the poor are always sick. They would be, if you think. I once went round the cottages with Edgar, and I was too sensitive to go a second time. Yes, I was too sensitive even to set my eyes on the things which other people actually suffered, and I maintain that that was very sensitive.'

'Self-knowledge speaks ill for people,' says Hope Cranmer. 'It shows they are what they are almost on purpose.'

'I feel that to know all is to forgive all,' says Terence Calderon, 'and other people seem to forgive nothing. And no one can say they don't know all. I have never thought of any way of keeping it from them.'

Nor are the tyrants themselves incapable of goodness. Some of them are even capable of acts of almost heroic virtue, following hard upon others of extreme baseness. Sophia Stace, Josephine Napier and Matilda Seaton, the most intelligent of them, have moments of inspired sympathy. Where angels might fear to tread, and where the *anima naturaliter Christiana*, if a simple soul, would be likely to blunder, they walk sure-footed. It is a truism that a good heart may often guide a poor head: they prove that the converse may also be true. In them a fine understanding can produce fine and generous behaviour; in certain subtle difficulties it would be to them that one would turn for support, sooner than to many better-hearted people. Their creator reminds us that Wisdom is, after all, an intellectual virtue, and that the children of this world can be wiser (and, so far, to be more commended) than the children of light.

Most of the tyrants receive and deserve some respect and affection, even from their victims: the tyranny never quite abolishes family feeling, and when a tyrant has a bad fall the victims are chivalrously ready to pick him up. Some of them secure friendship and deep affection from characters of complete integrity, who see their faults clearly, but are yet fond of them — and this friendship and affection is also at least in part deserved. The tyrants are never all bad, and therefore untragic. Their fate cannot be a matter of indifference; in the one instance of tyrannicide, in *Men and Wives*, the pity of Harriet's death is as moving as the horror of Matthew's crime.

The last scene between Matthew and his mother can hardly have been read by those who profess to find neither action nor passion in Miss Compton-Burnett's books. It is wonderfully eloquent, and shows that she has the distinction, unique among living English prose-writers, of being capable of tragedy.

'Matthew followed his mother upstairs, and was drawn by her into her room. "Matthew," she said, standing with her hand on his shoulder and her eyes looking up into his face, "I want you to do something for me; not a great thing dear; I would not ask that. I don't ask you to give up your work, or to give up your marriage; I know you cannot give up. I don't mean that any of us can; I am not saying anything to hurt. I only mean that I would not ask much of you. I just want you to put off your marriage for a few months, for your mother's sake, that she may have a little space of light before the clouds gather. I don't mean that my illness is coming again; I don't think it will come yet. And if it were, I would not use that to persuade you. I would not do what is not fair, while I am myself. I think you know I would not then. But I ask you simply, and as myself, to do this thing for me. I feel I can ask you, because I have seen your eyes on me tonight, and I have said to myself: 'My son does not love me, not my eldest son. And it is my fault, because mothers can easily be loved by their sons. So I can ask this from him, because I cannot lose his love, or lessen it. I have not put it in him.' And so I ask it of you, my dear."

"Mother, what a way to talk!" said Matthew. "Indeed your illness is not coming again. You could not be more at the height of your powers. Your speech was worth taking down. You may use it again. It was only I who heard it. My eyes show all this to you, when all my eyes are for Camilla at the moment, and if anyone knows that, it is you! I might tell you what your eyes show to me, and you would not have an answer. Now take one of your sleeping-tablets; I think I should take two; I have put them out on this table. And the marriage shall not happen until you sanction it. Camilla can get what she wants from this family, from you. She will have you as a friend before me as a husband. I daresay that will be the end."

Harriet stood with her eyes searching her son's.

He kissed her and left her, and turned from the door and gave her the smile that should safeguard for both of them this memory.'

It is not surprising that the only successful, living writer of English verse tragedy should show signs of Miss Compton-Burnett's influence both on the situation and the dialogue of *The Family Reunion* — though its action is more diffuse and less tragic than the greater moments in her novels. Perhaps it is not entirely fanciful to see Mr. Eliot acknowledging this influence when he names one of his characters Ivy, and gives another an invitation to stay at 'Compton-Smith's place in Dorset'.

The tragic aspects of Miss Compton-Burnett's work have been dwelt on at this length, because of their immense significance. They mark her divergence from Jane Austen, and her unique position and stature as a novelist, and they indicate the importance which she attaches to her implied view of life. Briefly, she holds with Mr. Forster that, to be good, people must be serious and truthful, and had better be intelligent; but she differs from him in adding that Charity begins at home. Her good and intelligent characters are not public-spirited, and her philanthropists are almost invariably prigs or bores, though delightfully entertaining.

Lydia Fletcher in *Pastors and Masters* has her men's class, her 'dear men things'. In *Men and Wives* there is an inimitable working-party. The village in *A House and Its Head* is cursed with three women, ruthlessly going about doing good to their neighbours.

For, like Miss Austen, Miss Compton-Burnett is a great comic writer.

'I am such a votary of the comic muse. "No," I have said, when people have challenged me, "I will not have comedy pushed into a back place." I think tragedy and comedy are a greater, wider thing than tragedy by itself. And comedy is so often seen to have tragedy behind it.'

This is true of her work, though it is an absurd character who says it. As well as humorously exploiting situations, and making use of epigrammatic brilliance in dialogue, she is a great creator of comic characters. Many of them play an active part as the philanthropic busybodies or the tyrant's parasites, to whom reference has been made — roles which are often combined. Others, like Mrs. Christy who has just been quoted, have a more simply decorative function.

A scene from *Pastors and Masters* illustrates the simpler form of humour, rare in her later work, of several absurd characters in action together.

"Mrs. Merry," Miss Basden said, in a rather high monotone, "the boys are saying that the marmalade is watery. I am telling them that no water is used in marmalade, that marmalade does not contain water, so I do not see how it can be."

"I do not see how it can be, either; but of course I wish to be told if anything is not as nice as it can be. Let me taste the marmalade."

Miss Basden offered a spoon from the pot.

"It seems to me that it is very nice. Perhaps I am not a judge of marmalade. I do not care to eat it on bread with butter myself. One or the other is enough for me. But it seems to be very nice."

"Mother, don't water the boys' preserves," said Mr. Merry, nodding his head up and down. "Don't try to make things go further than they will go, you know. The game isn't worth the candle."

"I do not understand you, dear. There is never any extra water in preserves. They would not keep if they had water in them. There would not be any object in it. It would be less economical, not more."

"Oh, well, Mother, I don't know anything about the kitchen business and that. But if the marmalade is not right, let us have it right another time. That is all I mean."

"I do not think you know what you mean, dear."

"No, Mother, no; very likely I don't."

"The housekeeping is not your province, Mr. Merry," said Miss Basden. "You will have us coming and telling you how to teach Latin, if you are not careful."

"Ah, Miss Basden, ah, you saucy lady!"'

A source of amusement is the invariable curiosity of the minor characters about the central tragedy; this is dissembled by the dishonest, and frankly acknowledged by the more worthy.

'Our curiosity is neither morbid nor ordinary. It is the kind known as devouring.' (Evelyn Seymour, in *Daughters and Sons.*)

'We can't put gossip off until we return from London. It has a frail hold on life like all precious things.' (Julian Wake, in *Brothers and Sisters.*)

'I don't like things to pass me by, without my hearing about them. We are meant to be interested in what the Almighty ordains.' (Sarah Middleton, in *A Family and a Fortune.*)

The brilliance and wit of the dialogue have increased with each successive book. Even in the more conventional and easily detachable epigrams there are turns and rhythms which unmistakably show their author: 'Saying a thing of yourself does not mean that you like to hear other people say it. And they do say it differently.'

'Being cruel to be kind is just ordinary cruelty with an excuse made for it. And it is right that it should be more resented, as it is.'

The extraordinarily subtle humour of her finer writing would need illustration by a long, sustained passage, though it is suggested by such a passage as this from *More Women Than Men*, where Felix Bacon is talking to Josephine Napier about the staff of her school.

' "I hope they none of them presume upon their friendship?"

"I trust that they deal with me fully as a friend. I hardly understand that phrase, 'presume upon friendship'."

"I quite understand it. Shall we have a gossip about your staff?"

"No!" said Josephine. "When you have known me a little longer, you will know that my mistresses, in their presence and in their absence are safe with me. I hope I could say that about all my friends."

"I hoped you could not. But it is interesting that they would not be safe if we had the gossip. They must have treated you fully as a friend. I almost feel we have had it." '

It is not to be supposed that the characters in Miss Compton-Burnett's novels are only types, because they are easily classifiable. They are in fact very subtly differentiated. They are limited on the whole to certain broad categories, because the plot is to deal with certain kinds of happenings. Since the happenings come out of the people, that entails certain kinds of people. Happenings cannot come out of types, they must come out of real characters. The twelve tyrants, for example, all stand out distinct in the memory: though similarity of situation may sometimes cause them to speak alike, one could in nearly every case pick out the speech of one from that of all the others.

Critics who are unwilling to take the trouble that this very difficult writer requires, or who are not sensitive to subtleties of speech, complain that all her people talk alike. She herself has written in the *Conversation*: "However differently characters are conceived — and I have never conceived two in the same way — they tend to give a similar impression, if they are people of the same kind, produced by the same mind, and carried out by the same hand, and possibly one that is acquiring a habit.'

Each of her characters talks like the others in the sense that they all talk with maximum clarity and self-revelation, and in a polished bookish speech — in this they are all more alike than they are like any character by any other writer. But they have all been conceived with such clarity that with patience they are easily distinguishable. Moreover two practices of the author's which make her characters superficially more alike, in fact mark their difference. When one character tries to imitate another, who is a more brilliant conversationalist, we are at once aware of the imitation — this could not be the case unless both characters were very distinct in our minds. (Thus in *Brothers and Sisters*, Latimer imitates Julian; in *Men and Wives*, Kate imitates Rachel Hardisty.)

Her second device occurs in her later novels, and is an even greater *tour de force*. She brings out family resemblances, so that in *A Family and A Fortune*, the little boy, Aubrey, combines something of the peevishness of his maternal grandfather, Oliver Seaton, with more of the clear-headed fineness of his paternal uncle, Dudley Gaveston (whose manner of speech he also consciously imitates). Nevertheless all three characters remain entirely distinct in the reader's imagination, and Aubrey is one of the most moving child characters in fiction. This sort of achievement is perhaps unique — it is much more than mere technical virtuosity, it is real character creation.

Her treatment of children is particularly admirable. Children in fiction have been more sentimentalized, lied about and betrayed than any other class of being. The more intelligent the writer, the better he treats them. Henry James and Proust have written better about them than anyone. An author so unsentimental and intelligent as Miss Compton-Burnett might be expected either to leave them alone, or to deal with them perfectly, as she has done. Although her narrative takes place almost exclusively in the form of very highly developed conversation among remarkably articulate people, she has all the same managed to draw shy and even very young children brilliantly — and she knows, what most people forget, how extremely early the character is distinct. Nevill Sullivan in *Parents and Children* is only three, and a very definite character, with his own kind of independence and protective cunning.

There are few more triumphant revelations of the child mind in English literature than in the scenes in *Elders and Betters* where Julius and Dora Calderon practise their extraordinary private religion. Their prayer to their God, after the death of their aunt and the suicide of their mother is often quoted.

'O great and good and powerful god, Chung, grant that our life may not remain clouded, as it is at this present. And grant that someone may guide us in the manner of our mother, so that we may not wander without direction in the maze of life. For although we would have freedom, if it be thy will, yet would we be worthy of being our mother's children. And if there is danger of our inheriting the weaknesses of our mother and our aunt, thy late handmaids, guard us from them, O god, and grant that we may live to a ripe old age. For it would not be worth while to suffer the trials of childhood, if they were not to lead to fullness of days. And we pray thee to comfort our father and our brother and sister; and if they are in less need of comfort than beseems them, pardon them, O god, and lead them to know the elevation of true grief.'

Miss Compton-Burnett's novels are certainly of permanent value, though they may never be 'popular classics'. Her work continues to become increasingly attractive to serious students of literature. Many will find her style rebarbative on a first approach: all must find it difficult. Only repeated re-reading can extract all the treasure from her finest work; and it is hard to persuade people to give the attention to a major novelist that they are ready to squander on minor poetry. It does not seem too much, or nearly enough, to claim for her that, of all English novelists now writing she is the greatest and the most original artist.

Some Principles of Fiction

APOLOGY

Any general examination of the novelist's art must appear arid and theoretical. It cannot fail to be directed towards the more formal elements in that art, while criticism of individual novelists can deal more adequately with the life they are trying to create. A book of this sort is doomed to appear excessively schematic, and some people may object that profitable things can be said about this or that novel, but hardly about the Novel; for as Lawrence said: 'all rules of construction hold good only for novels that are copies of other novels'.

That a great many things cannot be said in a book of this sort must be obvious to anyone who has ever given any thought to the novel. One can isolate for the purpose of analysis such an element as Plot, for instance – but in many novels that do not lack unity, the principle of cohesion is something we cannot call Plot, something to which we cannot do justice except in individual studies of these books or of their authors.

But though much must be left unsaid, something can be said – and a generalization may be useful even if it does not cover every instance. One of the purposes of such an examination is to help writers; and it is very difficult indeed to help writers except over formal problems. The only useful help many writers have ever given or received has been over small points such as punctuation, or the phrasing of a sentence.

The present book deals with other aspects of the novel than those dealt with in my former treatise. It aspires only to an internal consistency. It is not a correction or a defence or a completion of the former book, but has an independent existence of its own. If anything said here implies a slightly different view from that expressed in the first book (and this must sometimes be the case), I have not thought it required mention.

I

THE SUBJECT OF FICTION

§ 1. THE DIFFICULTY OF CHOOSING A SUBJECT AT THE PRESENT DAY

There is, no doubt, too much written and said about the present day, too much speculation about what the novelist *must* do today, and will *have* to do tomorrow. In the arts it is not very important to be up-to-date, and nothing looks more out-of-date today than the book that was up-to-date a year or two ago. And it is not an intelligent exercise to ask such questions as: 'What is the future of the novel?' or: 'Has the novel a future?'

A very few words on this point should be enough. While English remains a living language, in which prose can be read and written fluently, and so long as people live, and there are personal relations between them — then English fiction is possible. Reasons may make it more difficult to write at one time than another — it is probably now, for several reasons, as difficult as it has been at any time since the life-time of Richardson. It is especially difficult to find a suitable subject.

§ 2. THE INSECURITY OF LIFE

The chief difficulty today is caused by the crushing impact of public affairs. 'There is no private life which has not been determined by a wider public life,' says George Eliot — but since her day the determination has been very much more rigid. No one in Middlemarch, after all, ever had to join the armed forces, ever had to leave Middlemarch if he did not like it. And those who remained in Middlemarch never had to fear that their lives might be cut short or their homes destroyed by a bomb.

Nowadays, if a hero and heroine marry at the end of a book, and live happily ever afterwards – although we know that fictional characters are only puppets, and that the toy-box is shut at the end of the book, yet we cannot help asking how long that happiness is likely to last. Writer and reader alike feel an insecurity: we only half believe in the happiness or unhappiness of real persons, and therefore of fictional characters which are their *simulacra* – it seems such a frail thing.

On the other hand, if we read one of those bluff, middlebrow writers who seem to pride themselves on having escaped the jaded nerves of our epoch – then we believe even less in the characters or in the world that they have created. They seem to have been incapable of sensitively imagining what it is like to be alive today.

Already, after the first world war, Katherine Mansfield was complaining of writers who wrote as if it had not occurred. 'I don't want (God forbid!) mobilization and the violation of Belgium, but the novel can't just leave the war out. There must have been a change of heart.'[1]

Today we do not ask for pages about the Spanish war (God forbid!) or the Munich agreement – which loom too large as it is in contemporary fiction.

What we do demand of an author is rather, perhaps, a feeling of sadness, a lack of faith in simple or easy solutions to human problems, a sense of the frailty of life . . . no loud, hearty songs of innocence, but quiet songs of experience; and a great part of the experience of our time is expressed in a few, sad little words of Mr. Stephen Spender's:

Who live under the shadow of a war,
What can I do that matters?

There is no attempt here to lay a moral or social duty upon the writer; it is an attempt to define an artistic duty for the novelist who is trying in any way to represent contemporary life. One can hardly write truthfully about characters living in this age without showing that many of them live in perpetual fear that their world is in imminent danger of falling to pieces round their ears. It would be like writing a novel about the Middle Ages, and leaving out the fear of Hell. This is not to suggest that the novelist could or should have a scheme for saving the world; if he thinks he knows how to save the world, then he had better go to work about it, and leave off writing fiction, for fiction will not hold the world together. Nor do we much want to read the views of his characters upon public events, for they will be very stale by the time the book is in print. We only require sadness, scepticism and a feeling of insecurity.

Those novels which people used to write at one time, about consumptive patients in sanatoria, would not be a bad model for present-day novelists, if they were better novels—for all characters nowadays are sick, with 'this strange disease of modern life', and it will probably carry them off. Whether characters are, for example, *Munichois* or *anti-Munichois* is only a question of which way they have got the disease: we do not want to know, for clinical details are boring.

In this unfortunate age in which we live, since everything is insecure, some people think it does not much matter how they behave — these people become criminals. Others, less extreme in their application of a similar point-of-view, still think that it does not very much matter what any individual does or suffers:

these people are apt to be impatient with fiction. What can it matter, they argue, what an imaginary person does or suffers, when the world's fate hangs in the balance? Are not novelists fiddling while Rome is burning?

This is not so sensible an attitude as it might at first appear. The fate of the world, after all, is only important in so far as it affects the people in it. We may speak, if we like, of Poland, Spain or wherever suffering; but of course it means nothing: it is only Poles, Spaniards or whoever that can suffer. Moreover we cannot even say that two Poles, for example, can suffer twice as much as one. Suffering is not a thing that can be added up or multiplied, like horsepower. There is never more suffering, or worse suffering at any one time in the world than the worst that can be contained in one human consciousness.

If we think that it does not matter what happens to the individual, then we have no reason to think that it matters what happens to the world, for it is the individual who feels what happens to the world.

If we think the individual matters, then our sympathy can as easily be extended to the imaginary individual — for other people are to us for the most part imaginary individuals. And if the novelist seems to be fiddling while Rome is burning, it may be a useful service to play to the firemen while they have their luncheon.

St. Augustine says that he could not weep for his sins, which might plunge him into Hell, but he could weep for Dido's unhappy love. He thought this a sign of his own perversity, but we may also regard it as a sign of Vergil's artistry: Vergil made him weep for Dido. A novelist may still hope to make us weep for his heroine, and to forget for a while the things that may plunge us in ruin; but his Dido, if she is a woman living in the world of today, will have a shakier throne to sit on, and a more unstable background than that of the Queen of Carthage. This is one of the things that will make her story more difficult to tell. The novelist not only has to keep his eye on his character, and no interesting characters keep still for very long — he has also to keep his eye upon a surrounding world that will not keep still, as it kept (comparatively) still for Jane Austen or for Trollope — to see steadily what is, itself, unsteady.

§3. THE STANDARDIZATION OF LIFE

Not only is life insecure, it may also be said that it is less interesting than it used to be, and that people are not so interesting as they used to be. When people profess to find that Dickens's characters are wild exaggerations, and when they say that they have never seen anyone remotely like Mrs. Gamp or Mr. Pecksniff, it is to be feared that they are often telling the truth — they haven't. Those of us who have been more fortunate, must sorrowfully admit that the most Dickensian people of our acquaintance are now elderly, or in their graves.

The standardization of life, alas, requires no proof. The progress of machinery has made the working-lives of industrial labourers infinitely less interesting, as everyone knows. It may be possible to avoid the uglification of life — well-designed things can be made by machines; it may be possible, by use of machinery, so to cut down working hours that industrial labourers may (on the balance) be happier. This is no consolation to the novelist as such, who does not care whether they are happy or not, or whether what they make is beautiful or hideous. He would like their working-lives to be interesting and significant as a subject for fiction — and that they will never be again. If we look, on the contrary, at the lives of stone-masons or woodlanders in the Wessex novels, we can see at once how rich their working-lives were in material for the novelist.

Again, big businesses, multiple stores and the like may be able to do much for their work-people, but one thing they cannot give them, an interesting working-life. Yet for anyone who had worked for Mrs. Todgers or for Poll Sweedlepipe or for any of the little shops and businesses in Dickens, life would have been full of drama.

The standardization of life does not only blight people's working-lives, but also their amusements. A big household, like that of Mansfield Park, would be unlikely today to get up private theatricals — with all those wonderful scenes of jealousy and passion that result. The Bertrams, and Rushworths, and Crawfords, and Fanny Price and Mrs. Norris would drive into Northampton, and go to the cinema. The wrong people might sit together, or Henry Crawford might press Fanny's hand in the dark: but there is little there for a novelist to get his teeth into.

§4. THE REMOVAL OF OBSTACLES TO LOVE

There has been in this century such a relaxation of people's ideas about sexual morality, and, in particular, about marriage, that most people's emotional lives are very much freer and less complicated than they used to be. People may or may not be happier or better for this change — but for the novelist as such it is a change for the worse, for life is less interesting.

In *Sense and Sensibility* Edward Ferrars is unhappy through three-quarters of the book because, while he was under twenty-one, and not even legally bound by his promise, he had offered marriage to an underbred young woman, who has since appeared a worthless character to his more mature judgment. Life with Lucy must be unhappy; moreover Edward has now fallen in love seriously, and with a very superior woman in his own class, and has reason to believe that she is attached to him — but he may take no steps to break off his engagement.

Much later in the nineteenth century, it is thought dishonourable for the hero of *The Spoils of Poynton* not to fulfil his engagement to a most odious young woman, after he has come to dislike her as she deserves. He may not even play a waiting game, and hope that she will tire of him and give him up, though there is every chance of success in this line. He has to behave as if he were even impatient to marry her.

These two great novels must today be read with a 'willing suspension of disbelief' in the standards of honour maintained. Neither of these situations could occur today — or, if they did, the man would be thought so absurdly scrupulous that he would forfeit all sympathy.

It seems easier now, at any rate in fiction, to put an end to a marriage, than it was then to put an end to an engagement — and the social consequences are less disagreeable. It is therefore harder for a novelist to convince his readers by a picture of a desperately unhappy married life. Formerly husband or wife might cry: '*I can't get out!*' like Sterne's starling. That is not true any more: the door is open. Formerly there was no way out but Death, and that door could only be forced by Suicide or Murder — wonderful climaxes to a plot. A husband or wife who escapes by Suicide is now thought feeble; if either rids himself of a partner by Murder, it looks brutal and pointless.

There is a very good essay on this subject by Mr. Aldous Huxley, called *Obstacle Race*. He begins by a brief analysis of that strange novel by Stendhal, *Armance*, in which religion, convention, honour, delicacy and money one after another keep the lovers apart.

'Poor Octave!' says Mr. Huxley, 'Unhappy Armance! Their whole life was a kind of obstacle race — a climbing over and a crawling under barriers, a squeezing through narrow places. And the winning-post? For Octave the winning-post was a dose of laudanum; for Armance, a cell in a nunnery.

'If they had run their course today, they would have run it on the flat, or at any rate over a course irregular only by nature, not artificially obstructed. The going is easier now.'

Mr. Huxley went on to give as an example of flat-racing the love-stories of a Russian writer, whose sexual morality was merely that of the farmyard. Since the date of Mr. Huxley's essay, those who direct the destinies of Russia are said to have ordered many changes in these things — so much the better for the future of the Russian novel.

The most beautiful and skilful obstacle-racing in English fiction is probably to be found in *The Wings of the Dove.* The lovers' meeting in the park, at the beginning of this novel, is one of the most splendid in prose literature, simply because of the obstacles in their way. They themselves are fully aware of them, and Kate Croy almost glories in them — she is about to devise yet another obstacle, and one which will in the end, though she little knows it, keep them permanently apart. 'Yes,' she says, 'we're hideously intelligent. But there's fun in it too. We must get our fun where we can. I think our relation's beautiful. It isn't a bit *banal.* I cling to some saving romance in things.'

In too many recent novels the characters have only the most banal and unbeautiful relationships, and couple like animals, without the intelligence ever coming into play. There is no 'saving romance'.

Some French novelists have avoided the banality of flat-racing. Proust and Gide deal with sexual abnormality, which is still ringed round with complications; M. Mauriac deals with Catholics, who still recognize the existence of obstacles. Here are two fields for obstacle-racing indeed, but they have disadvantages. Those who write about Catholic or homosexual characters usually are consciously, rather too self-consciously, presenting them to a public which is neither homosexual nor Catholic, and from which a more or less 'willing suspension of disbelief' is therefore required: the difficulty of tone is quite exceptional. These are probably safer fields for French writers: a French novelist can without so much difficulty regard Catholic standards as a norm — and he is not awed by British criminal laws, or by British methods of banning books. It is sad to see these promising courses for obstacle-racing being levelled by some novelists into the dullest of flat race courses.

§5. THE REMOVAL OF SOCIAL OBSTACLES

Social life, as well as sexual life, is now very much less of an obstacle race than it used to be; most of the class-barriers are down. Our place in the social hierarchy is much less firmly fixed at birth. We are no longer confined by class in our choice of a profession. At one time Cabinet ministers were always gentlemen — today this is no longer the case. At one time gentlemen never became dentists — it is more than likely that there are now exceptions to this rule.

The lowering of barriers may, on the whole, be a good thing: but there is something to be said on the other side, and Burke has said it.

'I do not hesitate to say, that the road to eminence and power from obscure condition, ought not to be made too easy, nor a thing too much of course. If rare merit be the rarest of all things, it ought to pass through some sort of probation. The temple of honour ought to be seated on an eminence. If it be opened through virtue, let it be remembered too that virtue is never tried but by some difficulty and some struggle.'[2]

If this be applied to fiction, it is certainly true — for if the hero is to rise from obscure condition, it is the difficulties and struggles, precisely, that make the story. We are interested in the probation through which his virtue passes more than in his virtue itself — just as our interest in *Pamela* disappears when virtue is rewarded — and if it should happen to be the story of a failure and not a success, the experience conveyed may be no less significant.

It may be said that life today is freer and should be more interesting for people have more choice. The Brontës, daughters of a poor clergyman, had only two alternatives in life: to marry other clergymen, or to become governesses. Charlotte did both; her sisters died.

Today Charlotte Brontë might have edited a newspaper, might have sat in Parliament, might have toured the world on one or other of a hundred missions — she would probably have done some or all of these things. She would probably not have written so well.

A writer does not need wide experience so much as deep experience — and the wider experience is, the shallower it is likely to be. Even if there had still been that dramatic home at Haworth, and that drunken brother in the background — if Charlotte Brontë had been to a hundred other places, and had done a hundred other things as well as being a daughter at home — then that dramatic home at Haworth and that drunken brother would have sunk further into the background, would have mattered much less to her, and would not have been the same potent force of inspiration.

If Charlotte Brontë had been an important woman journalist, where would have been that pathetic dream of running a little school of her own with her sisters, which was only just impossible of realization, and was finally realized in that charming novel *Villette*?

§6. THE DEATH OF THE ORGANIC COMMUNITY

The organic community, which still exists as a permanent background to the novels of Jane Austen or Hardy, is no longer a living thing — and every modern novelist feels or exhibits its loss.

Jane Austen or Hardy looked out at country villages inhabited by labourers and landowners, by clergymen and doctors and their female dependents, by people who belonged there, and were functionally connected with the place. In Wessex there are already some strays: Lucetta at Casterbridge or Mrs. Charmond at Hintock, but they are not Hardy's more successful characters.

Today a number of houses may be inhabited by people whose real life and work is in the town, who live in the country only from Saturday to Monday, or who sleep there at night to be away from the noise, or merely because they cannot find room in the town. They may move house tomorrow — their tie to the place is feeble, and their relations with the other inhabitants are unreal and can be lightly broken.

If Jane Austen had been asked where she came from, she would at once have answered Hampshire — if Hardy had been asked, he would have answered Dorset — but many Englishmen, if asked what is their *pays,* do not know what to answer. Their parents have moved about, and so have they.

In consequence, their life has lacked depth and continuity. Many people in adult life know no one who was a child with them, no one who knew their parents. Social life is impoverished by restlessness and rootlessness — people do not live in one place for life, but are as transient as the English used to be in India, or as diplomats are *en poste* — life is therefore probably less interesting to live; it is certainly less interesting to write or to think about.

Jane Austen delighted to get her characters grouped in a village, where they were all fixed — at least for the time. If newcomers arrived, like the Dashwoods at Barton, the Crawfords at Mansfield, or Mr. Frank Churchill at Highbury, they came because they had connections with the place, and they were known and talked of before they appeared. Their visits were generally of some duration, and were likely to be repeated: they did not appear from nowhere, take a house furnished for three months, and then disappear without leaving a trace.

The modern novelist is often forced to resort to the most fluid and inorganic communities, that have been formed by no necessity, are kept together by no duties or loyalties, and will be broken up tomorrow — because he can find no more permanent group. A house-party in a country house used to be a popular subject — even that had the connection that all the guests must know at least their host or hostess, and some of them might antecedently know each other. There are fewer country house parties than there used to be, and novelists have gone on to show their people more loosely grouped in a hotel — or, worse, as travelling on the same train or ship.

There cannot in such circumstances be time or opportunity

for interesting relations to develop between them, or for any real, deep complication of motive.

The modern loneliness which results from the death of the organic community, in which nearly everyone had his place, is an interesting phenomenon — but it is the sort of phenomenon that is hard to exhibit in fiction, which gets its better effects from showing people together rather than in isolation. Nevertheless, like any other real experience, it is a possible theme for the novelist — and a better theme than contemporary social life often supplies. If we compare two novels of M. Sartre, we can see at a glance the great superiority of *La Nausée*, with its poignant picture of loneliness and isolation, to *L'Age de Raison*, where the people are indeed connected by personal relations of a sort, though these are of little strength or interest.

It may be said that nowadays it is easier to get about, and to meet a great number of people — and that this ought to help the novelist in his study of human nature. It is no compensation for the death of the organic community. There is much more to be learned from living in a constricted neighbourhood, and from seeing the same people again and again, year after year — in that way they force themselves on our attention. If we see too many people we cannot trouble to focus our eyes and minds upon them. Lazy focusing, which is said to be bad for the physical eyesight, is certainly bad for the mental vision.

Katherine Mansfield in her letters said that she wanted to know only a very few people: her husband, the friend she calls 'L. M.', a servant called Mrs. Honey. They helped her to people many of her best stories.

For the novel is a form of story-telling, and has a close affinity with a very humble intellectual activity, Gossip. You can only gossip effectively about people whom you know well, or people you know a great deal about. And gossip, and leisurely, gossippy letter-writing is the best breeding-ground for the novelist. It was the chat, and the chatty letters of a big family, that helped Jane Austen to develop into what she was: it was servant-girls' gossip that formed Samuel Richardson. Gossip is local, and it is not great travellers who have been the best letter-writers — it is people who have stayed at home, and have talked about their neighbours.

§7. WHAT REMAINS FOR THE NOVELIST

In the present age, man's inhumanity to man is less, if looked at from the private and social aspects, which alone interest the novelist; it is infinitely greater if looked at from a public or national aspect. Many obstacles are gone, and we can do a good deal of far and fast flat-racing; but we and our race course may be blown to bits by an atomic bomb. The atomic bomb may be devastating, but it is not at all interesting: it can only figure in one place in a plot — at the end. The obstacles, however, were really interesting, and might appear at any moment; moreover, they were a valuable stimulus to human ingenuity: there were all sorts of ways of dodging or of overcoming them. Our attitude to the atomic bomb can only be passive.

We must look for comfort where comfort is to be found. People are still human, and to be human is to err, and the world is not yet so mechanical that there is no room for human error. Individuals can (fortunately for the novelist) still do a great deal of harm, and cause a great deal of suffering — and though it is easier to escape from them than it used to be, there will always (or at least for a very long time) be people who cannot entirely escape from their neighbours' cruelty. And since it is individuals who feel the results of the misdeeds of the state, these misdeeds, though often not very interesting in themselves, may be interesting in their consequences — and from the cruelty of the state it is very much more difficult to escape than it used to be.

Moreover, although the human heart changes, it changes slowly. Most civilized people today would certainly say that Othello was a brutal fool — but though they would think it monstrous to murder Desdemona, however guilty she were, yet they would still think that, if Desdemona were guilty, Othello had the right to be very seriously annoyed. A dramatic critic who complained some years ago that the play was about nothing, was probably in the minority. However, a woman once told M. Mauriac that she could not understand *Phèdre*. 'What a lot of fuss about nothing!' she said. 'As if it wasn't the most natural thing in the world to fall in love with one's stepson!'[3]

People no doubt object to adultery very much less than they did — even a religious man might well, before he thought twice, be more angry if he were suspected of beating his own wife, than if he were suspected of seducing his neighbour's. Nevertheless people do object to it. If a time should come when no one objects — gone will be a favourite subject for the novelist. Even so, moral standards could, for a limited time, survive in fiction their extinction elsewhere — just as some ideals of honour have lingered on in drama after they were dead in everyday life.[4] Even in a Huxleyan brave new world a novelist might be able to write historical novels about ages in which the human race had still been human — if he and his readers retained sufficient semblance of humanity.

And even now, if we feel over much grieved at the collapse of obstacles, at the tediousness of most people's working-life, at the death of the organic community, it is in our power to revive all these things by placing the action of our novels a few years back into the past. This is what Miss Compton-Burnett has done. She is thus enabled to depict a world unshaken by modern warfare, a community rooted in a single place, and lives still ruled, and even laid waste, by family tyranny. She can do this, because she need only take a period fifty years ago, when she was herself already alive – therefore she can recreate this age without the artificiality and falsity of the historical novelist. Younger writers can hardly do the same thing, and she is, too probably, the last person who can do it successfully. Already this device causes some readers to make the mistake of dismissing her novels as 'Quaint' – but in time their date of publication may cease to be relevant, and they may come to seem novels of English life between 1888 and 1910, which might have been written at any time. It is to be hoped that this will be the case; it would be a sad thing if a novelist whose powers are little, if at all, inferior to Jane Austen's, should be forced, owing to the unpropitious age in which she lives, to occupy no higher place in the history of the novel than that of, say, Peacock. There is reason to hope for the happier alternative: contemporaneity is not very important to the novelist, and Jane Austen, Scott, Dickens, Thackeray and George Eliot did their best work with no regard to it.

This for our wisest . . .

We others have still nooks and crannies of life to pry into, and oddities to bring to light. The modern novelist might say, with one of Miss Compton-Burnett's characters: 'It is little, unnatural corners of the world that appeal to me. I am very over-civilized.' Good minor work may be raised on these little, unnatural corners – and given a fortunate combination of the man, the experience, and the 'objective correlative', good major work is by no means impossible. Balzac built some of his best work on just such little, unnatural corners of the world – it should still be possible to write such a book as *Le Curé de Tours*, and who has the right to wish to write anything better?

Of little, unnatural corners of the human mind, more is known; psychology may help us to investigate some of them. And though we lose infinitely much by the relaxation of tabus about what people may do, we may gain a little by the relaxation of a few tabus about what people may say. Subjects hitherto denied to us may no longer be withheld. Thackeray complained that no novelist since Fielding had been permitted to exhibit the whole man; now we have all Fielding's freedom and more. Thackeray would have liked to give Arthur Pendennis something of the sex-life of Tom Jones; but Fielding had been reticent about some aspects of Tom Jones's life – he did not, for example, explore his digestion as James Joyce has explored that of Bloom. Yet we have not, perhaps, gained so very much in gaining the freedom of the character's alimentary canal: it can tell us a great deal about the character, but things that might have been learned more interestingly from his words and behaviour – and even admiring readers of Lawrence must confess to boredom with the physical details of his people's loves.

Nevertheless, though the prospect is not very cheerful, there are probably as many subjects left in life as ever came out of it. It is not yet time to despair of the novel, or to decide that nothing but a serious operation can give it renewed life.

§8. THE MYTH OF THE DAUGHTERS OF PELIAS

The sorceress Medea cut an old ram into pieces, boiled them in a caldron of water with a few herbs, and out jumped a fine young lamb. She persuaded the daughters of Pelias to try a similar experiment upon their father, in order to rejuvenate him. It was a trick, and they found they had only made him into soup.

So, when we are invited to admire the 'broken time-scheme' or some other experiment, whether of Mr. Aldous Huxley, or Mr. Philip Toynbee, or anyone else – it is proper to inquire: Has the novel sprung with renewed life from their caldrons, or have they merely made soup of its poor old bones?

NOTES

[1] *The Letters of Katherine Mansfield*, ed. J. Middleton Murry, I, p. 278: November 10th, 1919.

[2] *Reflections on the Revolution in France.*

[3] *Le Roman*, p. 14.

[4] The standards of honour maintained in *The Spoils of Poynton* are no doubt already a survival.

II

FOUR RELATED QUESTIONS

§1. THE FOUR QUESTIONS

There are four questions of some importance in the criticism of fiction which are too seldom asked. No final answer to these questions can be expected, but this does not mean that it is merely idle curiosity to ask them: every time they are honestly raised, some small contribution towards solving them is likely to be made.

I. Can a good novel be a poor work of art?

And the converse:

II. Can a good work of art, which is in the form of a novel, be a poor novel (or poor as a novel)?

And two related questions:

III. Is it possible to say something significant, and yet write bad prose?

IV. Can prose be good when its content is insignificant?

Many people would answer all these questions unhesitatingly in the negative, and it is true that almost all the critical preconceptions that we have acquired in the second quarter of this century incline us to such an answer.

We have learned to repudiate the vicious distinction between 'style' and 'subject-matter', and the admiration for 'beautiful English', in which many of us were brought up by old-fashioned school-masters. In all branches of literature we have been shown the inseparability of the thing said from the way we say it — and of course philosophers have always known, even if men of letters have sometimes forgotten, that a thing said in two different ways is never precisely the same thing said, and that if we say a thing beyond a point badly, we have failed to say it. Mr. I. A. Richards in *Practical Criticism*, and other critics who have adopted his methods, have taught us to look very closely at the texture both of prose and verse, and few will dissent from Mrs. Leavis when she writes: 'the essential technique in an art that works by using words is the way in which words are used'.[1]

Moreover Mr. T. S. Eliot has maintained against William Archer that a play cannot be a good play and yet be bad literature, and that in poetic drama poetry and drama are the same thing[2] — he has even given us the impression that the better the poetry is the better the drama will be[3] (though, if he ever held this view, he must have revised it before writing *The Cocktail Party*). We are likely to reason for ourselves that a novel cannot be a good novel and yet be bad literature, and that in prose fiction the prose and the fiction are the same thing — we may even go further and opine that the better the prose is, the better the fiction must be (or vice versa).

§2. WHETHER DISTINCTIVE NAMES FOR DIFFERENT LITERARY GENRES ARE OF USE

It may first be pertinently inquired if there is any value at all in the traditional names for the different literary genres: drama, the novel, the essay, biography, etc. Should we confine ourselves to some general term, such as 'Literature', for the art that works by using words; and is it not enough in each work that comes under our notice, to examine the way in which words are used? Even such broad distinctions as Poetry and Prose might be done away with, since no two people are in agreement about them any more than they are over the meaning of the word 'gentleman'. Moreover the existence of 'Free Verse' has blunted the more easily drawn distinction between Verse and Prose: for who will presume to say how free Verse can be, and yet remain, Verse?

The traditional names for the genres are often misleading in literary history: we find 'histories of the novel', for instance, which neglect the influence of Dryden on Richardson, because Dryden was not one of his 'precursors in the novel'. While in many important activities of criticism, such as the assignment of merit, these names have often no help to give.

This speech of Mrs. Gamp's, for instance, may be called prose or verse.

Which, Mr. Chuzzlewit, is well beknown to Mrs. Harris
As has one sweet infant (though she *do* not wish it known)
In her own family by the mother's side,
Kep' in spirits in a bottle;
And that sweet babe she see at Greenwich Fair,
A travelling in company with the pink-eyed lady, Prooshan
    dwarf, and living skelinton,
Which judge her feelin's when the barrel-organ played,
And she was showed her own dear sister's child,
The same not bein' expected from the outside picter,
Where it was painted quite contrairy in a livin' state,
A many sizes larger,
And performing beautiful upon the Arp,
Which never did that dear child know or do:
Since breathe it never did, to speak on, in this wale!
And Mrs. Harris, Mr. Chuzzlewit,
Has knowed me many a year, and can give you information
That the lady which is widdered can't do better

And may do worse than let me wait upon her,
Which I hope to do.
Permittin' the sweet faces as I see afore me.

If this is prose, with the eighteenth-century novelists to set the standard, or subtle, dramatic verse, in which Jacobean comedy lives again, it hardly matters — it is magnificent, whether verse or prose. While the death of little Nell is contemptible writing, whether it be regarded as prose or verse.

Unlike the productions of the plastic arts, we can never say of a literary work that its creator mistook his medium — as when a sculptor makes out of bronze a statue that would have been more appropriate in porcelain. The literary artist has only one medium: words. Nor, as in Music, can we ever say that a literary work has been wrongly scored, for there is only one instrument that could ever perform it, the human voice — and whether soprano or baritone, spoken aloud or in the head, makes no difference at all.

Literary works cannot be differentiated by the medium in which they are executed, or by the instruments for which they have been written. Can they, like architectural monuments, be differentiated by the purpose for which they are made?

Function is less valuable an artistic criterion than it has sometimes been thought. 'The first qualification for judging any piece of workmanship from a corkscrew to a cathedral is to know *what* it is,' writes Mr. C. S. Lewis, '— what it was intended to do and how it is meant to be used . . . as long as you think the corkscrew was meant for opening tins or the cathedral for entertaining tourists you can say nothing to the purpose about them.'[4] This sounds disarmingly reasonable, and indeed the general form of corkscrew or cathedral is determined by its function — the necessity to get a good grip on a cork or (among other things) to provide a sizable choir and a number of altars for the use of a college of canons. But these functions can be served equally well by beautiful or ugly corkscrews or cathedrals. And a significant work of art can often, in later times, be put to purposes for which its creator never intended it. The builders of Salisbury cathedral were equally far from supposing that it would ever be used for the choral offices of the Church of England, for organ recitals of eighteenth-century music, or for the entertainment of American tourists — for all of which purposes it is exquisitely well adapted. And so long as any literary work continues to delight (whether or no it was once also meant to instruct) we cannot call it a failure.[5]

The analogy of Architecture does suggest that while we can certainly say of a theatre, for example, that it is a pretty building, but an inefficient theatre — or that it is an admirable theatre, but a hideous building, it may not be absolutely impossible to make some sort of parallel distinction in Literature. But any parallel between the arts is misleading if drawn too far — works of Literature have a more obvious duty to delight and a less obvious duty to be useful than most works of Architecture, and works of Architecture fall more disastrously to the ground if they are ill constructed.

§3. THE INCONVENIENCE OF REJECTING THESE NAMES

If we repudiate the traditional names for the literary genres, and refuse to speak of the drama, the novel, etc., then our first two questions disappear. We have only to ask of a literary work if it is, or is not, a good work of art. But as long as we retain these names, then these questions are at least not meaningless, and can certainly be asked, even if they should turn out to be no more than questions about the meaning of words.

But it does not seem so easy to get rid of all these names. Some could indeed go without much loss: the ode has long been divorced from any idea of a public, ceremonial performance, and lyric poetry has nothing more to do with the lyre. But drama has not yet lost all suggestion of an action performed before an audience seated in a theatre — and good art which would not please an intelligent and sensitive audience under those conditions may reasonably be called 'undramatic'. And Mr. Eliot finds himself forced to admit a distinction between dramatic and purely poetic values when he writes: 'Heywood's versification is never on a very high poetic level, but at its best is often on a high dramatic level.'[6]

It is unlikely that drama is the only name that must be retained: it looks as if each name should be retained or rejected on its own merits. And perhaps it is a convenience to have a name for prose fictions, for the narrative representation of character in action.

Though we do not, before the event, have to have names for the things we are going to do, yet we generally have to find names for the things we are going to make. A sinner, for example, will probably not say to himself: 'I am now going to commit fornication; I shall now perpetrate calumny,' or the like. But a writer does not sit down to make a literary work any more than a cook stands up to make a work of culinary art — the writer proposes to make, say, a novel, and the cook a soufflé.

Moreover no good writer ever directly aims at self-expression, or the criticism of life, when engaged in creative work — he wants to make a definite work, through which he may indeed be found to have expressed himself, and to have commented on the world around him. And if the work he has tried to make involves the representation of characters in action, then the critic may properly inquire how he has represented characters in action, and not only how he has used words. It is certain that a man may use words very well indeed, and yet be quite incapable of representing characters in action: it is not quite so certain that a man can use words clumsily or ill, and yet succeed in this — but it may be so.

§4. THE CHILD-MIND IN FICTION

It may be so; and, if it is so, then a form of criticism entirely directed towards 'the way in which words are used' will come to grief. It may be so, because the creative artist in Literature is not always a person of the highest intelligence — any more than the creative artist in the other arts. His mind is imaginative rather than philosophical — like Rickie Elliot in Mr. Forster's novel *The Longest Journey* (himself a creative writer), he fills imaginary pastures with imaginary cows, plashing knee-deep by the brink of impassable rivers, while the abstract mind is inquiring whether external objects exist when they are not seen. Lower parts of the mind are the novelist's province — memory, for example, which is sometimes despised by the abstract thinker as merely mechanical, and rather bad mechanism at that. ''Tis better to own a Judgment,' wrote Glanvill, 'Tho' but with a *curta supellex* of coherent notions; then a *memory*, like a Sepulchre, furnished with a load of broken and discarnate bones.' But the novelist does not require so very much judgment — he waits for breath to come from the four winds and breathe upon the dry bones, that they may rise again, but combined in a new way, and so his fiction is born.

The novelist's sensibility may be greater than his intelligence, but even this is limited — the highest sensibility is more likely to appreciate than to create. Some very primitive factors are involved in creation — in particular, cruelty. Drama is more akin to mimicry, the novel to gossip and even scandal-mongering, than either of them are to Science or Philosophy — and the primitive factors in Literature cannot be neglected or despised, they are the forces that make it live. (This does not mean that a novelist should not educate such intelligence and sensibility as he possesses as well as he can.)

A child, or an otherwise immature mind, can be observant and also creative about human beings and the relations between them — can even be extremely subtle and penetrating about more highly evolved beings than itself, even if it is in the dark about many of their interests. 'What a creator of character needs', says Mr. Eliot, 'is not so much knowledge of motives as keen sensibility; the dramatist need not understand people; but he must be exceptionally aware of them.'[7] For this reason the advance of psychology has done very much less for fiction than people, not novelists, expected it would: it can help us to understand people, but it cannot increase our awareness of them.

Henry James's Maisie did not even know what are so often and so oddly called 'the facts of life' — and yet she anxiously and shrewdly followed the couplings and uncouplings of her immoral parents and step-parents, with a sensitive awareness of which the Queen's Proctor is unlikely to have been capable.

Any intelligent book about an intelligent child is likely to make the same point. 'I could observe', says David Copperfield of his youthful self, 'in little pieces, as it were; but as to making a net of a number of these pieces, and catching anybody in it, that was, as yet, beyond me!' Nevertheless we see the pieces beginning to cohere — and they are always sharply observed.

It is not only sentimentality to say that 'children always know', and perhaps the same proposition about animals is less ridiculous than it is often thought. If we know what we mean, then we may say that (some) children and animals 'know': for this reason it is much more humiliating to be rebuffed when we court the friendship of these creatures, than to find ourselves getting on badly with a journalist, for example, or a society woman whom we have met for the first time.

§5. THE CASE OF CHARLOTTE YONGE

Charlotte Yonge, who is as probably in heaven as any novelist, if not a little child, was not much more grown up than a pious schoolgirl, whose favourite treat is a missionary meeting. We cannot call hers an interesting mind, no abstract speculations of hers could hold us for a moment, and it is unlikely that she would ever influence us in matters of taste. But in practical matters she knew the difference between Right and Wrong, and she was unusually observant and sensitive about people and the relations between them. If she and Galsworthy, to name no living novelist, were both present at some occasion of human interest, it is surely to her that one would go for an eye-witness account, or from her that one would prefer to receive a letter about it — just as there are school-children with whom one would rather gossip than with first-rate literary critics.

Therefore her biographers may well speak of her 'ageless books, marked by an understanding of the constant elements in human nature',[8] and it will often be found that other novelists enjoy reading them — they are uninteresting only to those who are not interested in people.

It is instructive to compare her famous novel, *The Heir of Redclyffe*, with *Amabel and Mary Verena*, a sequel by Mrs. Hicks

Beach. The earlier writer was incomparably the more creative: she has given a splendid vitality and idiosyncracy to her characters, otherwise Mrs. Hicks Beach would not have wished to write more of them, and would not have found any readers if she had. The characters of *The Heir of Redclyffe* live, but live in our minds like people we ourselves knew in adolescence (if we were very observant), or like people who have been described to us by observant but simple gossips. And, after all, the simple narrator has often been chosen by novelists, and has been a successful literary device: we owe much of our knowledge of the happenings at Wuthering Heights and at Thrushcross Grange to Nelly Dean, and Esther Summerson has kept us similarly informed about the happenings at Bleak House. One advantage in the simple narrator is that the reader feels that he does not know all, and therefore the characters have the mysterious vitality of living people: we can therefore take sides about the fictitious characters, as we can about people in real life, and in history — it is possible to read *Wuthering Heights* from a pro-Heathcliff, or a pro-Linton point of view, accepting either the romantic values of Wuthering Heights (by a willing suspension of disbelief) or the values of Thrushcross Grange, which are those of any sane morality. Similarly, in *The Heir of Redclyffe*, Guy and Amy may be our hero and heroine, or Philip and Laura.

There is, however, a great difference between the simple narrator, and the simple author. Nelly Dean and Esther Summerson are controlled by the higher intelligence of their creators, and therefore *Wuthering Heights* and *Bleak House* are significant works of art — a term which one cannot apply to a work in which no more developed mind than that of Charlotte Yonge is in evidence.

The sequel to *The Heir of Redclyffe*, by Mrs. Hicks Beach, is a most interesting commentary. A less creative but far more intelligent writer has understood Charlotte Yonge's characters more profoundly than she could have done herself, for much of their lives lay outside her range. Charlotte Yonge could never have 'gone behind' Charles, nor could she have revealed Philip's limitations; he was at any rate cleverer and better educated than she was, and had gained over her much the same ascendancy as he enjoyed over most of the women in the book. When reading *Amabel and Mary Verena*, we feel that we are revisiting in maturity people whom we have intimately known but imperfectly understood in early life — they seem smaller perhaps, even as places are said to shrink when revisited.

It is hard to avoid the conviction that Charlotte Yonge has presented character with some success, and that in a limited, but not negligible, sense *The Heir of Redclyffe* is a good novel, though not a significant work of art.

§6. THE GOOD BOOK WHICH IS A BAD NOVEL

If, however, we have to maintain that a significant work of art, which happens to be a novel, must be a good novel, then we are not far from the position of Miss Jenkyns in *Cranford* — we have no argument to oppose to her.

She had unwillingly been obliged to listen to poor Captain Brown reading the account of the 'swarry' which Sam Weller gave at Bath.

'When it was ended, she turned to me, and said with mild dignity — "Fetch me 'Rasselas', my dear, out of the book-room."

'When I had brought it to her, she turned to Captain Brown —

'"Now allow *me* to read you a scene, and then the present company can judge between your favourite, Mr. Boz, and Dr. Johnson."

'She read one of the conversations between Rasselas and Imlac, in a high-pitched, majestic voice: and when she had ended, she said, "I imagine I am now justified in my preference of Dr. Johnson as a writer of fiction." '

It is pleasant to reflect that Dr. Johnson would not probably have shared this preference. Though his remarks about Fielding are hostile, he could not have been insensitive to the quality of his writing; and though he may have felt Richardson's vulgarities less than Lady Mary Wortley Montagu did, they are likely to have struck him more forcibly than they strike most readers today — and yet he could declare: 'Sir, there is more knowledge of the heart in one letter of Richardson's, than in all *Tom Jones*.'

And yet *Rasselas* hardly succeeds as a novel — if, indeed, it was ever intended to do so — though worthy of all Miss Jenkyns's admiration as a book. As it is a book couched in the form of a novel, with characters and actions, then it would probably be an even better book if we could take any interest in those characters and actions — if, for example, the misfortunes of Pekuah had any power to move us. It is only through its brevity that it remains readable, and escapes that 'violent tediousness' which even such an admirer of D. H. Lawrence as Richard Aldington finds in his novels.

It is often objected, and with reason, that criticism which speaks of Form and Content, Plot and Character, Colour and Design, and the like is vicious — for it is putting asunder what God has joined; it is an artificial separation of what is, in each case, a single process, for the sake of a fruitless analysis. But only too often the single process, which is characteristic of the satisfactory work of art, has not taken place — the fatal split between two parts of what should have been a single process can only too often be discerned. It is when Form and Content, Plot and Character, etc., are straining apart, or are in some way incompatible, that it is still worth talking about them.

§7. BAD PROSE WITH A SIGNIFICANT CONTENT: HARDY

We may proceed to the second two questions, even more fundamental, about the separation of prose from its subject matter.

A passage from Hardy provides a convenient object-lesson.

'To persons standing alone on a hill during a clear midnight such as this, the roll of the world eastward is almost a palpable movement. The sensation may be caused by the panoramic glide of the stars past earthly objects, which is perceptible in a few minutes of stillness, or by the better outlook upon space that a hill affords, or by the wind, or by the solitude; but whatever be its origin, the impression of riding along is vivid and abiding. The poetry of motion is a phrase much in use, and to enjoy the epic form of that gratification it is necessary to stand on a hill at a small hour of the night, and, having first expanded with a sense of difference from the rest of civilized mankind, who are dreamwrapt and disregardful of all such proceedings at this time, long and quietly to watch your stately progress through the stars. After such a nocturnal reconnoitre it is hard to get back to earth, and to believe that the consciousness of such majestic speeding is derived from a tiny human frame.'

Lord David Cecil has chosen this passage from *Far From the Madding Crowd* for especial praise. 'Its detail', he writes of Hardy's vision of the natural world here expressed, 'endows it with the concrete recognizable actuality of something we know. It has also the compelling imaginative power of a picture which exhibits something known in a new, grander perspective, extending our field of vision so that we see what we know in relation to the greater conditioning forces we do not know. Incidentally, the passage is an illustration of how a strong creative imagination can make use of what might seem the most intractable material. The scientific view of the universe, introduced in the Victorian age, is a grim affair. Hardy was only too well aware of this . . . But the poet in him was undefeatable, and revealed through his eyes, it becomes the opportunity for a new sort of poetry — an awe-inspiring vision of infinite spaces and mysterious, irresistible forces — as compelling to the fancy as any primitive belief in the gods of wind and earth and fire.'[9]

This passage has a grand and cosmic beauty, one is ready to agree, and yet Mr. Denys Thompson has picked it out for especial condemnation. 'Strained, lumbering, creaking with polysyllables because the author thinks them "literary" ',[10] is his comment — and this also is true.

How horrible some of the phrases are! 'A palpable movement . . . The poetry of motion is a phrase much in use . . . to enjoy the epic form of that gratification . . . disregardful of all such proceedings . . . nocturnal reconnoitre.' Not to mince words, this is ugly, bad writing — and many persons of taste could easily rewrite such a passage to its great improvement — though they could never have seized the original feeling that inspired it, to which Lord David Cecil has done justice. This is another proof, if proof were required, that we need both 'academic' and 'practical' criticism — critics who see the wood, as well as critics who see the trees.

Hardy has said what he has to say very badly, but not so

badly that he has failed to say it: his meaning is significant, and can be apprehended as significant, though expressed in very bad prose. And if some of the blemishes were removed from this passage, the slight changes that we should make in the meaning (for a change of word is a change of meaning — and we have learned that there are no synonyms) would actually improve the meaning. For example, if we were to begin the third sentence thus: 'To enjoy the poetry of motion in its epic form'; if we were to omit the weak and clumsy phrase 'disregardful of all such proceedings', and to substitute such a word as 'adventure', or 'experience' for 'nocturnal reconnoitre' — the meaning on the whole would be clearer and sharper, and nothing that mattered would have been lost.

A significant meaning has to be apprehended through the ugly texture of the prose in the work of other mature writers — very often in that of George Eliot. And good writers, not yet mature, often know what they want to say, before they know how to say it — for example, it is sometimes difficult to make out how sensitively a complicated situation has been handled by L. H. Myers in *The Orissers*, because the book is not well enough written.

§8. EUPHONY

It must not, however, be thought that by some divine system of pre-established harmony the best meaning is always expressible in the best words, and that the prose-writer has only to be quite clear in his mind about what he wants to say. Euphony has also to be considered — and Flaubert's patient toil, removing repetitions, and assonances, and double genitives, was not a waste of time. The simplest and most lucid expression of a meaning may well be ungainly.[11]

It is sometimes best to write ungainly prose. A philosopher who wishes to express very fine shades of meaning, and whose aim is at all costs to be understood, and not at all to give pleasure, is justified in making a total sacrifice of euphony. Moreover, the use of precise, but ugly, philosophical jargon sometimes prevents the philosopher, as well as his readers, from getting into a muddle – Locke wrote euphonious English, and in consequence we do not always know, and it seems that he was not always sure, what precise meaning he attached to the word 'idea'.

The creative artist, novelist as well as poet, seldom has such a fine point of sense to convey as the philosopher – but his task in the use of words is no easier – he has often to convey a fine point of feeling. And here ugly but precise psychological jargon is no help to him at all, but quite the contrary. His art is that of rhetoric rather than dialectic – without some degree of euphony, and without great sensitiveness in the choice of words, he cannot make the reader feel the feeling that he wishes to convey. For we apprehend Sense no matter how ugly its expression is, so long as it is lucid and grammatical: from this point of view, the notices of births and deaths in the newspapers are perfectly adequate. It is when the advertisers have the bad taste to advertise also their feelings about these events that we are embarrassed – for feelings cannot be conveyed without art, though facts can.

§9. STYLE AND MEANING

We can perhaps return to the position that Style is not separable from Meaning, if by Meaning we understand the total Meaning – which Mr. I. A. Richards has analysed into four parts: Sense, Feeling, Tone and Intention — Feeling being the writer's attitude to the Sense he wishes to communicate; Tone, his attitude towards the readers with whom he wishes to communicate; and Intention the aims which he wishes to promote.[12]

With this for our definition of Meaning, we can endorse Flaubert's teaching, as reported by Maupassant: 'whatever the thing is that one wishes to say, there is only one word to express it, one verb to animate it, and one adjective to qualify it. Therefore one must search until one has found them, this word, this verb, this adjective.'[13]

The writer has to struggle with the claims of Sense, Tone, Feeling and Intention, which may not always be pulling the same way, and finally he has to wrestle with the angel of his language, and he must not let it go until it has blessed him — and Euphony is one of the blessings in its gift.

It is natural that many writers have seen all writing as translation. 'The duty and task of a writer', says Proust, 'are those of a translator.'[14] And Conrad writes: 'To render a crucial point of feelings in terms of human speech is really an impossible task. Written words can only form a sort of translation. And if that translation happens, from want of skill or from over-anxiety, to be too literal, the people caught in the toils of passion, instead of disclosing themselves, which would be art, are made to give themselves away, which is neither art nor life.'[15]

Poetry may sometimes be the 'original', but Prose is almost always 'translation' — and while Poetry, even when it is not great Poetry, has often reached its final state, Prose, as Katherine Mansfield discovered, 'is never finished'.

§ 10. CAN PROSE BE GOOD WHEN ITS CONTENT IS INSIGNIFICANT?

We are now in a better position not to answer the fourth question, for such questions cannot be answered, but to discover lines along which an answer may be sought.

Even when we know better, we are still prone to identify Meaning with its first part, Sense. If we give Meaning this limited meaning, then Form and Content are very much more easily separable: all that belongs to Feeling, Tone and Intention will be reckoned as part of the Form. It will then be easy to find very good prose which has no significant content. Letters, for example, by Cowper, and other excellent letter-writers, are often ostensibly about nothing — but while the Sense they convey is negligible, they are exquisite little masterpieces of Tone and Feeling.

We have been taught, by ancient works on Rhetoric, to recognize the merit of writing in which Intention is the prime element — when the orator wishes to urge his hearers to action, to resist Philip or to condemn Verres. We still lack a Rhetoric of Tone and Feeling.

But before we rise to the study of Rhetoric, there is the humble, essential and too much neglected study of Grammar to be made. 'Beautiful English' is an unfortunate conception, and unhappy are those who try to write it; 'Dignified English' is a language into which the Greek and Latin classics are too often translated — it is much the same thing as the jargon described by Fowler as 'Wardour Street'; but there is such a thing as 'Good English' — and it is Grammar that tells us what it is, and it can be learned and taught.

§ II. GRAMMAR MAY BE ABSENT FROM GOOD PROSE

We can and should admire such a speech as Mrs. Gamp's, in which Grammar (the wider term also includes Syntax) is set at naught. Its relation to a beautiful speech by an illiterate person in real life is much the same as the relation we discussed between the narrative of a simple narrator directed by a great artist (Nelly Dean or Esther Summerson) and the narrative of a naturally simple narrator (Charlotte Yonge).

Mr. Herbert Read is right in asking us to admire Vanzetti's great speech to Judge Thayer. 'If it had not been for these thing, I might have live out my life, talking at street corners to scorning men. I might have die, unmarked, unknown, a failure. Now we are not a failure. This is our career and our triumph. Never in our full life can we hope to do such work for tolerance, for joostice, for man's understanding of man, as now we do by an accident. Our words — our lives — our pains — nothing! The taking of our lives — lives of a good shoemaker and a poor fish peddler — all! That last moment belong to us — that agony is our triumph!'[1]

Mr. Read is right in saying that though this speech is devoid of all 'artistry' and of all deliberate structure, it has the elements of great prose. It would be barren pedantry to deny that this great tragic speech had the elements of great prose; it would be sentimentality to say that it was great prose. But the great comic speech of Mrs. Gamp has a very great artist behind it, moulding its deliberate structure — it is great prose. A great artist in prose must know his grammar, even if he chooses to play tricks with it.

§12. LE STYLE EST L'HOMME

If we take Meaning to be the total meaning: Sense, Feeling, Tone and Intention — and if Style is the Expression of that Meaning, and inseparable from it — then we can give new life to the old cliché *le style est l'homme*, for we are what we mean.

We are not the same at all times, and we probably ought to take care to purify ourselves from our worst passions before writing — or at any rate we ought not to write for the public when we are at our worst, any more than we should write private letters in a temper.

'A certain transfusion takes place upon paper', wrote the Abbé de St. Cyran, 'of the spirit and heart of the writer, and is the cause of one perceiving, so to speak, his image in the picture of the thing which he represents . . . The smallest cloud in our heart will spread on our paper, like a bad breath that tarnishes the whole surface of a mirror, and our smallest indisposition will be like a worm that passes into our writing, to gnaw the heart of those who read it to the end of the world.'[17]

This is, of course, exaggerated scrupulosity — and if a novelist were to accept Jansenist direction, he must throw down his pen; we know well enough the words of Pierre Nicole: 'A writer of novels and a dramatic poet is a public poisoner, not of bodies but of the souls of the faithful, and should regard himself as guilty of an infinite number of spiritual homicides.'[18]

It is in the spirit of Nicole that the English laws about obscenity have been framed, and most enlightened people think them rather a pity. We are not responsible for the effects of our writing on other people further than our intention goes — Benjamin Constant was wrong in being shocked when Goethe told him that he did not care if *Werther* were dangerous reading for fools, for Goethe was not writing for fools. But for our intention we are totally and gravely responsible, and it is a most serious duty to keep it pure. It would be better if contemporary criticism were more exacting about authors' purity of intention, and troubled less about their idealogies. And purity of intention is to be deduced by the methods of literary criticism, and no others, from style not biography — for a vicious man can sometimes remain a virtuous writer.[19]

All the same, a writer had better be as good as he can be, were it only for the sake of his writing. Fowler, in *Modern English Usage*, has clearly shown that many faults in writing spring from real faults in feeling and character; they are not only due to bad taste and to literary ill-breeding, but to moral faults, such as envy, hypocrisy, vanity and cowardice. If the style is the man, the man has always room for improvement.[20]

And conversely, the man may be improved by the improvement of the style; for improvement can proceed both from the heart outwards, and from without inwards to the heart. The thought need not surprise us: anyone who has heard sermons is familiar with the duty of controlling that unruly member the tongue — and everything that we have been told about the tongue is equally true about our eleventh finger, the pen, except that the pen is much easier to control. If we could as easily go back and erase or emend our speeches, our lives would be happier: our writing need never be hurried, ill-considered, or ill-tempered.

If, with Fowler for our director, we were to rid our style of vanity, envy, hypocrisy and cowardice, we should have gone a long way towards being more courageous and more truthful.

NOTES

[1] *Fiction and the Reading Public*, p. 232f.
[2] *Selected Essays*, pp. 110ff.
[3] Ibid., pp. 50ff.

[4] *A Preface to Paradise Lost*, p. 1.

[5] What are we to say of such works as the novels of Amanda Ros, which are supposed to give delight because they are so bad? The authoress certainly did not intend them to give the kind of delight that they give, but they cannot be said to be a failure. It is surely some strange kind of excellence that gives delight, not badness, which is merely dull.

[6] Loc. cit., p. 175.

[7] Ibid., p. 132, and see chap. v, s.v. 'Knowledge of Motives'.

[8] *Victorian Best-seller: the world of Charlotte M. Yonge*, by MARGARET MARE and ALICIA PERCIVAL, p. 5.

[9] *Hardy the Novelist*, p. 73.

[10] *Reading and Discrimination*, ad fin. Cf. the criticisms of Hardy in GEORGE MOORE's *Conversations in Ebury Street*.

[11] For a discussion of Euphony, see *The Summing-Up*, by W. SOMERSET MAUGHAM.

[12] *Practical Criticism*, pp. 179ff.

[13] *Le Roman* (preface to *Pierre et Jean*).

[14] *Le Temps Retrouvé*, II, p. 41.

[15] Preface to *Within the Tides*.

[16] *English Prose Style*, p. 165.

[17] Cit. SAINTE BEUVE, *Port Royal*, II, ix.

[18] Ibid., VI, x. Cf. 'Nous savons d'expérience que le même ouvrage qui aide au salut de beaucoup d'âmes en peut corrompre plusieurs autres. Cela est vrai, même de l'Ecriture.' FRANCOIS MAURIAC, *La Roman*, p. 78.

[19] Cf. *A Treatise on the Novel*, p. 50 and note.

[20] It has been pointed out to me, however, by M. Cyril des Baux, that the Devil should be given his due: he has inspired some works of art. He adds that certain works of Gide owe their quality to hypocrisy.

III

SUMMARY

§ 1. SUMMARY

All narrative art is made up of Summary and Scene: if there were no Summary it would be dramatic and not narrative, and if there were no Scene, as we shall see, it would not be art.

Even Drama itself finds difficulty in getting on without Summary. When it is read, and not seen on the stage, some form of stage directions are necessary — whether they are the brief indications of the speakers' names which sufficed in the great ages of Drama, or the long descriptive passages to which we have become accustomed in the decadence of that art in the hands of Barrie and Shaw.

Even in great ages of Drama it was necessary to put stage directions from time to time into the mouths of characters — to disguise, in fact, this form of Summary as Scene.

Examples leap to the mind:

There stands the castle by yon tuft of trees . . .

or the lines in *Bérénice*, that so much amused Horace Walpole:

De son appartement cette porte est prochaine,
Et cette autre conduit dans celuy de la Reine.

Stage representation can nowadays replace that sort of thing in most cases, but it can do nothing to obviate the tiresome process, necessarily narrative and non-dramatic, which Henry James called 'Harking back to make up'.[1]

This process has been admirably parodied by Sheridan:[2]

SIR WALTER You know, my friend, scarce two revolving suns
And three revolving moons have closed their course,
Since haughty Philip, in despite of peace,
With hostile hand hath struck at England's trade.

SIR CHRISTOPHER I know it well.

SIR WALTER Philip, you know, is proud Iberia's king!

SIR CHRISTOPHER He is.

SIR WALTER His subjects in base bigotry
And Catholic oppression held, — while we
You know, the Protestant persuasion hold.

SIR CHRISTOPHER We do.

Dangle. Mr. Puff, as he *knows* all this, why does Sir Walter go on telling him?

Puff. But the audience are not supposed to know anything of the matter, are they?

Sneer. True, but I think you manage ill: for there certainly appears no reason why Sir Walter should be so communicative.

Puff. 'Fore Gad, now, that is one of the most ungrateful observations I ever heard — for the less inducement he has to tell this the more, I think, you ought to be obliged to him; for I am sure you'd know nothing of the matter without it.

The cinema can flash upon the screen a printed summary of any information needed by the audience. Elizabethan drama could tell us things in the soliloquy (though First and Second Gentlemen or Citizens did a good deal of 'harking back to make up'). And in Greek drama the Gods themselves could appear in the prologue to supply necessary information. It is only in a realistic play on a modern picture-stage that this process is merely absurd. It requires a good deal of ingenuity to avoid, and even very competent playwrights sometimes fail. In *The Circle*, for instance, by Mr. Somerset Maugham, characters sit round and inform each other about facts in their family history of which, being close relations, none of them could well be ignorant.

Fiction, which still has the resource of Summary undisguised, has very little excuse for employing Summary badly disguised as Scene, when it needs to 'hark back to make up'. And yet in one form or another this fault still occurs. The device, for instance, of 'the tale within a tale' — not necessarily, but commonly a disaster — is not yet dead. It was one of the devices Jane Austen made fun of in her comic synopsis of a novel, designed to suit the tastes in fiction of the Prince Regent's librarian: 'Book to open with father and daughter conversing in long speeches, elegant language, and a tone of high, serious sentiment. The father induced, at his daughter's earnest request, to relate to her the past events of his life. Narrative to reach through the greater part of the first volume. . . .'

§2. FICTION MAY BE NEARLY ALL SCENE

The most vital part of a novel is always in the form of Scene, and Scene is the condition to which narrative seems always to aspire. In *Emma* Jane Austen seems to have tried to use the minimum amount of Summary, and very much less has been used by Henry James in *The Awkward Age*, and by Miss Compton-Burnett in all her novels.

But characters by Henry James and Miss Compton-Burnett do not talk like other people. In their speeches, often long, and usually unrealistic, they show a subtlety quite foreign to the stage — for which Henry James proved unfit, and for which

Miss Compton-Burnett has said she has no inclination. They are able to 'go behind' their characters, as Henry James would say. Older Drama could do this, in the soliloquy – modern prose drama on a picture-stage cannot do this – and it was this advance in realism, as much as anything else, that was the death of Drama as an art-form.

Miss Compton-Burnett's novels, moreover, abound in stage directions: if she makes her characters speak more than any other writer's, no other writer tells us more precisely how the people speak, or how they move when they speak.

They raise their eyebrows, stand squarely, look around, fall into open mirth (or into rather doubtful mirth); they give a yawn, draw themselves up, press their fingers to their brow, look faintly startled, or step impetuously forward. . . .

They may speak in a strident, self-confident voice; or in a colourless tone; a low, quick tone; an even tone; an open, considering tone; husky, languid tones; or a tender, almost shaken tone; on an urgent note; quietly; with a roguish eye; with an indulgent smile; or with a faint frown; with a touch of firmness, a touch of grimness, or a touch of earnestness; spacing their words; in a condoning manner; or even in a manner of saying what should be said, whether or no with hope of result. These examples have been picked, more or less at random, from one, only, of her novels; it is no exaggeration to say that her whole work would probably yield hundreds more.

Of course the way in which they say things modifies considerably what they say. This truth has been recognized by a very different writer when he says: 'In civilized life domestic hatred usually expresses itself by saying things which would appear quite harmless on paper (the *words* are not offensive) but in such a voice, or at such a moment, that they are not far short of a blow in the face.'[8] Miss Compton-Burnett will not allow an evil speech to appear harmless on paper — and that is one of her great and almost unique distinctions as a writer of dialogue.

The characters in *The Awkward Age*, who have more intangible things to convey, are even more subtle in their shades of expression. They faintly gasp, appreciatively sigh, ever so graciously smile, and protestingly moan their speeches. Now they are delightfully positive, now they speak with utter detachment, and now with an argumentative sharpness. Now they give little wails of baffled imagination, now their gaiety deepens, or they veer a little to indulgence. They can glare and grin and muse (all at once, so it would appear); they are indeed, as their creator often tells us, wonderful.

§3. SUMMARY IS NEEDED TO CONTROL THE TEMPO

A novel is not, like a statue or a picture or a building or a short lyric poem, all there at once — it is an experience that unfolds in time, like a play or a musical composition. A playwright or a composer can control the speed at which his works are performed, can at least indicate the speed he desires — and is able to provide for pauses. But the novelist writes for private reading, which may take place at any speed, and he has no reason to suppose that the end of a chapter will necessarily hold up the reader. He must therefore carefully keep such control as he can over the narrative tempo by structural means — for the tempo must be important in any art that cannot make an instantaneous effect.

'The object of a story is to be long,' wrote Stevenson, who was putting the process in its simplest terms, 'to fill up hours; the story-teller's art of writing is to water out by continual invention, historical and technical, and yet not seem to water; seem on the other hand to practise that same wit of conspicuous and declaratory condensation which is the proper art of writing. That is one thing in which my stories fail: I am always cutting the flesh off their bones.'[4]

It is not only that a story has to go on for a certain length of time — but that events in a story must occur at the proper place. In a child's composition the dénouement of a story is likely to take place in the first or second sentence, and more self-conscious writers do not always sufficiently prepare their events. Henry James took Mrs. Humphry Ward to task for this fault: 'I think your material suffers a little from the fact that the reader feels you approach your subject too *immediately*, show him its elements, the cards in your hands too bang off from the first page — so that a wait to begin to guess *what and whom the thing is going to be about* doesn't impose itself: the ante-chamber or two and the crooked corridor before he is already in the Presence.'[5]

It must generally be the work of Summary to guide the reader down the crooked corridor, or to entertain him in the ante-chambers — Scene is a more precious effect reserved for more important uses, and liable to debasement if put to servile tasks like these — it is also liable to become artificial or tedious.

Moreover the subject of a novel is often, in itself, a gradual process — the gradual formation, for example, or disintegration of a character. This is a subject almost impossible for a dramatist to handle: he must fasten on crucial incidents. Thus Racine, in the twelve-hour day of *Britannicus*, is able to show the first fatal steps by which Nero began his career of tyranny; and in the twelve-hour day of *Phèdre* he shows the final consequences of her long repressed passion. For a more complete unfolding of either process, Summary would have to give its aid. Even a rapid, if gradual, process like inebriation needs in part to be described by Summary. In *Savonarola Brown* Lucrezia Borgia hands a cup of wine to a gaoler, and he immediately becomes helplessly drunk – this instantaneous effect is not worthy of imitation; and there are too many dreary drinking scenes in dramatic literature, in which the process is as slow as in life, or slower; not the least dreary is that in *Guy Domvile*.

Henry James, in later life, was conscious of having got the time-scheme wrong in *Roderick Hudson*; of having gone too fast. 'Everything', he says, 'occurs . . . too punctually . . . Roderick's disintegration, a gradual process, and of which the exhibitional interest is exactly that it *is* gradual and occasional, and thereby traceable and watchable, swallows two years in a mouthful, proceeds quite *not* by years, but by weeks and months, and thus renders the whole view the disservice of appearing to present him as a morbidly special case . . . at the rate at which he falls to pieces, he seems to place himself beyond our understanding and our sympathy.'[6]

In an art that unfolds itself in time (and no metaphysical speculations about the nature of Time are here necessary – ordinary everyday time, that we measure with our watches, is meant) things must happen (or seem to happen) at the right time, and must take (or seem to take) the right time to happen.

'Life', says Maupassant, 'precipitates events, or drags them out indefinitely. Art consists, on the contrary, in making use of precautions and preparations, in arranging cleverly disguised transitions, in throwing the light on the essential happenings by skill in composition alone, and throwing all other happenings into suitable relief according to their importance.'[7]

In a novel in which Summary is almost totally lacking, time

sometimes seems to stand still. Miss Compton-Burnett's characters have to go away from their home circles at times: some of them teach or learn at schools or universities, others have one or another sort of 'London life'. But when we open one of her novels we are as certain to find them all at home as we are to find everyone in *Grandison* in the cedar-chamber. This is not a fault: the characters appear to feel that their family life goes on all the time, that there is no real escape from it, and that whatever they have done or suffered elsewhere is of little significance in comparison – this kind of continuity is indeed almost the worst terror of that kind of life.

For this reason, perhaps, she contents herself with very short passages of summary, short enough to be telling.

'Clement remained at the window after his brother had left him. He was to stand there several times in the next two months. At the end of them he came to the room where his sister was alone.'

Summary has also to be used to tell the history of happy people who have no history – happiness is seldom dramatic enough to be given in scenes. And yet one would be sorry to say that there is no room for happiness in fiction. People like reading about it, understandably. 'Why write about imaginary unhappiness,' they often say, 'when there is so much real unhappiness in the world?' It is a common plea of Circulating Library subscribers, and rather harder to take into account than their preference for 'Love without Sex'. But it expresses a feeling that even sophisticated novel-readers must share, if they are human. Sainte Beuve evidently shared it, and he must have included happiness in 'the good' that was too entirely absent from *Madame Bovary*. 'Is it, however, the office of art to wish not to console, to refuse to admit any element of gentleness and sweetness under colour of being more true?

For truth, if that were all that one were after, is not entirely and necessarily on the side of evil, on the side of stupidity and human perversity.'[8] The desire for some comfort from literature is not wholly to be mocked at and flouted — the scenes of Levin's country life in *Anna Karenina* may cause what Henry James calls a 'leak in its interest', but add immensely to the geniality in which that book gains so much over Flaubert's novel. Nor are the convalescences of Lucy Snow and of Marianne Dashwood, in *Villette* and in *Sense and Sensibility*, the least good things in those admirable books.

Even if it were not (in moderation) a good thing in itself in fiction, happiness would earn a place there as a necessary preparation for trouble. *O mors quam amara est memoria tua homini pacem habenti in substantiis suis!* The novelist needs a little space to show the man of substance in peace, and some passages of summary in which to do it. Hardy has done this so well in several chapters of *The Mayor of Casterbridge*, that it is a real tragedy — we feel the decline and fall of Michael Henchard, because we can believe that things could have continued to go well with him, whereas Tess, with whom nothing could ever have gone right, fails to move us so greatly. In life, as well as in art, the persistently afflicted are more tedious than pitiful — even more bored with than they are sorry for themselves.

In general, we may say of the happiness of fictional characters very much what Proust says about their authors' happiness. 'As for happiness, it has almost only a single use, to make misfortune possible. In happiness we must form very sweet and very strong ties of confidence and attachment so that their rupture may cause us that so precious heart-rending called misfortune. If one had not been happy, were it only in prospect, misfortunes would have been without cruelty, and, in consequence without fruit.'[9] Just as love is for fictional characters, as Flaubert said it was for the artist, principally valuable as a source of suffering — its procreative function is so very unimportant in fiction.

Another history that has to be reported in summary (if it is reported at all) is the history of public events that have been going on while the characters in the novel have lived their private lives. This kind of summary is a temptation to the novelist: it is restful and easy to do, it fills up space, and makes his book look 'important'. But Jane Austen got on perfectly without mention of the Napoleonic wars, which must have been of interest to several characters in her novels: contemporary novelists are apt to make extensive reference to public events that are of much less importance to their characters — it is a satisfaction to the reader when he can catch them out in errors of chronology, he feels it serves them right.

The unpretentious news reels of Mr. John Dos Passos are probably as good a device as any for reporting news — if it must be done. Though the reader feels uncomfortably that an arbitrary selection of news items has been put in front of him, and that other selections would have served the author's purpose just as well — and this destroys completely the illusion of inevitability, so necessary for making us think that what we are reading is a work of art. However, they are so arranged that the reader can easily omit them, and get on with the story — this is, perhaps, a low sort of merit, but it is not altogether to be despised: too many excrescences on fiction cannot be spotted on a first reading — Dickens and Scott are very much better reading when we know them well enough to be able to skip.

It seems strange to mention Virginia Woolf in this company, but she had as a device a special use of summary designed to mark the passage of time, and to make pauses in her narrative.

She may have hoped that it would do for her novels something of what the chorus does in Greek tragedy – a suspension of time in timeless poetry, not altogether remote from the feelings and thoughts of the play. Unfortunately the central chapter in *To the Lighthouse*, and the passages about the waves in *The Waves* are failed poetry: this fact has been obscured because too many critics, unable to understand them, have not ventured to rate them at their proper worth.[10] Sensitive admirers of Virginia Woolf's work, who have been embarrassed by these passages, probably let their eyes travel very lightly over them on re-reading these books – and so they will be briefly held up, and the tempo will have been controlled, even if it has not happened quite in the way that the author intended.

§4. FICTION THAT IS ALL SUMMARY

Fiction that is all Summary can hardly be called art at all. 'The art of fiction does not begin', writes Mr. Percy Lubbock, 'until the novelist thinks of his story as a matter to be *shown*, to be so exhibited that it will tell itself. To hand over to the reader the facts of the story as so much information – this is no more than to state the "argument" of the book, the groundwork upon which the novelist proceeds to create. The book is not a row of facts, it is a single image; the facts have no validity in themselves, they are nothing until they have been used.'[11]

Novelists sometimes are content to state the argument of a book, and to leave it at that, without even touching the difficult part of their art, indeed that part which alone deserves the name of art. Critics and readers are sometimes deceived into thinking that the resulting novels show a fine line or an artistic economy – whereas they are merely empty. Many short-story writers are forced by the exigence of space into this vice of synopsis writing; Mr. Somerset Maugham has not altogether escaped it. And the novels of Maurice Baring generally consist of little but groundwork, on which that novelist seldom built anything.

'The novelist who doesn't represent, and represent all the time is lost',[12] as Henry James says; he even speaks as if Summary ought to be ruled out altogether: 'Processes, periods, intervals, stages, degrees, connections may be easily enough and barely enough named, may be unconvincingly stated, in fiction, to the deep discredit of the writer, but it remains the very deuce to represent them.'[13] Perhaps it is not always necessary that processes, periods, intervals, stages, degrees, connections should be represented — if they are briefly stated in summary, and their consequences represented in scenes, the novelist may have done enough. The reader will not feel that he has been requested to take something on trust — 'the very death'[14] of the art of fiction.

As we have already seen, fiction is a rhetorical art, and seeks to communicate Feeling quite as much as Sense — and Feeling is not to be communicated in a bare summary. So that those who criticize adversely readers of fiction for being deeply moved by the woes of fictional characters while they are comparatively unmoved by accounts in a newspaper of an air crash, or a mine disaster, show a great insensitiveness to the power of words. St. Augustine (who himself used words magnificently) was temporarily forgetting their power when he blamed himself for weeping for Dido, and not for his sins. What is Hecuba to us? The mobled queen is everything that the poets of two thousand five hundred years have represented her to be — while yesterday's victims, whom war, dearth, age, agues, tyrannies, despair, law, chance, hath slain are less lamentable — *carent quia vate sacro*. At best, we can use our imaginations upon them, and ourselves become their poets: but Homer and

Vergil were better poets than we are. 'The facts are nothing [to us] until they have been used.'

'Representation' is of such importance that the reader feels particularly badly cheated if a big scene is avoided. Henry James rightly complains that in *The Bride of Lammermoor* there is a deviation of interest from the centre of the subject towards the frame — 'which is, so to speak, beautifully rich and curious' — because the central subject has never been represented in a scene. 'The situation represented is that Ravenswood loves Lucy Ashton through dire difficulty and danger, and that she in the same way loves him; but the relation so created between them is . . . never shown us as primarily taking place. It is shown only in its secondary, its confused and disfigured aspects — where, however, luckily, it is presented with great romantic good faith.'[15] We have never seen Edgar and Lucy in any way loving; we are merely told they love.

It is all the more unfortunate if a scene has been led up to, has been promised, as it were, to the reader, and then never takes place. A 'messenger's speech' is not at all sufficient, for in fiction, where we do not *see* the scene, the rules of classical decorum do not apply: Medea may kill her children before the people (i.e. the readers), though on the stage it would be revolting. Indeed she had better do so.

One would not like to say that nothing should ever be 'left to the imagination'. Fiction would then be severely limited; and George Moore was probably right in saying that 'there are scenes in life that cannot be written, even if they can be proved to have happened'[16] — though he may not be right in picking upon Willoughby's repentance in *Sense and Sensibility* as such a scene. Characters would lose in verisimilitude if the novelist lost his 'negative capability', and was not allowed to be in doubt about some of their motives — even the omniscient

Proust uses this power. And Henry James would then not be allowed his power of 'adumbration',[17] whereby he suggests more evil in *The Turn of the Screw*, and in one or two other stories, than is actually stated. The reader is encouraged to frighten himself thoroughly:

> *Like one, that on a lonesome road*
> *Doth walk in fear and dread,*
> *And having once turned round walks on,*
> *And turns no more his head . . .*

Nevertheless Henry James sometimes overdid 'adumbration'. We feel uneasy about the frightful apparition in the haunted room that killed Owen Wingrave. And when our fears have not been played upon, the adumbration is even less successful. We cannot at all believe in the something (unspecified, but dreadful) that Louisa Pallant tells a young man to discourage him from marrying her daughter.

'There may be such a state of mind brought about on the reader's part, I think, as a positive desire to take on trust', wrote Henry James, 'but that is only the final fruit of insidious proceedings, operative to a sublime end, on the author's side.'[18] When the reader sees through the insidiousness of the author's proceedings, trustfulness vanishes. It is not easy to trust the narrator in *The Figure in the Carpet* when he tries to make us believe that there was a cryptic *something* at the heart of Hugh Vereker's work, essential to its understanding, and unperceived even by the most intelligent critics. (It has become no easier to believe in this since people have busied themselves with the Figure in Henry James's carpet, and have propounded theories in which it is very difficult to believe.[19] We should remember George Corvick's words in this story: 'that if we had Shakespeare's own word for his being cryptic he would at once have accepted it. The case was altogether different — we had nothing but the word of Mr. Snooks.' We have not Henry James's own word for his work being cryptic.)

We are annoyed at things being left to our imagination, when we feel that the author's imagination has not worked hard enough: this suspicion, invalid in the case of Chekov himself, is only too valid in the case of most Chekovian short-story writers. Katherine Mansfield possibly entertained this suspicion about herself. 'What I chiefly admire in Jane Austen', she wrote, 'is that what she promises, she performs, i.e. if Sir T. is to arrive, we have his arrival at length, and it's excellent, and exceeds our expectations. This is rare; it is also my weakest point. Easy to see why. . . .'[20]

We are told that we should promise to perform virtuous actions when we intend to do them and are unlikely to be prevented (we give our future beneficiaries the pleasure of expectation, we further bind ourselves to do what we ought, and we acquire the extra merit of having fulfilled a promise — which is rightly denied to those mean people who say: 'I never make promises'). All this is no doubt applicable to fiction as well as to life, and we see that Jane Austen does indeed acquire an extra merit in this way — over and above the surpassing merit of Sir Thomas Bertram's return.

§ 5. SUMMARY INTO SCENE

At this stage it is time to hazard a definition of Summary and Scene. Scene is that part of a novel in which the novelist makes things happen under the reader's eyes. Summary is that part of a novel in which the novelist says that things are happening, or that they have happened — and sometimes there is a prophetic summary at the end of the book about things that will happen.

Scene cannot quite be equated with Dialogue, though Dialogue should probably not be used for purposes of Summary — the conversation between Sir Walter Raleigh and Sir Christopher Hatton shows what can happen if it is used in this way. There are, however, scenes that are not wholly in Dialogue — and various fusions of Summary and Scene.

For example, there is Scene in Indirect Speech — and since indirect narration is the form used, a great deal more can be said than what passed in dialogue between the characters. Nevertheless the novelist keeps near enough to Scene for the whole passage to have value as 'Representation'; he has 'represented' his processes, periods, intervals, stages, degrees, connections, or he has persuaded the reader that he has done so — which is nearly the same thing.

In the following passage from *The Spoils of Poynton,* far more is conveyed than a dialogue between Fleda and Mrs. Gereth could convey, but without much tiresome 'harking back to make up' — words and phrases of actual speech are reported, to give greater vividness.

'She hated the effacement to which English usage reduced the widowed mother; she had discoursed of it passionately to Fleda; contrasted it with the beautiful homage paid by other countries to women in that position, women no better than herself, whom she had seen acclaimed and enthroned, whom she had known and envied; made in short as little as possible a secret of the injury, the bitterness she found in it. The great wrong Owen had done her was not his "taking up" with Mona — that was disgusting, but it was a detail, an accidental form; it was his failure from the first to understand what it was to have a mother at all, to appreciate the beauty and sanctity of the character.

She was just his mother as his nose was his nose, and he had never had the least imagination or tenderness or gallantry about her. One's mother, gracious goodness, if one were the kind of fine young man one ought to be, the only kind Mrs. Gereth cared for, was a subject for poetry, for idolatry. . . .'

Flaubert, who needed a great deal of summary, wished nevertheless to represent everything. 'This should be six or seven pages at most, and without one *reflection* or one *analysis*,'[21] is one observation of his. Again he says: 'I persecute metaphors, and finally banish moral analyses.'[22] Yet by extreme skill in transition from Scene to Summary, by the insertion of vivid, photographic pictures to give life to narrative passages, he was able to use more Summary than appears to the casual reader. Moreover he will write what appears to be Scene in the imperfect tense ('they used to . . .'); another device which requires skill to use, but which used with his great skill enables him to convey a great deal of necessary information in such a way that it seems hardly separable from the happenings, which he produces before our eyes.

NOTES

[1] *The Art of the Novel*, p. 321.
[2] *The Critic*, II, p. 2.
[3] C. S. Lewis, *The Screwtape Papers*, iii.
[4] *The Letters of Robert Louis Stevenson*, ed. Sidney Colvin (London, 1900), II, p. 93.
[5] *The Letters of Henry James*, ed. Percy Lubbock (1920), I, p. 330.
[6] Loc. cit., p. 12.
[7] Preface to *Pierre et Jean*.
[8] *Causeries du Lundi*, XIII, 4 mai, 1857.
[9] *Le Temps Retrouvé*, II, p. 65.
[10] Cf. 'We all know that *The Waves* is a poem and a masterpiece, but we dare not read it; we cannot; we can no more read it than we can walk like flies, on the ceiling; we are too heavy, we sink, we fall. I say "we", but I make a very humble and tentative exception for myself! Having an insatiable passion for the sea, and having spent last winter with its waves coming in at my window, I fell in love at first sight with those matchless inter-chapters . . . and would not admit I could not read the book till, having read every page at least five times, I very nearly

did understand it.' B. DE SÉLINCOURT, cit. DENYS THOMPSON, *Reading and Discrimination*, p. 106.

[11] *The Craft of Fiction*, p. 62.

[12] *The Art of the Novel*, p. 94.

[13] Ibid.

[14] Ibid., p. 224.

[15] Ibid., p. 68.

[16] *Avowals*, ch. 1.

[17] Loc. cit., p. 175.

[18] Ibid., p. 224.

[19] e.g. Mr. Edmund Wilson's theory about *The Turn of the Screw*, and Mr. Quentin Anderson's interpretation of *The Wings of the Dove*.

[20] *Journals*, January 2nd, 1922.

[21] *Correspondance*, II, p. 205.

[22] Ibid., III, p. 11, 10 mai, 1855.

IV

DIALOGUE

§ I. THE LATE APPEARANCE OF DIALOGUE

'We have seen', wrote George Saintsbury, of conversation in fiction, 'how very long it was before its powers and advantages were properly appreciated; how mere *récit* dominated fiction; and how, when the personages were allowed to speak, they were for the most part furnished only or mainly with harangues – like those with which the 'unmixed' historian used to endow his characters. That conversation is not merely a grand set-off to a story, but that it is an actual means of telling the story itself, seems to have been unconscionably and almost unintelligibly slow in occurring to men's minds; though in the actual story-telling of ordinary life by word of mouth it is, and always must have been, frequent enough.'[1]

Drama perhaps, in its great days, was monopolizing conversation. If fictitious characters wanted to talk, it was perhaps thought that the stage was there for that purpose – while, between the covers of a book, with no impatient audience to curb them, they could safely indulge in long set speeches.

Yet, though a late development, and a mark of growing sophistication in the art of the novel, there is nothing about conversation that makes it a particularly sophisticated taste. It was Alice who observed: 'What is the use of a book without pictures or conversations?' Fortunately she decided that it was of no use, and fell into her wonderful dream.

§2. THE ABUSE OF DIALOGUE

Some writers, and many readers have, however, felt and expressed some caution about conversation in fiction. Of course, like every other fictional device, it can be abused, it may become boring. Edith Wharton went so far as to maintain that only significant words should be said. 'The vital dialogue is that exchanged by characters whom their creator has really vitalized, and his instinct will be to record only the significant passages of their talk, in high relief against the narrative, and not uselessly embedded in it.'[2] This is an extreme, but an understandable, view.

Anthony Trollope has defined the place of conversation in the novel as well as anyone: he was no aesthetician, but he had great good sense.

'The dialogue is generally the most agreeable part of a novel; but it is only so as long as it tends in some way to the telling of the main story. It need not seem to be confined to that, but it should always have a tendency in that direction. The unconscious critical acumen of the reader is both just and severe. When a long dialogue on extraneous matter reaches his mind, he at once feels he is being cheated into taking something which he did not bargain to accept when he took up that novel. He does not at that moment require politics or philosophy, but he wants his story.'[3]

Too often we are given politics or philosophy, and with little relevance to the story, either because the novelist wishes to write propaganda for or against some point of view, or merely out of vanity — because he thinks he has something entertaining to say on these or other subjects. Sometimes it is out of laziness, for nothing is easier than writing dialogue on extraneous matters. It is the least exacting way of discussing art or thought, for as soon as a speaker gets into difficulties he can be interrupted, and all awkward questions can be left unanswered. The author remembers, conveniently, that his dialogue is intended to be dramatic and not Socratic, and he evades the obligations of philosophical dialogue just as he has ignored those of fiction.

This is not to say that fictional characters may not speak well, and on subjects of general interest — but it will be better if all the time their creator is asking himself, of all their utterances: 'does this further the plot?' or: 'does this reveal the speaker's character?' or: 'in what way does this tend to the telling of the main story?'

A resolution which André Gide noted in his journal is here in point. 'Don't go in for politics and hardly ever read the newspaper; but do not lose a chance of talking politics with no matter whom; it tells you nothing about public affairs, but it admirably informs you about people's characters.'[4]

The novelist can only give us stale information, and probably only second or third hand ideas about public affairs: what we ask him to give us, through the mouths of his people, is information about their characters.

It need not be the besetting sin of every fictional character that he shows off in conversation — a trait almost universal in Mr. Aldous Huxley's characters. There are people in real life who do not so show off — and they are sometimes found among people whose talk is polished and witty.

§3. THE MOST PLEASING FORM OF DIALOGUE

Two novelists who abound in dialogue, Henry James and Miss Compton-Burnett, generally give us the highly polished conversation of very sophisticated and clever people. But their clever people are clever dramatically; their good things appear to proceed from the moment, and not from previous study. They cannot easily be detached from their context for quotation, and the whole context is brilliant, not merely a setting for a few flashy gems.

It was into such a world of civilized talk that Marivaux's heroine Marianne entered. 'It is certain', she said, 'that they had more wit than other people, and that I heard them saying excellent things; but they said them with so little effort, they were seeking so little for effect, it was so easy and uniform a tone of conversation that I might well have believed they were uttering complete commonplaces . . . Witty people are often accused of wishing to shine; oh there was no question of that here! And, as I have already said, if I had not had a little natural taste, a little feeling, I could have been mistaken, and I should have noticed nothing.'

It is this sort of circle that is most attractive in fiction. We do not only wish to read about characters who resemble the sort of people we should like to have for friends, we also like reading about silly, dishonest, rude and cruel people — but, if we are to listen to their converse, some of the same rules apply in fiction as in life. 'The company of clever, well-informed people, who have a great deal of conversation' is the best company.

As in real life, we will tolerate, and even enjoy the presence of some eccentrics and Malaprops — we can also appreciate the rustic simplicity of peasant speech — but the general level of conversation that we shall prefer will be that of educated people. So it is in the novels of Jane Austen and Henry James, in Stendhal and Proust and Tolstoy — so it is in the majority of the best modern novels, among others in those of Lawrence,

Virginia Woolf, Mr. Forster, Miss Compton-Burnett and Miss Elizabeth Bowen, and in those of MM. Gide, Mauriac and Camus.

§4. THE VICE OF 'SCUDÉRYSME'

In easy and well-bred fictitious conversation, there is not any ground for the uncomfortable suspicion that the characters think each other very clever, and that the author is indirectly complimenting himself through their mouths on his own cleverness. For all the cleverness they have is necessarily derived from himself — apart from such quotations from other writers as he allows them to let fall, and from such bits of out-of-the-way knowledge as they evince. These are dragged in from his *arrière-boutique*, or perhaps from the Encyclopaedia Britannica, or other reference books.

The sin of self-praise, when thus practised by novelists, may be called for convenience *Scudérysme*, after Mademoiselle de Scudéry, who was so much addicted to it. Sainte Beuve writes of her: 'In most of her dialogues, making her people talk, she finds a way, after every good thing she gives them, to make the one who replies say: "all you say is so well said" . . . Or, to use a word she is fond of: "that is very well made out". This indirect compliment she pays herself recurs endlessly, and she is inexhaustible in formulas for praising herself.'[5]

A more artful and self-conscious novelist, like Proust, is more likely to make ironic use of the praise of one character's wit by another character. The Duchesse de Guermantes is complimented on her *bien redigés* anecdotes, out of snobbery, by characters who are sometimes too simple to understand them, and are at any rate too simple to see how empty her wit is. Madame Verdurin, who prides herself on having a *salon*, exalts the pitiable wit of some of her guests, such as Cottard or Brichot. The same device is even applied below stairs, in the servants' hall of the narrator's home. For Proust wishes to show the paltriness of every kind of society, just as he wishes to show that every kind of love is a sickness. Of nearly every conversation in his book, we are to feel that it would be almost intolerable to take part in it — and yet it must be absorbingly interesting to read. This is perhaps the most difficult problem that dialogue raises for the novelist.

§5. THE NEED FOR STYLIZATION

Words strain,
Crack and sometimes break, under the burden
Under the tension, slip, slide, perish,
Decay with imprecision, will not stay in place,
Will not stay still.

The written word is hard enough to control. Only by hard work and by re-writing, can we sometimes make words say what we mean, or an approximation to our meaning — only thus can we choose the right words, and place them in an elegant or witty order.

This cannot be done on the spur of the moment. Conversation in real life is therefore not often very good. The 'good talker' dominates it, like a professional soloist hired to perform with an amateur orchestra — and his phrasing is more competent than delicate. The civilized interchange of chamber music is sometimes found in drama or fiction, it is regretfully mentioned in some memoirs — but who has ever heard it? Conversation of that sort is often called a lost art, but it is quite likely that it never really existed — like the brilliance of Madame de Villeparisis's salon, which Proust tells us never existed except in her memoirs. When such conversation has been preserved in a record, it has naturally been recorded by the pen which selects, retouches and creates -- never by the merciless dictaphone. As for the 'excellent things' that Marianne heard her friends saying, one may suspect that they contained a good deal of *marivaudage*. And the 'good talkers' — Dr. Johnson or Wilde — 'talk like a book': in a book one is more tolerant of their arrogance and vanity than one might have been in real life.

Moreover talkers have to tune up, and being tuned up they have to make an occasional concession to their audience. They must utter a few platitudes or nothings, refuse or accept cups of tea — it is selection, not strict verisimilitude that the recording Boswell will aim at — and we all know by now that Boswell was a great artist.

Selection, Arrangement, Stylization — it is these that turn talk into the art of conversation, and this is a literary art. Everything that people say is not interesting — but a fictional character must not bore the reader, even though it is his character to be a bore, and we may have to watch him boring other characters.

Very good criticism of fictional dialogue is that expressed by the Sultana in *Le Sopha*, by Crébillon fils. Almanzéi was telling his story, and used a large proportion of dialogue.

'This way of treating things', she said, 'is agreeable; it depicts the characters one puts on the stage better and more universally, but it is subject to some disadvantages. From wishing to get to the bottom of everything, or to seize every shade of expression, one risks falling into minutiae which are perhaps subtle, but which are not important enough to justify one's pausing at them, and one wears out the listener with tedious detail. To stop precisely where one should, is perhaps a more difficult thing than to create.'

'O if I knew how to omit,' wrote Stevenson, almost echoing the Sultana, 'I would ask no other knowledge. A man who knew how to omit would make an *Iliad* of a daily paper.'[6]

§6. THE BORE IN FICTION

Perhaps a man who knew how to omit could make a good comic character out of every bore of his acquaintance. This is unlikely: there is no reason to suppose that 'everyone is interesting' — this is one of the unproved dogmas of that sentimental philanthropy which for many people replaces religion, and it is no more credible than the related doctrines that everyone is really nice, or that everything is everyone's business.

Yet a man who knew how to omit and to combine, and where to stop, should be able to make at least one good comic character out of his experience; and it is from the bores that he would make it.

Nearly every great comic character is a 'flat' character — and in real life nearly every 'flat' character must be a bore. 'Flat' characters lack the charm of surprise, they are summed up in the stock phrase which they repeat at every entrance like a *leitmotiv*: it is for the novelist to see that their entrances are not too frequent, and that the *leitmotiv* is not allowed to drive us to distraction. As Macaulay said: 'It is a very hazardous experiment to attempt to make fun out of that which is the great cause of yawning, perpetual harping on the same topic. Sir Walter Scott was very fond of this device for exciting laughter: as witness Lady Margaret, and "His Sacred Majesty's disjune"; Claude Halcro, and Glorious John; Sir Dugald Dalgetty, and the Marischal College of Aberdeen; the Baillie, and his father, the deacon; old Trapbois, and "for a consideration". It answered, perhaps, once, for ten times that it failed.'[7] Life, alas, places even fewer restrictions than Scott upon the many people we know as 'flat' characters.

Moreover the bore in fiction has a dramatic function: in Trollope's words, his speech must, like that of every other character, 'tend in some way to the telling of the main story'. This gives him a prodigious advantage in interest over the bore in real life, who often seems only to interrupt the telling of the story.

It would need a detailed analysis of *Emma* to show how much of the story is in fact told by Miss Bates. Her knowledge of Highbury was, of course, incomparable, and she was not the sort of person to keep it to herself. In all innocence it was she who first furnished Mr. Knightley (and the reader) with a clue to the private understanding between her niece Jane Fairfax, and Frank Churchill.

Frank Churchill mentioned a rumour that Perry, the doctor, meant to set up a carriage: he believed that he had heard this from his stepmother, Mrs. Weston, who regularly wrote him news of Highbury. Mrs. Weston, however, had never heard of any such plan. Frank Churchill, guiltily aware that he must therefore owe the information to his clandestine correspondence with Jane Fairfax, tried to pass it off as something that he must have dreamed.

'Why, to own the truth,' cried Miss Bates, who had been trying in vain to be heard the last two minutes, 'if I must speak on this subject, there is no denying that Mr. Frank Churchill might have — I do not mean to say he did not dream it — I am sure I have sometimes the oddest dreams in the world — but if I am questioned about it, I must acknowledge that there was such an idea last spring; for Mrs. Perry herself mentioned it to my mother, and the Coles knew of it as well as ourselves — but it was quite a secret, known to nobody else, and only thought of about three days. Mrs. Perry was very anxious that he should have a carriage, and came to my mother in great spirits one morning because she thought she had prevailed. Jane, don't you remember grandmama's telling us of it when we got home? — I forget where we had been walking to — very likely to Randalls; yes, I think it was to Randalls. Mrs. Perry was always particularly fond of my mother — indeed I do not know who is not — and she had mentioned it to her in confidence; she had no objection to her telling us, of course, but it was not to go beyond; and, from that day to this, I never mentioned it to a soul that I know of. At the same time, I will not positively answer for my having never dropt a hint, because I know I do sometimes pop out a thing before I am aware. I am a talker, you know; I am rather a talker; and now and then I have let a thing escape me which I should not. I am not like Jane; I wish I were. I will answer for it *she* never betrayed the least thing in the world. Where is she? — Oh! just behind. Perfectly remember Mrs. Perry's coming — extraordinary dream indeed!'

What a thing Miss Bates has now popped out! What a thing she has let escape her! In all her rambling speech, the essential points are not lost. The Perrys' plan was known only to the Bates and the Coles — from 'the worthy Coles' it would not get to Mr. Frank Churchill. It was made known to Miss Bates and Jane Fairfax on their return from Mrs. Weston's house — therefore the unlikelihood of their having dropt a hint to her is much increased. Miss Bates ends, with unconscious irony, by praising her niece's discretion, just as she has begun with unconscious irony: 'if I must speak on this subject', when she has had to struggle for a hearing.

This speech is one of the many instances of that concealed art whereby Jane Austen reveals character and advances her story at the same time.

Sir William Lucas, in *Pride and Prejudice*, is only one of her minor bores; he is overshadowed by his wonderful son-in-law. Yet Sir William twice intervenes to set the story going. At his own house, he once forces Darcy to invite Elizabeth to dance — her refusal increases her value in Darcy's estimation, and when Miss Bingley accosts him, he is meditating on Elizabeth's fine eyes. At the Netherfield ball it was Sir William who put into Darcy's head the idea that Bingley and Jane Bennet were commonly thought to be attached to one another — giving Darcy the feeling that he ought to try to preserve his friend from an unfortunate connection. Darcy was too lofty to have observed the attachment for himself, and Sir William was perhaps the only person sufficiently insensitive to dare to tell him of it.

§7. THE SPOKEN WORD TRANSCENDED; JANE AUSTEN AND HENRY JAMES

The first part of *Pride and Prejudice* exhibits an even finer and more complex art; while Darcy and Elizabeth misunderstand each other the conversations between them, with the inevitable ambiguities — the words which are understood in one way by the speaker, in another by the hearer, and in a third way by the reader — are of a comic delicacy that is probably unique in literature. 'Cross answers and crooked questions' are common enough on the stage, and are an almost necessary element in farce — and at the opposite extreme, the subtle misunderstandings of Jamesian characters in such an empty novel as *The*

Sacred Fount, do little more than obscure the lack of meaning in the situation. The talk in the drawing-room at Netherfield shows a quite different skill.

'After playing some Italian songs, Miss Bingley varied the charm by a lively Scotch air; and soon afterwards Mr. Darcy, drawing near Elizabeth, said to her:

' "Do not you feel a great inclination, Miss Bennet, to seize such an opportunity of dancing a reel?"

'She smiled, but made no answer. He repeated the question, with some surprise at her silence.

' "Oh," said she, "I heard you before; but I could not immediately determine what to say in reply. You wanted me, I know, to say 'Yes', that you might have the pleasure of despising my taste; but I always delight in overthrowing those kind of schemes, and cheating a person of their premeditated contempt. I have, therefore, made up my mind to tell you that I do not want to dance a reel at all; and now despise me if you dare."

' "Indeed I do not dare."

'Elizabeth, having rather expected to affront him, was amazed at his gallantry, but there was a mixture of sweetness and archness in her manner which made it difficult for her to affront anybody, and Darcy had never been so bewitched by any woman as he was by her. He really believed, that were it not for the inferiority of her connections, he should be in some danger.

'Miss Bingley saw or suspected enough to be jealous. . . .'

In a very sensitive essay on *Pride and Prejudice*, Mr. Reuben Brower comments on the inadequacy of any possible stage rendering of the scene: we hear so much more with the mind's ear than any possible voice rendering could give. 'Elizabeth', he writes, 'hears his question as expressing "premeditated contempt" and scorn of her own taste. But from Mr. Darcy's next remark and the comment which follows it and from his repeating his question and showing "some surprise", we may hear in his request a tone expressive of some interest, perhaps only gallantry, perhaps, as Elizabeth later puts it, "somewhat of a friendlier nature". We could hear his "indeed I do not dare" as pure gallantry (Elizabeth's version) or as a sign of conventional "marriage intentions" (Miss Bingley's interpretation), if it were not for the nice reservation, "He believed, that were it not for the inferiority of her connections, he should be in some danger." We must hear the remark in a tone which includes this qualification.'[8]

Probably one should go even further than Mr. Brower: he seems to imply that while Mr. Darcy's frame of mind was complex, Elizabeth shifted from one simple point-of-view to another, and Miss Bingley's point-of-view remained steady. It is likely that there was a good deal of ambiguity in the ladies' minds. In consequence, in the mind's ear, the attentive reader does not only hear one voice, but a lovely polyphony of voices saying: 'Indeed I do not dare.'

In spite of the skilful irony of Henry Tilney's speeches in *Northanger Abbey*, and the complicated misunderstandings in *Emma* — it is only the plot of *Pride and Prejudice* that, in the earlier part of the book, enables Jane Austen to use this skill to perfection.

Though the misunderstandings between Henry James's characters are sometimes merely tiresome, yet he is the artist who has perhaps most subtly shown understanding between two people. The kind of communication between the two lovers at the beginning of *The Wings of the Dove* is another proof of the superiority of fiction over the drama. No two speaking voices could so entirely give the body and soul of the two people.

They are much in love, but they are kept apart because her

family wishes and even needs her to marry for money. They meet in Hyde Park, and, out of pride, in full view of Kate's aunt's house.

'Everything between our young couple moved today, in spite of their pauses, their margin, to a quicker measure – the quickness and anxiety playing lightning-like in the sultriness. Densher watched, decidedly as he had never done before.

' "And the fact you speak of holds you!"

' "Of course it holds me. It's a perpetual sound in my ears. It makes me ask myself if I've any right to personal happiness, *any* right to anything but to be as rich and overflowing, as smart and shining, as I can be made."

'Densher had a pause. "Oh you might by good luck have the personal happiness too."

'Her immediate answer to this was a silence like his own; after which she gave him straight in the face, but quite simply and quietly: "Darling!"

'It took him another moment; then he also was quiet and simple.

' "Will you settle it by our being married tomorrow – as we can, with perfect ease, civilly?"

' "Let us wait to arrange it," Kate presently replied. . . .

'He gave rather a glazed smile. "For young persons of a great distinction and a very high spirit we're a caution!"

' "Yes," she took it straight up; "we're hideously intelligent. But there's fun in it too – we must get our fun where we can." '

For young persons of a great distinction and a very high spirit they certainly are a caution, they are hideously intelligent – that is where they get most of their fun, and where the reader gets his. That is also why their situation is so moving – we are more moved by such a burst of feeling between persons whose communication is so intelligent and so witty. And in scenes such as this we are shown the relation between them as primarily taking place — we are not told that Kate and Densher love, as Scott tells us about Ravenswood and Lucy Ashton — we see and feel them loving.

§8. VERBAL FLUX; HENRY JAMES AND BRADSHAW

Alas, it is only too easy to find passages where Henry James incurs the strictures that the Sultana of *Le Sopha* pronounced against Almanzéi. He wishes to get to the bottom of everything, or to seize every shade of expression — and he falls, in consequence, into minutiae which are perhaps subtle, but which are not important enough to justify one pausing at them, and he wears out the reader with tedious detail.

Henry James was once very cross with someone who parodied his style in a skit called: 'If Henry James had written Bradshaw.' But he himself has shown us Charlotte and the Prince in *The Golden Bowl* consulting a railway time-table.

'He could only keep his eyes on her. "And have you made out the very train — ? "

' "The very one. Paddington — the 6.50 'in'. That gives us oceans; we can dine, at the usual hour, at home; and as Maggie will of course be in Eaton Square I hereby invite you."

'For a while he still but looked at her; it was a minute before he spoke. "Thank you very much. With pleasure." To which he in a moment added: "But the train for Gloucester?"

' "A local one — 11.22; with several stops, but doing it a good deal, I forget how much, within the hour. So that we've time. Only," she said, "we must employ our time."

'He roused himself as from the mere momentary spell of her; he looked again at his watch while they moved back to the door through which she had advanced. But he had also again questions and stops — all as for the mystery and the charm. "You looked it up — without my having asked you?"

' "Ah my dear," she laughed, "I've seen you with Bradshaw! It takes Anglo-Saxon blood." '

By this time the exhausted reader wants to knock Charlotte's and the Prince's heads together.

A thesis might be written — and this is not the place to develop it — about the use of the railway time-table in fiction: the witty handling of it in *Zuleika Dobson*, the superb genius with which Proust has dealt with *le plus envirant des romans d'amour, l'indicateur des chemins de fer.* We have seen Henry James with Bradshaw; for all his Anglo-Saxon blood, it was a fatal temptation to him.

§9. TRIVIAL DIALOGUE

The over-elaboration of dialogue must not tempt us from the certitude that Selection, Arrangement and Stylization are necessary to dialogue in fiction. If we doubt this for a moment, we shall be easily convinced by our next glance into a book where the conversations are not characterized by Selection, Arrangement and Stylization. It would be invidious to choose a book — one picked at random from a station book-stall should do. We shall find talk that does not reveal character nor tell the story — speeches that might be changed round from one speaker to another without any loss. Whereas in the work of a great writer of dialogue — in Jane Austen, in much of Dickens, in Proust — we should always know who was speaking, even if the names were left out. It seems a thing to aim at, as a condition of achieving any distinction at all, that each character should have a 'voice' of his own. In too much modern fiction no individual voice is heard – though one or two novelists introduce a lisp or a stammer.

It is of course natural and necessary for characters, at times, to say things of little significance, in which no special voice can be heard. 'It is very warm today', or 'will you pass me the butter, please?' Such remarks may sometimes be necessary, in order to elicit more interesting replies from other characters.

How, asked Flaubert in despair, is one to make trivial dialogue which is *well written*?[9] His own answer was patient work, and careful art – and Stevenson's words suggest a course to take: 'O if I knew how to omit!' Omission can be learned.

The novel has here a great advantage over drama – not everything need be said, characters can be present without opening their mouths – we are not conscious of them standing round dumbly like people at a party who do not know the other guests. They can come and go without a reason being given for their exits and their entrances. If they eat or drink, light or throw away cigarettes, powder or blow their noses, they can perform these entirely uninteresting actions without our being informed of them – it would generally be better if we were not so informed; unfortunately some novelists (and many dramatists) seem to labour under the delusion that these entirely uninteresting actions are Action.

There is, however, Euphony to be considered, as well as Sense. Rhythm must be taken into account, and the right tempo must be maintained. Moreover the reader sometimes wants a pause. There is no way of creating a blank space in a book, as in Architecture, nor of writing a rest, as in Music. Perhaps there is nothing to do but to put in something entirely uninteresting.

§10. TRAGIC DIALOGUE

Nor is it only trivial dialogue that is hard to write well. We do not, at tragic moments in our lives, commonly speak with tragic grandeur. We do not even write very well at such times. The letters that suicides leave behind them shock, more often than not, by their vulgarity — and yet the writers are doing much to prove the sincerity of the sentiments which they have so ill expressed; man can hardly do more.

Conrad writes of his pitiful heroine, in *The Secret Agent*: 'as so often happens in the lament of poor humanity, rich in suffering but indigent in words, the truth — the very cry of truth — was found in a worn and artificial shape picked up somewhere among the phrases of sham sentiment'.

Perhaps it is just as well that poor humanity, being so rich in suffering, should be indigent in words, otherwise we might suffer too much when we were told of other people's sufferings. Wordsworth was perhaps right when he said that we could bear more in verse than in prose, because of the 'small, but continual and regular impulses of pleasurable surprise from the metrical arrangement'.[10] Because these impulses were there lacking, he found 'the distressful parts of *Clarissa Harlowe*' too painful. He was evidently much of the opinion of the Rhyming Butler in *Lovers' Vows* (so well known to us from *Mansfield Park*) who said: 'Loss of innocence never sounds well except in verse.'

Tragic dialogue, then, is probably better when kept brief — and it is a case for recourse to Summary. 'Because in a novel comment is possible, it does not impoverish the feelings to reduce the language of the characters to that of ordinary speech. Their feelings can still be defined by description so that they are seen to be delicate and not coarse, precise and not vague'[11] —

nevertheless, for the sake of unity of tone and style, and of the readers' feelings, the less impoverished language there is, the better.

§11. HISTORICAL NOVELS

The beginning of *Ivanhoe* will serve as an object lesson. After a few pages of false history, a forest-scene is revealed in which two preposterous characters are discovered, Gurth the swineherd, and Wamba the jester. Their fancy dress is described at some length, before they engage in a dreary and frigid piece of dialogue. The story is said to derive from an ancient chronicle, appropriately called *The Wardour Manuscript* – the language is that called 'Wardour Street' by Fowler, after that street 'Mainly occupied by dealers in antique and imitation-antique furniture'.

Here is some humorous dialogue between Gurth and Wamba.

' "How call you those grunting brutes running about on their four legs?" demanded Wamba.

' "Swine, fool, swine," said the herd, "every fool knows that."

' "And swine is good Saxon," said the Jester; "but how call you the sow when she is flayed, and drawn, and quartered, and hung up by the heels, like a traitor?"

' "Pork," answered the swineherd.

' "I am very glad every fool knows that too," said Wamba, "and pork, I think, is good Norman-French; and so when the brute lives, and is in the charge of a Saxon slave, she goes by her Saxon name; but becomes a Norman and is called pork, when she is carried to the Castle-hall to feast among the nobles; what dost thou think of this, friend Gurth, ha?"

' "It is but too true doctrine, friend Wamba, however it got into thy fool's pate." '

Scott was trying to write a language that should be intelligible rather than archaeologically correct, to give a vague mediaeval atmosphere, while avoiding the sort of antiquarian excesses committed by Strutt, who in *Queenhoo Hall* wrote such gibberish as this:

' "That same borel knight," said Hugh, "Benemp him how ye may, was a tall man and a brave — "

' "He a tall man!" cried Hob, "the foul fiend affray him, he is a carle, a princox. I'll tell ye, my hearts, this tall man, with his gay train as crank as a peacock's, passed my doors without giving me the good-day, or hansling a single cross with me for luck's sake."

' "Marry, that was a shrewd ill guise of his!" '

But Strutt was not the only example Scott had to learn from. He owns that Gurth's and Wamba's speech, having been in Anglo-Saxon, must here be translated — what then was to prevent him from translating it into the idiom of 1817? There was a precedent for this in *The Castle of Otranto*, where the dialogue is said to be translated out of Italian, and is genuine eighteenth-century English.

There are several ways in which tolerable historical dialogue has been written.

First, the dialogue of a past age may be faithfully reproduced — of which method Scott's border novels are the finest example. This is only possible when the age is not far distant.

Secondly, a kind of negative archaism can be used — the writer writes in the language of his own time, denying himself any words or references that are startlingly contemporary. Thackeray's *Esmond* is an example of this method.

Thirdly, a writer may straightforwardly use the language of his own time — as the Elizabethan dramatists did, whatever age they were representing — and as Horace Walpole did.

But one thing that is never endurable is the language of Wardour Street. Scott, who could tell a good story even in this abominable jargon, did much to make it popular. It did incalculable damage to the English language in the nineteenth century, and it is not dead yet; it has so completely permeated English letters, from translations of the Greek and Latin classics, down to advertisements, that many people are incapable of seeing anything objectionable in it. To those who have freed themselves from it, perhaps it is more repellant than it should be — perhaps one should be able to read *Ivanhoe* and *The Talisman* with pleasure in spite of it.

§12. DIALECT

In an age of universal literacy, when the whole country is overlaid by a stereotyped culture; when everyone reads the newspapers, listens to the wireless, and speaks or hears Board School English; then, for independence and freshness of speech we must go to people independent of this stereotyped culture, if they can be found — whether they would be said to be above it or below it.

From the practice of writers in the past, we may collect that much the same rules are here applicable as those we discerned in historical fiction.

A dialect may be faithfully reproduced — but this is only possible when it is not too far remote from 'standard English' to be readily understood.[12]

Or a writer may exercise an economy in his choice of words, omitting words that his rustic characters could not have used, and limiting himself to their syntactical forms.

The worst, and most common expedient, is to use a kind of

'Doric', of which it is as certain that it was never spoken in any place, as it is certain that 'Wardour Street' was never spoken in any age.

NOTES

[1] *History of the French Novel* (1919), p. 340.

[2] *A Backward Glance* (1934), p. 203.

[3] *An Autobiography* (1883), II, pp. 38-9.

[4] *Journal* (Americ-Edit., 1943), I, p. 54.

[5] *Causeries du Lundi*, 12 mai, 1851.

[6] *The Letters of Robert Louis Stevenson*, ed. Sidney Colvin (1900), I, p. 289.

[7] *Journal* for November 9th, 1832, cit. *The Life and Letters of Lord Macaulay* by Sir G. O. Trevelyan, Bt.

[8] *Scrutiny*, xiii, no. 2, pp. 101-2.

[9] *Correspondance* (Bibliothèque-Charpentier, 1920), II, p. 132.

[10] Preface to *Lyrical Ballads*. Even if we disagree with Wordsworth about *Clarissa*, yet it is surely sound criticism to object that some things in fiction may be too painful for us to bear. It is a sign of an author's power if he can make us bear a great deal – as Dickens makes us bear a great deal in the first part of *David Copperfield*. But it is possible to go too far, so far that a book cannot be read with any pleasure: I think the author of *Poil de Carotte* has gone too far.

[11] M. C. Bradbrook, *Themes and Conventions of Elizabethan Tragedy* (Cambridge, 1935), p. 43.

[12] The faithful reproduction of a stammer or of an odd accent is to be deprecated, when the result is even more painful to the eye than the oddity represented could have been to the ear: e.g. Balzac's Baron de Nucingen. Henry James was wiser: 'The language spoken by M. Nioche was a singular compound, which may not here be reproduced in its integrity . . . The result, in the form in which he in all humility presented it, would be scarcely comprehensible to the reader, so that I have ventured to attempt for it some approximate notation.'

V

TERMS AND TOPICS

Accidents

'The number of people on this earth who die accidentally every day is considerable. But can we make a tile fall on the head of a principal character, or throw him under the wheels of a carriage, on the pretext that we must allow for accidents?'[1]

An accident makes a particularly unfortunate effect when the novelist has a very strong motive for getting rid of a character, and the reader must sometimes feel inclined to return a verdict of wilful murder against Hardy, for instance. Lord David Cecil's plea that Hardy aimed at exhibiting the helplessness of man in the grip of a rigid and hostile fate, is an eloquent plea for mercy — and it might avail if the accidents were less frequent and convenient. Characters must not die off like the brides of George Joseph Smith.

It is probably wiser to use an accident for the removal of a minor character — the results of his accidental death, and the reactions of the principal characters may be interesting: there seems no reason for a novelist to deny himself a moderate use of this theme.

Aim

'Mérimée once said to me something very true and sensitive: "In the little that I do, I should blush not to address myself to *my betters*, not to try to satisfy them." That is really the mark of every fine and sincere artist. One may make mistakes, but one must aim at satisfying one's equals (*pares*) or one's superiors, and not write for those who have less taste and wit than oneself; in a word, one must aim high, not low.'[2]

As well as analysing passages in terms of 'Sense, Tone, Feeling and Intention' we may also sometimes inquire what was the writer's Aim. His 'Tone' reflects his 'attitude to his listener',[3] his 'Aim' indicates his choice of listeners – not exactly the same thing.

BACKGROUND

'The setting of a novel is a thing of very small importance; the best is that which we know best, and not the most uncommon.'[4]

'Happy lovers are ready to put up with any kind of frame; they have in themselves the power of beautifying a desert. A luxuriant nature no doubt serves them better and enchants them; the grandeur of nature admired with another is the finest accompaniment of a noble love. But it is not right for the poet to insist upon it more than the lovers would be likely to do themselves.'[5]

'The material description of things and places is not, in the novel, so we understand it, description for description's sake. It is the means of transporting the reader into a certain setting favourable to the moral emotion which should spring from these things and places.'[6]

'For them [Elizabethan audiences] the actors were very plainly on the stage, but the characters might, half the time, be nowhere in particular. It was, for the dramatist of that day, a privilege akin to the novelist's, who may, if he chooses, detach characters, through page after page, from fixed surroundings... [Shakespeare] will always have, of course, as the novelist has, the whereabouts of his characters in mind, and casual allusion to it will crop out. There may also be the demands of the action for a house-door, a balcony, a tree or a cavern to be satisfied; but these things will have rather the utility of furniture than the value of scenery. And — this is the point — he need never give more attention to his play's background than he feels would be dramatically profitable. Moreover, he can give it — yet again as does the novelist — the exact sort of attention he chooses.'[7]

The picture-stage, which localized characters, robbed the dramatist of his privilege of leaving them nowhere in particular. This was probably the chief factor contributing to the ruin of drama — for it made soliloquy and formal speech appear absurd in prose drama. The novelist is unwise if he surrenders his privilege of delocalization.

Baggy Monsters

'A picture without composition slights its most precious chance for beauty . . . There may in its absence be life, incontestably, as "The Newcomes" has life, as "Les Trois Mousquetaires", as Tolstoi's "Peace and War", have it; but what do such large loose baggy monsters, with their queer elements of the accidental and the arbitrary, artistically *mean*? We have heard it maintained . . . that such things are "superior to art"; but we understand least of all what *that* may mean, and we look in vain for the artist, the divine explanatory genius, who will come to our aid and tell us. There is life and life, and as waste is only life sacrificed and thereby prevented from "counting", I delight in a deep-breathing economy and an organic form.'[8]

It has been argued that the analogy with a picture is misleading. 'A painting must be imagined in such a form that it establishes itself in existence, only in existence, at a glance; a novel, making its impression through the medium of language, can and does allow itself time for the last word to be absorbed by its reader.'[9] It may be allowed that a novel's composition is not quite the same thing as that of a picture – but composition there must be, if it is to be a work of art; a symphony is not a success, if it is a 'baggy monster'.

See FLUID PUDDINGS.

BLASPHEMY

By derivation the word means simply 'injurious speaking', by usage it has come to mean 'injurious speaking about sacred subjects'. Writers who are also believers in a traditional religion, or who have at least been educated in such a belief, will be likely to use the word correctly. To them only sacred things are sacred. Other writers should use the word with caution – it might help them if they could obtain a copy of the list of subjects not to be spoken ill of, which is circulated in Greece by the Anti-Blasphemy Society, with the reminder that Blasphemy is an offence against God, a sign of bad manners, an abuse of the Greek language, and punishable by the civil code. This organization sometimes holds Anti-Blasphemy weeks in the provinces.

To speak of *Blasphemy* against Life, Love, Motherhood or any other human subject, is a sentimental abuse of a fine word. Mr. C. S. Lewis, in particular, ought to have known better than to censure the young woman who found Charissa suckling her babies in *The Faerie Queen* as revolting a figure as Error vomiting, for 'blasphemy against life and fertility'[10] – for there is nothing essentially numinous about life and fertility. And the

Anglican bishop who once called hard words about the League of Nations 'blasphemy against the Holy Ghost', ought to have pointed out what he thought was the connection between the League and the third person of the Holy Trinity.

This is not to say that one cannot write or speak offensively about other than sacred subjects — there is probably no subject about which offensive words cannot be spoken or written. *Blasphemy*, however, is not then the word for the offence, and another should be found. Perhaps what is said is in bad MORAL TASTE (q.v.), or merely cynical, flippant, or vulgar.

CARNALITY

'She [Jane Austen] faces the facts, but they are not her facts, and her lapses of taste over carnality can be deplorable, no doubt because they arise from lack of feeling.'[11]

It would be easier to defend Jane Austen against a definite accusation — but her critics seldom hazard a definite accusation against her. We are left to wonder what lapses of taste Mr. Forster found in her work; we are at a loss to guess what meaning Mr. Stephen Spender could attach to the word 'vulgarity' when he applied it to her. They have not told us.

Jane Austen would probably answer that Mr. Forster was being 'missish'. He goes on to show much more sensibility than sense over her harmless jest, in a private letter to her sister, about the still-born child of Mrs. Hall of Sherborne. Jane Austen had lost sisters-in-law in childbed; its facts were her facts more than they can be any man's, except a man-midwife's.

She was far from lacking a sensitive awareness to the 'facts of life'. Her frank account of that scene at Lyme, when William Eliot shows signs of being sexually attracted by Anne, and this causes Captain Wentworth to look at her again with interest, may be contrasted with a far more 'missish' account in *Howard's End* of Margaret Schlegel's being attracted by a young waiter. And the 'almost animal emotion that consumed Marianne when she went up to London in search of Willoughby'[12] has been left out of Helen Schlegel, although her story requires something of the kind to be intelligible.

CLINICALISM

'Thus, in their desperate eagerness to hide nothing, these writers reveal things about their heroes that a man rarely learns about his fellows except from case-histories of their patients published by doctors. Is there room for surprise then, that these so-called heroes appear as so many clinical cases? It is not an equal who is offered to the reader's sympathy, but something like the insect whose entire behaviour the naturalist observes, behind a glass. The nature of the information we are given about him almost diverts us from regarding him as one of those beings like ourselves that we are in the habit of meeting in life and, in consequence, in literature. For, even when it has been given elevation by the author's talent, this information is still just like that which we are in the habit of receiving from specialized, one might say technical, research, carried out by scientists. Man is there necessarily treated as a thing; that is, without respect or shame. . . .

'It is best for us to know and ignore about fictional characters pretty much the same as we should be likely to know or ignore about them, if they were living people and we met them. A complete account degrades them and humiliates them. It robs everyone of the possibility of feeling for them that indispensable sympathy on which, for the most part, the illusion of fiction rests. We are invited to feel for a hero about whom we know things it is impossible to know in life about anyone — unless we are doctors and he is our patient, or unless he is a criminal, and we are appointed to judge him. In a word, we know things about him that no one must ever learn about us.'[13]

Documentation

'The novel since Balzac', wrote the Goncourts, 'has nothing left in common with what our fathers understood by the novel. The actual novel is made with *documents*, related from life, or heightened; just as history is made with written documents. The historians are the narrators of the past, the novelists of the present.'[14]

The originators of 'Mass-Observation' once said that their findings ought to be helpful to novelists: the Goncourts were precisely the sort of novelists who would have thought them helpful — and their novels would have been even more lifeless in consequence.

'They could never conceive that the happenings ought to proceed from a character, and not a character from the happenings. They would have been capable, in a historical novel about the Revolution, of grouping round an imaginary person everything that resulted from a Marat or a Robespierre, without understanding that, take away these real characters, something would no doubt have happened, but not these same things. They did not see that what happened to one person would not have happened to another, because in the same situation their reactions would have been different. They practised — and the old Goncourt even more than the two Goncourts — the mutual independence of the man and the human anecdote: it is what is called the literature of documentation. It is not compatible with fiction. The same anecdotes, which in the

Journal have such an air of freshness and freedom, wedged into their novels acquire an indefinable awkwardness, and an air of having been forced.'[15]

Dovetailing

'I have but done as the painters do — made compositions by dovetailing different sketches together.'[16]

The word *conflation* is sometimes used for the creation of fictional characters out of disparate observations. *Dovetailing*, though an even clumsier word, may help to describe the analogous construction of episodes or plots.

Escapism

'Escapist literature is enervating when it leads one into wishful thinking about problems which must be faced. On the other hand, certain ageless books, marked by an understanding of the constant elements in human nature but concerned with problems no longer urgent, can be as restful as dreamless sleep after a day of heavy toil.'[17]

If 'Escapism' can ever be properly used as a term of reproach, it must mean 'a tendency to try to escape from that which we ought not to (or cannot) escape from'. On this definition, the novels of Charlotte Yonge are less 'escapist' now than ever they were. In 1853, if anyone had then spoken that horrible jargon, there might have been some sense in asking for 'socially conscious' novels, when the lot of the poor was so bad. Nowadays when the wealthier classes are compelled by taxation willy nilly to do their duty, and perhaps rather more than their duty, to their poorer brethren, and when everyone is 'socially conscious', we need to be reminded of the duties of private life.

There is no doubt that from these duties there are 'escapists' — Mrs. Jellybys who think that charity begins in Borioboola-Gha. And the journalist who did public penance in his column for his share in the murder of Gandhi — because he happened to be living when it occurred — could have found faults, no doubt, that ought to have weighed much more heavily on his conscience, and for which it would have been much less fun to do appropriate penance, if he had been given to that kind of self-examination that a reading of *The Heir of Redclyffe* might have prompted.

Ficelle

Henry James described Maria Gostrey (in *The Ambassadors*) and Henrietta Stackpole (in *The Portrait of a Lady*) as 'cases, each, of the light *ficelle*, not of the true agent'.[18]

'Each of these persons is but wheels to the coach, neither belongs to the body of that vehicle, or is for a moment accommodated with a seat inside. There the subject alone is ensconced, in the form of its "hero and heroine", and of the privileged high officials, say, who ride with the king and queen.'[19]

'Half the dramatist's art, as we well know — since if we don't it's not the fault of the proofs that lie scattered about us — is the use of *ficelles*; by which I mean in a deep dissimulation of his dependence on them.'[20]

The 'ficelle' is a character belonging not to the 'subject' of the novel, but to the 'treatment'.[21] Henrietta, for instance, seems to be there as part of the author's 'provision for the reader's amusement';[22] a part, he says, 'of my wonderful notion of the lively'.[23]

Figures to be Let

'Annibale Caracci thought twelve figures sufficient for any story; he conceived that more would contribute to no end but to fill space; that they would be but cold spectators of the general action; or, to use his own expression, that they would be *figures to be let*.'[24]

Nobody would suggest taking the rule over, just as it stands, to the criticism of fiction, but the principle behind it is worth consideration. The term *figures to be let* could well be applied to FICELLES (q.v.) who do not somehow justify their presence.

'It is by the analogy that one art bears to another, that many things are ascertained, which either were but faintly seen, or, perhaps, would not have been discovered at all, if the inventor had not received the first hints from the practices of a sister art on a similar occasion.'[25]

Fluid Puddings

'Don't let anyone persuade you . . . that strenuous selection and comparison are not the very essence of art, and that Form is [not] substance to that degree that there is absolutely no substance without it. Form alone *takes*, and holds and preserves, substance — saves it from the welter of helpless verbiage that we swim in as in a sea of tasteless tepid pudding, and that makes one ashamed of an art capable of such degradations. Tolstoi and D[ostoievsky] are fluid puddings, though not tasteless, because the amount of their own minds and souls in solution in the broth gives it savour and flavour, thanks to the strong rank quality of their genius and their experience. But there are all sorts of things to be said of them, and in particular that we see how great a vice is their lack of composition, their defiance of economy and architecture, directly they are emulated and imitated; *then*, as subjects of emulation, models, they quite give themselves away. There is nothing so deplorable as a work of art with a *leak* in its interest; and there is no such leak of interest as through commonness of form. Its opposite, the *found* (because the sought for) form is the absolute citadel and tabernacle of interest.'[26] See also BAGGY MONSTERS.

War and Peace seems to be held in such superstitious veneration by some people, that any suggestion that it is not self-evidently a perfect masterpiece, and the greatest novel in the world, is apt to be met with scorn and anger. It may be all that people say — those who cannot read Russian will never be quite certain what they have missed. But whatever it is, it does not look like a good model for an intending novelist (though no worse in itself for that). Anyone may, perhaps everyone should, sit down to write a *good* novel: no one should sit down to write a *great* novel.

Freedom

'It is a general prejudice, and has been for these sixteen hundred years, that arts and sciences cannot flourish under an absolute government; and that genius must necessarily be cramped where freedom is restrained. This sounds plausible, but it is false in fact. Mechanic arts, as agriculture, manufactures, etc., will indeed be discouraged where the profits and the property are, from the nature of the government, insecure. But why the despotism of a government should cramp the genius of a mathematician, an astronomer, a poet or an orator, I confess I never could discover. It may indeed deprive the poet or the orator of the liberty of treating certain subjects in the manner they could wish; but it leaves them subjects enough to exert genius upon, if they have it.'[27]

'Heaven preserve you from a liberty of the press established by edict! Nothing contributes more to rendering a nation coarse, to destroying taste, and debasing eloquence and every sort of intellect. Do you know my definition of the *oratorical sublime*? It is the art of saying everything without being sent to the Bastille, in a country where it is forbidden to say anything. . . .'[28]

The despotism that is really destructive to letters is one that imposes commands, not prohibitions — that orders the treatment of certain subjects, and in a certain manner.

Geometry

'Really, universally, relations stop nowhere, and the exquisite problem of the artist is eternally but to draw, by a geometry of his own, the circle within which they shall happily appear to do so.'[29]

We have to draw the line somewhere — we cannot treat all our characters' friends, business associates, distant connections, friends of the family, and friends of friends. Just as in real life we have to draw the line, and say: 'I will help you, but not your friends.'

In good fiction, characters move in a smaller circle than people in real life — they have only friends or habitual associates, and few acquaintances. It is unfortunate for fiction that contemporary life provides most of us with many acquaintances, and few friends or habitual associates.

Henry James drew the circle very tight. Edith Wharton once asked him: 'What was your idea in suspending the four principal characters in *The Golden Bowl* in the void? What sort of life did they lead when they were not watching each other, and fencing with each other? Why have you stripped them of all the *human fringes* we necessarily trail after us through life?'

She tells us that, after a pause of reflection, he answered in a disturbed voice: 'My dear – I didn't know I had!'[30]

Imitatio Christi

Here are the views of three eminent novelists on the *Imitation*.

'It is impossible not to be gripped by the *Imitation* which is to dogma what action is to thought . . . This book is a sure friend. It speaks to all passions, all difficulties, even those of this world; it resolves all objections, it is more eloquent than all preachers, for its voice is your own, that rises in your heart and that you hear in the soul. In short, it is the gospel translated, made appropriate to every age, imposed on every situation.'[31]

'Why, you dear creature – what a history that is in the Thos à Kempis book. The scheme of that book carried out would make the world the most wretched useless doting place of sojourn – there would be no manhood no love no tender ties of mother and child no use of intellect no trade or science – a set of selfish beings crawling about avoiding one another, and howling a perpetual miserere.'[32]

'It was written down by a hand that waited for the heart's prompting; it is the chronicle of a solitary, hidden anguish, struggle, trust and triumph – not written on velvet cushions to teach endurance to those who are treading with bleeding feet on the stones. And so it remains to all time a lasting record of human needs and human consolations: the voice of a brother who, ages ago, felt and suffered and renounced – in the cloister, perhaps, with serge gown and tonsured head, with much chanting and long fasts, and with a fashion of speech different from ours — but under the same silent far-off heavens, and with the same passionate desires, the same strivings, the same failures, the same weariness.'[33]

Knowledge of Motives

'. . . A character, to be living, must be conceived from some emotional unity. A character is not to be composed of scattered observations of human nature, but of parts which are felt together . . . A "Living" character is not necessarily "true to life". It is a person whom we can see and hear, whether he be true or false to human nature as we know it. What the creator of character needs is not so much knowledge of motives as keen sensibility; the dramatist need not understand people; but he must be exceptionally aware of them.'[34]

'I am not certain whether to know the world and to know human nature be not two distinct branches of knowledge, which while they may coexist in the same heart, yet either may exist with little or nothing of the other. Nay, in an average man of the world, his constant rubbing with it blunts that fine spiritual insight indispensable to the understanding of the essential in certain exceptional characters, whether evil ones or good. In a matter of some importance I have seen a girl wind an old lawyer about her little finger. Nor was it the dotage of senile love. Nothing of the sort. But he knew law better than he knew the girl's heart. Coke and Blackstone hardly shed so much light into obscure places as the Hebrew prophets. And who were they? Mostly recluses.'[35]

Litterature Engagée

'Those who live by Letters, by the love of books and of study . . . can grant for a moment a corner of their existence and lend it to public thoughts and affairs — they ought to do so in urgent cases; but, the emergency over, they have the full right to return to their domain.

'This domain is a certain decent liberty, hard to define, but very easy to feel, which means that one is not on any side, that one is not always attacking or on the defence, that one seeks for the good, the beautiful, the agreeable in more than one place, that one's mind is like a window open to the sunbeam that enters, to the passing bird, the smiling morning. . . .

'Those who believe that Truth is one not only in Ethics, but also in Religion, Politics and everything, who believe they possess this Truth and that they can demonstrate it to everyone by clear and manifest signs, want all the time that literature should never stray from the exact lines they have laid down for her; but as in every age there is more than one sort of leading spirits (not to speak of charlatans and imposters) who think they are in possession of this unique and absolute truth, and are equally anxious to impose it, and as these spirits are in opposition to each other, it follows that literature, that freedom of poetic or scientific thought, pulled in different directions, would be much embarrassed in the choice of an allegiance.'[36]

The Looking-Glass

'It sounds too fantastic for truth, but it is true, that the ultimate defence of Elizabethan drama offered by many writers on it, is that it holds up so faithful a glass to the "bustling, many-sided life of that wonderful time".'[37]

Such writers Rupert Brooke calls 'wretched antiquarians'. There seems no reason why we should have any higher esteem for writers who want the novel to hold up a faithful glass to the 'bustling, many-sided life' of our own dolorous times.

Great novelists have, however, believed themselves to be holding up a glass. 'A novel', says Stendhal, 'is a mirror which goes along a high road. Sometimes it reflects the blue of the sky to your eyes, sometimes the mud and filth of the road.'[38] But he has to assume the presence of a man to hold the glass: 'And the man who carries the mirror on his back will be accused by you of being immoral! His mirror shows the filth, and you accuse the mirror! Rather blame the road where the mud is, or still more the road inspector who lets the water stagnate and the mud form.'

Yet if the glass reflects mud, that is not only the responsibility of the road inspector: the man who carries the glass is responsible, for he can turn it where he likes (it is ridiculous to think of it as strapped on his back). It may or may not be desirable and necessary to reflect mud: let us not evade responsibility, and say that we carry a glass, and cannot help ourselves.

The Marvellous

'A marvellous event is interesting in real life, simply because we know that it happened. In a fiction we know that it did not happen; and therefore it is interesting only as far as it is explained.'[39]

The Mill-Stone

' "Politics", says the author, "is a stone tied to the neck of literature which sinks it in less than six months. Politics in the middle of imaginary interests, is a pistol shot in the middle of a concert. The noise is harrowing without being effective. It doesn't harmonize with the sound of any of the instruments. This politics is going to offend half the readers mortally, and to bore the other half who found it far more particularly and effectively in the morning paper. . . ."

' "If your people don't talk politics," rejoins the publisher, "they're no longer Frenchmen of 1830, and your book isn't a looking-glass any more, as you claim." '[40] But for this claim see THE LOOKING-GLASS.

'I hate politics. It is the cause of all I love being in danger, it threatens happiness, it disturbs me at my work. I believe with all my heart in art and literature. This faith is absolutely foreign to the preoccupations of politics.'[41]

Moral Taste

Jane Austen tells us that Henry Crawford had enough 'Moral Taste' to appreciate Fanny Price's affection for her brother William – in 'Principles' he must have been deplorably deficient, or he would not have eloped with a married woman. His sister Mary, on the other hand, though her want of 'Principles' was never proved, destroyed Edmund Bertram's affection by her disgusting lack of Moral Taste.

Some very bad characters, both in life and in fiction, have preserved their Moral Taste. Lovelace still worshipped Clarissa's moral grandeur, even while he was plotting to drag it in the dust – but the Présidente de Tourvel in *Les Liaisons Dangereuses* was pathetically mistaken in thinking that Valmont, her Lovelace, retained any love of virtue. And Proust tells us that Madame de Villeparisis, herself not at all a good character, spoke with exquisite sensibility about modesty and kindness — virtues which her parents had actually practised.

A novelist may be deficient in Principles, that is his own affair — but the values he consciously or unconsciously maintains will go wrong if he is deficient in Moral Taste. (No doubt Moral Taste will not long survive the total death of Principle, but that is a question for the moralist — so is the converse, for Moral Taste may be the first to go, as in Mary Crawford.) And it is surely by Moral Taste that we know 'what it feels like to be a man much better than ourselves' — though Mr. C. S. Lewis says that we do not know this.[42]

One of the many reasons why great fiction is difficult to write at present, lies in the almost universal decay of Moral Taste which always characterizes an irreligious age. People are not necessarily less moral, but there is no universal standard of Moral Taste — even among Principled persons — to which a writer can appeal.

Notebooks

'The literary instinct may be known by a man's keeping a small notebook in his waist-coat pocket, into which he jots down anything that strikes him, or any good thing he hears said, or a reference to any passage which he thinks will come in useful to him.'[43]

Samuel Butler had that instinct, and in consequence overloaded his novel with note-book material, *obiter dicta* about heredity, music, etc., which he had not been able to work off elsewhere. Such passages are both the best thing in the book, and its greatest defect — for they stand out like 'purple patches', and they intolerably hold up the interest. It is doubtful if notebooks are ever a safe quarry for a novelist: they did the Goncourts little good (see DOCUMENTATION).

Proust is decided on the subject: 'The man of letters envies the painter, he would like to make sketches, to take notes; he is lost if he does. But when he writes, there's not a gesture of his people, a twitch, an accent which has not been brought to his inspiration by his memory.'[44]

And memory does not serve the writer least well by its gaps and inaccuracies.

Maria Edgeworth is of the same opinion about the harmfulness of notebooks to the creative writer. (Of course the critic and the historian must have his 'Collections' – and without them the compilation, e.g. of such a book as the present, must be impossible.)

'I was averse to noting down,' she wrote, 'because I was conscious that it did better for me to keep the things in my head, if they suited my purpose; and if they did not, they would only encumber me. I knew that, when I wrote down, I put the thing out of my care, out of my head; and that, though it might be put by very safe, I should not know where to look for it; that the labour of looking over a note-book would never do when I was in the warmth and pleasure of inventing; that I should never recollect the facts or ideas at the right time, if I did not put them in my own way in my own head: that is, if I felt with hope or pleasure "that thought or that fact will be useful to me in such a character or story, of which I have now a faint idea," the same fact or thought would recur, I knew, when I wanted in right order for invention.'[45]

And again: 'I could never use notes in writing Dialogues; it would have been as impossible to me to get in the prepared good things at the right moment in the warmth of writing conversation, as it would be to lug them in in real conversation, perhaps more so – for I could not write dialogues at all without being at the time fully impressed with the characters, imagining myself each speaker, and that too fully engrosses the imagination to leave time for consulting note-books; the whole fairy vision would melt away, and the warmth and pleasure of invention be gone.'[46]

Particularity

'How to get over, how to escape from, the besotting *particularity* of fiction. "Roland approached the house; it had green doors and window blinds; and there was a scraper on the upper step." To hell with Roland and the scraper!'[47]

To hell, indeed, with the scraper, unless it serves some purpose in the story, e.g. to trip up Roland – and he establishes what D. H. Lawrence calls a 'lively relation'[48] with it.

It was this particularity that disgusted Paul Valéry with fiction. He could not induce himself to write: 'the Marquise arrived at nine', when she might equally well have been a Comtesse, and might equally well have arrived later. And yet it would not do to write: 'the titled lady arrived during the evening'.

A writer on another art has some help to give: 'I am ready to allow that some circumstances of minuteness and particularity frequently tend to give an air of truth to a piece, and to interest the spectator in an extraordinary manner. Such circumstances therefore cannot wholly be rejected; but if there be anything in the Art which requires peculiar nicety of discernment, it is the disposition of these minute circumstantial parts; which, according to the judgment employed in the choice, become so useful to truth, so injurious to grandeur.'[49]

See SUPERFLUOUS INFORMATION.

PERFECTION

'... Perfection is only one of the qualities of the work of art, and there is a quality superior to perfection itself, and that is life. Perfection can be considered as a full stop in the evolution of forms. Flesh is become marble, and that is the end ... Perfection is then no longer the criterion according to which we shall judge a work of art. We shall ask of it beauty, a certain logical order, purity of language, originality of style and freedom of thought.'[50]

Nevertheless the idea of perfection in a work of art includes the presence of life, and the suggestion that a work would be better for the admission of more life at the cost of a little perfection is a dangerous one. For in a work of art Art is Life to that degree that there is absolutely no Life without it. Art alone *takes*, and holds and preserves, Life.

See also FLUID PUDDINGS.

PHYSICAL DESCRIPTION

If a novelist says that one of his characters is wise or good, it is his duty to make that wisdom or goodness apparent: but he may bestow physical beauty with a stroke of the pen, and ask us to take it on trust. As we cannot see fictional characters, and no one has ever described a face so as to compel the imagination, beauty is very much less important in fiction than it is in life. It is quite difficult, for instance, to understand why no one in Middlemarch was provoked at least to threaten to wring Rosamund's elegant neck — we have to pause, and to remember that she had a physical beauty not only sexually attractive, but capable of influencing her parents, her brother, and a woman like Dorothea. In *The Rise of Silas Lapham* by Henry James's friend, W. D. Howells, we are expected to be surprised at finding that the hero is attached to the plainer of two sisters — on the stage it might surprise, but in that novel the other choice would seem almost incredible.

Beauty can only be shown indirectly in fiction, in its effect on people — when this is sufficiently moving then the beauty of, e.g., Helen or of Lucien de Rubempré can move the reader at one remove. It may therefore be said that a great artist like Homer or Balzac can make a more beautiful face than a lesser writer can.

If beauty is to stir the imagination directly the novelist must probably borrow some help from the plastic arts: Odette de Crécy was like Botticelli's 'Jethro's daughter'; Milly, in *The Wings of the Dove*, was a Bronzino — and this is helpful, even to readers who get thereby no exact picture. (An extra-illustrated Proust would be a valuable piece of Grangerism.)

Voices are often said, vaguely, to be musical — but Madame de Mortsauf in *Le Lys dans la Vallée*, in whose voice were all the intonations of the paschal *O Filii et Filiae*, had surely the loveliest voice in fiction: it is hard to tolerate her rival the Marquise de Dudley — even though she was born 'in Lancashire, where women die of love'.

Sottisier

The collection of a *sottisier* is a conceited and dangerous hobby — it invites attention to our own unwary sayings; moreover the collector, in his zeal, is apt to put in remarks that are not, after all, so very silly, otherwise his collection will look too thin. This heading is therefore reserved for two remarks of a particularly sinister stupidity.

'Has anyone observed that no virgin, old or young, has ever produced a work, or anything?'[51]

'I hold Flaubert and Goncourt responsible for the repressions which followed the Commune, because they wrote not a single line to prevent them.'[52]

Superfluous Information

'We meet [in Balzac] with artifices like those by which De Foe cheats us into forgetfulness of his true character. One of the best known is the insertion of superfluous bits of information, by way of entrapping his readers into the inference that they could only have been given because they were true. The snare is more worthy of a writer of begging-letters than of a genuine artist.'[53]

Sir Leslie Stephen instances as 'superfluous information' most of what Balzac tells us about the family history and homes of his characters, and all that he tells us about their armorial bearings.

Jane Austen was able to compress into fifty words the 'two handsome duodecimo pages' in the Baronetage devoted to the family of Elliot of Kellynch Hall, and found it unnecessary to tell us their arms and motto, though they would have known them (Sir Walter was proud of his supporters) and Mary Musgrove would have recognized them on Mr. William Elliot's carriage at Lyme, had not the panel been hidden by a greatcoat.

The Novelist's Touch

Mr. E. M. Forster, in his discussion of the 'flat' character, quotes Mr. Norman Douglas on 'the novelist's touch'.

'It consists, I should say, in a failure to realize the complexities of the ordinary human mind; it selects for literary purposes two or three facets of a man or woman, generally the most spectacular, and therefore useful ingredients of their character and disregards all the others . . . It follows that the novelist's touch argues, often logically, from a wrong premise: it takes what it likes and leaves the rest. The facts may be correct as far as they go but there are too few of them; what the author says may be true and yet by no means the truth. That is the novelist's touch. It falsifies life.'

Mr. Forster answers, perhaps too modestly, that the novelist's touch is bad in biography, for no human being is simple — but that in a novel it has its place. He suspects, however, on account of the greatness of Dickens, 'that there may be more in flatness than the severer critics admit'.[54]

And yet the novelist's touch may be good in biography, if it touch any character other than the subject. Nor is it a mere convenience in fiction. For fiction is not always about life as it is, but sometimes about life as it appears to such-and-such observers — even when the 'point-of-view' is not rigidly limited to what the narrator (David Copperfield, Mr. Overton or another) says and knows, or to the observations of a third-person, Henry Jamesian spectator.

And to everyone, in 'real' life, some human beings must appear as 'flat characters'. When we say that someone is a 'character', we almost always mean that he is a 'flat character'. And we say of some people that they have always been the same as they are now — which cannot be true, though it seems true to us. While we ourselves appear as 'flat characters' to some of our neighbours, whether we like it or not. We probably wish to appear 'flat' to many people with whom we do not care to be on terms of intimacy: we come out with our *leitmotiv* as soon as we meet them.

Fiction 'falsifies life', yes: but so does ordinary, everyday observation.

Once this principle is accepted, we shall have a slightly different approach to several problems, among others that of Obscenity. We know that everything can be done that is mentioned, for example, in the Kinsey report, and that every word can be said that is found in slang or dialect dictionaries. But many observers will never see or hear these things — there is no place for obscenity within the observation of Strether, or perhaps within that of Henry James — and therefore its omission from *The Ambassadors*, for example, is no more false to life than life itself.

Truth

What is Truth in Literature — for it is clearly not the same thing as historical truth? Perhaps the Cartesian definition is the best: 'whatever is clearly and distinctly apprehended is true'. And whatever Truth may be in Logic, in Literature Truth lies certainly in Coherence, and not in Correspondence with some outside set of facts.

It is always an artist's duty to tell the truth, it is never his duty to tell the whole truth; his function is to choose what truth is worth telling.

'Many truths are supremely boring. Half a man's talent lies in choosing out of the true that which can become poetic.'[55]

'To tell everything would be impossible, for it would need at least a volume a day, to enumerate the crowds of insignificant incidents that fill up our existence.

'A choice, then, is forced upon us — which is the first blow to the theory of the whole truth.'[56]

'And for the authentical truth of either person or action, who (worth the respecting) will expect it in a poem, whose subject is not truth, but things like truth? Poor envious souls they are that cavil at truth's want in these natural fictions; material instruction, elegant and sententious excitation to virtue, and deflection from her contrary, being the soul, limbs, and limits of an authentical tragedy.'[57]

NOTES

[1] MAUPASSANT, preface to *Pierre et Jean*.

[2] SAINTE BEUVE, *Causeries du Lundi*, XI, Notes et Pensées cxlvi.

[3] I. A. RICHARDS, *Practical Criticism* (1929), p. 182.

[4] REMY DE GOURMONT, *Promenades littéraires*, IV (1920), art. 'Maupassant'.

[5] SAINTE BEUVE, *Causeries du Lundi*, 29 oct., 1849.

[6] EDMOND et JULES DE GONCOURT, *Journal*, 8 août, 1865.

[7] HARLEY GRANVILLE-BARKER, *Prefaces to Shakespeare* (Second Series), pp. 135-6.

[8] HENRY JAMES, *The Art of the Novel*, ed. R. P. Blackmur (1935), p. 84.

[9] STORM JAMESON, *The Writer's Situation* (1950), pp. 43-4.

[10] *The Allegory of Love*, p. 316.

[11] *Abinger Harvest*.

[12] GEORGE MOORE, *Conversations in Ebury Street*, chap. XVII.

[13] ROGER CAILLOIS, *Babel* (1945), p. 147.

[14] *Journal des Goncourts*, 24 oct., 1864.

[15] REMY DE GOURMONT, loc. cit., V, p. 61.

[16] JOHN GALT, *Literary Life*.

[17] MARGARET MARE and ALICIA PERCIVAL, *Victorian Best-Seller: the world of Charlotte M. Yonge*, p. 5.

[18] HENRY JAMES, loc. cit., p. 55.

[19] Ibid., p. 54.

[20] Ibid., p. 322.

[21] Ibid., p. 53.

[22] Ibid., p. 52.

[23] Ibid., p. 57.

[24] SIR JOSHUA REYNOLDS, *Discourses*, ed. Roger Fry (1905), pp. 88-9.

[25] Ibid., p. 209.

[26] *The Letters of Henry James*, ed. Percy Lubbock (1920), II, pp. 245-6.

[27] EARL OF CHESTERFIELD, *Letters*, ed. Bonamy Dobrée (1932), no. 1621.

[28] ABBÉ GALIANI, cit. SAINTE BEUVE, *Causeries du Lundi*, 15 oct., 1849.

[29] HENRY JAMES, *The Art of the Novel*, p. 5.

[30] Cit. SIMON NOWELL SMITH, *The Lesson of the Master* (1947), p. 112.

[31] BALZAC, *Madame de la Chanterie*.

[32] THACKERAY, *Letters and Private Papers*, ed. Gordon N. Ray (1945), II, p. 616.

[33] GEORGE ELIOT, *The Mill on the Floss*.

[34] T. S. ELIOT, *Selected Essays*, p. 132.

[35] HERMAN MELVILLE, *Billy Budd* (Edinburgh, 1924), pp. 44-5.

[36] SAINTE BEUVE, loc. cit., 13 oct., 1851.

[37] RUPERT BROOKE, *John Webster and the Elizabethan Drama* (1917), p. 57.
[38] *Le Rouge et le Noir*, II.
[39] SIR LESLIE STEPHEN, *Hours in a Library*, art. 'Balzac's novels'.
[40] STENDHAL, loc. cit.
[41] JULIEN GREEN, *Journal*, 4 avr., 1932.
[42] *A Preface to Paradise Lost* (1942), p. 98.
[43] *The Way of All Flesh*, chap. LXXIII.
[44] *Le Temps Retrouvé*, II, p. 54.
[45] *Chosen Letters*, ed. F. V. Barry (1931), p. 240.
[46] Ibid., p. 244.
[47] *The Letters of Robert Louis Stevenson*, ed. Sidney Colvin (1900), II, p. 299.
[48] *Phoenix* (1936), p. 529.
[49] SIR JOSHUA REYNOLDS, loc. cit., p. 73.
[50] REMY DE GOURMONT, loc. cit., IV, art. 'Les deux Flauberts'.
[51] *Journal des Goncourts*, 27 avr., 1862.
[52] J. P. SARTRE, *Situations*, II (1948), p. 13.
[53] SIR LESLIE STEPHEN, loc. cit.
[54] *Aspects of the Novel*, pp. 97-9.
[55] BALZAC, *Le Message*.
[56] MAUPASSANT, loc. cit.
[57] GEORGE CHAPMAN, dedication to *The Revenge of Bussy d'Ambois*.

APPENDIX

'INTIMATIONS OF IMMORTALITY'

1. BRIGHT SHOOTES OF EVERLASTINGNESSE

The three authors here studied together have this in common, that we know a great deal about the sources of their inspiration. They have also this in common, that in the work of each of them *Bright shootes of everlastingnesse* are more than occasional accidents. Their work is built upon:

Those shadowy recollections
Which, be they what they may,
Are yet the fountain light of all our day,
Are yet a master light of all our seeing.

It may be useful to look at them, and to look at them together, even though no critical rule and no philosophical truth emerges: in their different ways, and with their greatly differing talents, they bear witness to something permanent in human nature — to our desire for our true country, which is not here.

For this desire, Christianity provides an explanation — but of these three writers Forrest Reid was defiantly unChristian, Proust apparently took little interest in the Christian explanation, and Alain-Fournier was only obscurely approaching it. Their evidence for the human desire for Heaven is all the more interesting, by reason of its independence.

This is a part of human experience much neglected in contemporary fiction. Secular novelists disapprove of people seeking those things which are above; religious novelists have developed a cult for 'evil', and those of their characters who have any spiritual perception (and these are often the most depraved) are usually more sensitive to smells rising from the bottomless pit, than to the clean airs of Heaven. This seems rather a pity — the worst thing about Hell is that it entails a final loss of Heaven. Alain-Fournier, Forrest Reid and Proust were certainly not such good Christians as Georges Bernanos, M. Mauriac and Mr. Graham Greene — perhaps they were more Christian novelists.

II. LE DOMAINE PERDU

Sologne is an out-of-the-way province, not far from Blois, not far from Orleans, not far from Bourges. It contains no remarkable beauty-spot, and no important architectural monument — it has the distinction of being the nearest approach to a desert in Central France. For Henri Alain-Fournier, whose home was first the school-house of Epineuil, and later that of La Chapelle d'Angillon, the fir woods of the Sologne, the small *châteaux* lurking among them, the tarns, the swamp, the desert, the hidden roads, the quiet villages, the horizons as wide as the sea, were the country of his soul.

Among his earliest letters to his friend Jacques Rivière, later his brother-in-law, are two nostalgic pictures of his province. His grandparents' house at La Chapelle d'Angillon calls back the smell of hot bread, brought home from the baker's at mid-day, of the cheese eaten as an afternoon snack, of his grandmother's cherry brandy, and all the wholesome and delicious smells of larder and garden, to Henri Fournier, a young exile in London, famished between the perpetual ham and jam of the English. An even dearer place to him is Nançay, the country of his dreams — all his wishes are summed up in a wish to spend the end of that summer there, the beginning of the shooting-season — and one day to be buried there.

'You get there, after five leagues' journey by hidden ways, in old carts. It's a country lost in the Sologne; the roads are all dry; all the way there are the yellow points of firs, fir woods on the neighbouring plains, horse-flies in the air, game that stops your path. There are always stories of smashed carts, floods, a horse bogged in the ford where they tried to water him.

'There Uncle Florent has a big general shop – a kind of world in itself "like *David Copperfield*". Behind it is a huge kitchen, like that of a farmhouse, where the family has its meals, in a jumble of children, dogs and guns. There are long days shooting in the woods or on the moors – luncheon, perhaps, with the gamekeeper of some exquisite small country house, buried in this wild landscape. You come home at evening, through the shop, busy by lamp-light, and drop off to sleep from exhaustion on a kitchen chair, waiting for dinner. Old faded photographs are passed round – school groups of one's father's boyhood.

'The dream of finding a friend who can thrill to your own past . . . I believe that is what one seeks, above all, in love . . .' Perhaps this dream was one of Henri Fournier's chief impulses towards authorship.

The *châteaux* of the Sologne, and their mysteries, whether based on fact or fable, were to Henri Fournier what Yorkshire legends had been to Emily Brontë. There was the little *château* hidden in the woods, where the sick young English milord had lived – he who courted their grandmother years ago – till the village lads beat him up for trying to steal away the prettiest girl in the neighbourhood, and he fled, by night, in a closed carriage. There was the deserted *château*, like the home of the Sleeping Beauty, discovered by Henri and Isabelle Fournier, and their parents, one summer day in childhood. La Varenne, visited from Nançay with their cousin Robert, all its elegance hidden away under dust-sheets — and the silent lake where there had been boats and water parties. There was the *château* seen from the train, marking their approach to home — 'at the *château*, Mother used to say to us: "Look at me, darling," and with her handkerchief she wiped some of the dirt of the train off our faces'.

When love came to him, he pictured the beloved as 'a young lady, under a white parasol, opening the gate of a *château*, some heavy afternoon in the country . . .' So he wrote to his friend, René Bichet. 'To picture "the Young Lady," one must have been a peasant child oneself; one must have waited endlessly, on June Thursdays, behind the railings of a courtyard — near the great white gates at the end of the walks, on the edge of the woods of the *château*.'

His love-story would seem adolescent and banal but for two things, it was a love that lasted his life, and it inspired a great work of art.

On June 1st, 1905, Ascension Day, Henri Fournier had just been to an art exhibition in the Petit Palais. As he went down the big, stone staircase, between four and five in the afternoon, he saw a tall girl just in front of him on the steps. She was fair — trying to give his sister an impression of her extraordinary beauty, he hit on the image of a spray of white lilac. He followed until he saw her enter a house in the Boulevard St Germain; on the succeeding days, as often as he could get away from his Lycée, he went and stood under the windows. One evening she looked out, and smiled.

Next day, Whitsunday, he went back early, dressed as a schoolboy, so as not to create a false impression. He hoped to catch her on her way to an early Mass, perhaps at St Germain des Prés. She appeared, in her brown cloak. '*Vous êtes belle*,' he said.

He followed her into a tram, and they both got down at St Germain des Prés. 'Will you forgive me?' he said, and she answered: 'What do you want with me, sir? I don't know you – leave me.'

'She can't mind my going to Mass,' he told himself; but he did not see her anywhere in church. At last he discovered a Mass being said in a chapel behind the High Altar – and the hat with the roses bowed over her folded hands. He gave his last sou to the woman who came round collecting chair-money; he was one sou short, for chairs were two sous each. It was the eleventh of the month, he would not get his pocket-money from his parents till the fifteenth – and he had been ruining himself in tram fares for the last ten days.

They walked out of church together. If she were to take the tram, all would be up with him – he could not follow, as he was penniless. But she crossed the road, and walked towards the Seine.

'Then begins the great, beautiful, strange, mysterious conversation . . . she listens now as if she had realized who I am; her blue eyes rest on me with sweetness, almost with friendship. It is as if we had understood, each of us, who we are . . . No more defences, no more embarrassment; we walk . . . as if we were alone in the world, as if this admirable Whitsunday morning had been, from all eternity, prepared for us two. . . .'

But to all he said, she could only answer in a sweet and hopeless tone: '*A quoi bon? A quoi bon?*' – lifting her head a little at the *b* as she let it out. Then she bowed her head, and bit her lip.

'I told her my plans, my hopes . . . also that I had begun to write, poems, that my friends liked. She smiled a little. Then I took courage and asked in my turn: "And you, won't you tell me your name?" '

In his mind he had called her Mélisands — from now on he called her by the name which she bears in his novel, Yvonne de Galais.

At the Invalides they parted.

'We must separate,' she said. 'We are two children, we've been mad . . . .' She asked him not to follow, and he leaned on the balustrade of the bridge and watched her go.

Next year he went at the same hour to the same place on Ascension Day, in case she came again. He was disappointed, and yet he felt, if he had tried hard enough, somehow his feeling would have compelled her to come. Surely he had attained his greatest spiritual height, when he had been allowed that vision?

'Your griefs, desires, resignations of that day were your true life, that is to say, your true happiness. You owed them to a past perhaps . . . of no importance,' wrote Jacques Rivière, sensibly enough.

But Henri Fournier could not give up his private religion of Yvonne de Galais — though at times he might blaspheme against it himself, or doubt it altogether, or give her irreverent nicknames, such as 'Amy Slim'.

'How bitter all this would be', he wrote to René Bichet, more than three years after that meeting, 'if I were not sure that one day, by the power of my longing for her, I shall get to the point where we are reunited, in the big room, "at home", on a late afternoon when she has been paying calls. And while I watch her take off her big cloak, and throw her gloves on the table, and look at me, we shall hear "the children" upstairs unpacking the big toy-box.' Already the image of the *Demoiselle* is connected with the hidden voices of children: 'Quick, now here, now, always — ' another natural image of Paradise, our first world.

The Easter after the meeting, he had told his sister Isabelle: 'I am dreaming of a long novel that revolves round her, in a setting which will be Epineuil and Nançay – she's found, lost, found again . . . It will be called *The Wedding Day* . . . The young man, perhaps, will run away on the evening of the marriage, out of fear of this too-beautiful thing given him, because he has understood that Paradise is not of this world. . . .

'I don't know . . . the book is in me; it is forming, it reveals itself little by little. . . .'

Yvonne de Galais is not only the ideal beloved, she is the 'objective correlative' – round her, and the search for her, he can bring to life all his childhood, and all his adored Sologne – and in her loss he can express that sense of loss that is inseparable from recollections of early childhood, that may have something to do with our original nostalgia for Eden, and may not be quite unconnected with our hopes of Heaven.

Already, reading *Tess of the d'Urbervilles*, he had been deeply moved by the 'happiness after *too much* pain, and after the crime' – the brief, impossible happiness of Angel Clare and Tess, before their inevitable parting.

From early youth he had meant to write a novel. 'First it was only me, me and me! Then little by little it became depersonalized, began to be no longer the novel everyone has in his head at eighteen,' so he writes to Jacques Rivière. He wants to begin, somehow, from Laforgue, and yet to write a novel – a novel in which dreams cross: an old fantasy comes back, and meets a departing vision. He wants to do without character and plot, and yet to remain a novelist. Perhaps his book will be a continual *va-et-vient* between dream and reality. 'I want to express the mystery of the unknown world that I desire . . . . I want to make this personal world of mine live, the mysterious world of my desire, the new and faraway country of my heart

. . . a life recalled with my past life, a countryside that the actual countryside makes me desire.'

The departing vision is that of Yvonne de Galais – and the Laforgue from whom he begins is the timid Laforgue, who murmured:

Oh! qu'une d'elle-même, un beau soir, sût venir,
Ne voyant que boire à mes lèvres et mourir.

It is also the Laforgue of simple, poignant pictures:

Soeur faisait du crochet,
Mère montait la lampe . . .

And some of the melancholy of his Pierrot enters into the gipsy-life of Frantz de Galais, and his companion Ganache.

But Yvonne de Galais married, and was lost to Fournier's hopes – a loss to which he never quite resigned himself. 'I am suffering from "desolation",' he wrote. 'My country no longer wears the same face, reticent, mysterious and adorable. My paths don't lead any more towards the country of that soul, a country "curious" and mysterious like her. I've lost the delicious and the bitter "fancies" that she woke in me, and that were my whole life. Now I'm alone, at the centre of the earth.'

He speaks mournfully of the festival that will never take place – the wedding-day; he wants to write a book, or at least a chapter of a book, that shall be called 'The End of Youth'. His friend Jacques Rivière has married his sister Isabelle – and the union of the two people nearest to him leaves him, at least for a while, alone and in the cold.

Life offers him passing consolations, and he is not strong enough to refuse them, though they only bring a worse desolation — the pain of a man who longs for the purity of Eden, and whose life is not pure.

'Well, I've tried to live there, in Paris,' says Augustin Meaulnes in the novel, 'when I saw that everything was over and that it was not even worth the trouble any more, to look for the lost demesne . . . But a man who has once leapt into Paradise, how can he get used after it to the life of the rest of the world? What is happiness to others seemed mockery to me. And when one day I decided, sincerely and deliberately, to behave like other people, that day I piled up remorse enough for many a long day.'

Fournier's most personal confession is in a letter to René Bichet: 'At the deepest hour of the spring night, I am in the house of the fallen woman. I've slept in her bed: there's nothing more to say, I am going to go down the garden steps and to leave in the dark. But at the moment when it is time to end our secret interview, she holds me by the arm and falls back on the bed, saying: "Listen!" And a voice has burst out near us, in the garden; it mounts with a joy that raises, a purity that could disinfect this Hell. The nightingale is singing; and the woman smiles, like someone who has often seen the secret meeting of angels in a field, without talking about it, and reassures you as he goes across it with you — and she says; "he's there every night".'

The substitutes for Yvonne de Galais were one day to be conflated in the composite image of Valentine, the fiancée of Frantz de Galais, whom Meaulnes, in ignorance of her identity, made his mistress.

'She whom I met with her elder sister on a seat in a public garden, and as I spoke more gently to the elder, because the younger attracted me more, she said nothing and went away. . .' The dressmaker to whom Fournier sent his sister. The cast-off mistress who came back: 'she waited for me on a seat in the avenue, one night, two nights, ten nights. She said: "Time isn't long, when you're sure the person you're waiting for won't come."'

Henri Fournier was also to look for a substitute for Yvonne de Galais, further above her than Valentine had been below her. He found himself crying over 'a bad book about Bernadette and the pilgrims of Lourdes' (it was Huysmans's book). 'Lost companion, sister all-powerful, *turris eburnea, janua coeli*. Terrible queen, who smiled silently behind me as I read, and placed your hand on my shoulder with so much sweetness . . .' So he wrote to René Bichet; and he could not have forgotten another title of the Virgin: *hortus inclusus* or *le domaine mystérieux*. Two weeks later (after a visit to Lourdes) he wrote to Jacques Rivière, on the fourth anniversary of the apparition of Yvonne de Galais: 'Didn't I prove to myself the other day that every book led to some great triumph of the Virgin?' Yet so long as he lived he was never to find the lost demesne or its lady, on earth or in heaven, but only in his art. 'Perhaps,' Augustin Meaulnes was to say, 'when we die, perhaps Death alone will give us the key.'

When the experiences that went to the making of *Le Grand Meaulnes* are thus collected together, from Henri Fournier's letters to Jacques Rivière or to René Bichet, and from Madame Rivière's recollections of her brother, the novel seems almost their inevitable expression – but if it had not been for the novel, we should not have known which experiences to pick out as significant – a totally different novel of student life in Paris could very well be made from what is left over. Moreover his vocation as a novelist was known to him when he was very young, at an age when most future writers hope still that they are going to be poets – and Henri Fournier was already an artist when writing to his friends and talking to his sister.

'Novels without people, where the people are only the flux and reflux of life and its encounters.' This is one of his early notes. The chief people in *Le Grand Meaulnes* are only so far characterized as their functions require. Meaulnes is the big, silent boy who gets lost in the Sologne, and sees one December afternoon the tip of a grey turret above the fir trees: 'an extraordinary contentment uplifted him, a perfect and almost intoxicating tranquillity, the certitude that his end was now achieved, and that he had nothing but happiness now to expect'. He has taken his leap into Paradise. In hiding, he hears the voices of children talking of the mysterious wedding-feast of Frantz, at which they are to be masters of the ceremonies. He awakes to the unintelligible dialogue of Maloyau and Ganache, like that of a Shakespearian grave-digger and clown — they are going to reappear as Harlequin and Pierrot at the fancy-dress party, to which they invite him.

The chapters devoted to the strange wedding-feast are filled with an unearthly radiance. There is the dream-state of Meaulnes, come out of the surrounding cold into the warmth and light. Children are deputizing for the absent host, and most of the other guests are peaceable old people. Meaulnes was to say of them later: 'when one has committed some heavy, unpardonable offence, sometimes, in the midst of a great bitterness one thinks: "all the same, somewhere in the world there are people who would forgive me". One thinks of old people, of grandparents full of indulgence, who are convinced in advance that all you do is well done'. And the evening ends with the children sitting quietly, listening to Yvonne de Galais, the bridegroom's sister, playing old songs on the piano — a brown cloak thrown across her shoulders. Next morning, while the children were boating on the lake under a wintry sun, Meaulnes and Yvonne de Galais had the conversation that Henri Fournier had with the girl in the brown cloak on Whitsunday, by the side of the Seine.

But Frantz de Galais appears in the evening, in deep distress. The bride has failed to come with him, and the wedding will not take place. The feast breaks up in a hurry, and everyone goes home. Meaulnes gets a place in an old carriage, and falls asleep — in the morning he is set upon the road for Ste Agathe. He has, by sleeping, lost the track that leads to the hidden demesne — only a curious silk waistcoat, with mother of pearl buttons, part of his fancy dress, with which he has come away by mistake, remain to prove that it has not all been a dream.

François Seurel, the narrator, is the son of the school-teachers at Ste Agathe — as Henri Fournier was the son of the school-teachers at Epineuil. Meaulnes was their pupil and boarder, and François his closest companion. François is the uncharacterized narrator, distinguished only by lameness — a handicap which makes him fitter to share the adventure at one remove.

It is François who brings the book back from dream to reality after the wonderful adventure, and in the opening chapters he gives, with a few firm strokes, the setting of a school-house, in a Sologne village in winter, from which Meaulnes wandered by hazard into the mysterious wedding-feast. François keeps the level tone of a conscientious evangelist. 'The style to use', Henri Fournier had noted, 'is that of St. Matthew; *Christ's French*, as Laforgue said.'

When Meaulnes has gone to Paris in despair, it is François who discovers the way to the lost demesne. A school-friend speaks of a half-deserted property called Les Sablonnières. There, in the ruined chapel, he had seen a gravestone inscribed:

Ci-gît le chevalier Galois,
fidèle à son Dieu, à son Roi, à sa Belle.

There's only a farm, and a small villa – the only inhabitants are an elderly retired officer and his daughter – there was a son, who had peculiar ideas. . . .

Les Sablonnières was near Vieux-Nançay where, like Henri Fournier's 'Oncle Florent', François Seurel's 'Oncle Florentin' kept the general shop. Of course the Galais are his customers, and Yvonne herself comes on the old horse Bélisaire to do her shopping.

She talks to François about his future career – she also would like to teach children: 'I wouldn't give them the desire to run all over the world, as I dare say you will, M. Seurel, when you are a school-master. I would teach them to find the happiness that is right beside them, though it doesn't seem to be . . . So, perhaps there's a big, mad boy looking for me at the end of the world, while I'm here in Mme Florentin's shop, under this lamp, with my old horse waiting for me at the door. If this boy saw me, he wouldn't believe it, would he?'

'And perhaps I know that big, mad boy?' said François.

François went early next day on his bicycle, in search of Meaulnes, now passing his holidays with his mother at La Ferté d'Angillon. On the way he visited an old aunt – Henri Fournier's 'Tante Morenne' – who gave further authenticity to the mysterious wedding-feast, and attached it firmly to the real world. She had been there – she and her husband had been among the peaceable old people whom Meaulnes had met at dinner. On their way home they had met with the fugitive fiancée of Frantz de Galais. She was one of the daughters of a poor carpenter. 'She was convinced that so much happiness was not possible; that the young man was too young for her; that all the wonderful things he described to her were imaginary, and when at last Frantz came to fetch her, Valentine took fright. He was walking with her and her sister in the garden of the Archbishop's palace at Bourges, in spite of the cold and the strong wind. The young man, out of delicacy, and because he loved the younger sister, was full of attentions for the elder . . .' For a time the old woman took Valentine into her home, and then she went away to be a dressmaker in Paris, somewhere near Notre-Dame.

François finds Meaulnes about to set out on a long journey – he has a fault to repair, a fancied duty to help to find the fiancée of Frantz de Galais: 'when I discovered the nameless demesne, I was at a height at a degree of purity and perfection I shall never reach again. In death alone, as I once wrote to you, shall I perhaps find the beauty of that time once more'.

Oncle Florentin has organized a picnic, and Meaulnes and Yvonne de Galais are invited. Meaulnes learns from her of the ruin of Les Sablonnières, and of the poverty of her family – at the end of the day their last horse, old Bélisaire, is found to have lamed himself. It is a day of sadness and disappointment – but Meaulnes slips away from his friends at the end of the day, finds the road to Les Sablonnières, and offers marriage to Yvonne de Galais.

Frantz de Galais reappears on the evening of the marriage of Meaulnes and his sister. Frantz, like all the other characters in the book, but more than any, is a dream-figure, and more a symbol than a person. He is not a firmly conceived mediaeval symbol, standing for Weakness or Indecision – he is the symbolic figure of romantic literature, of which one cannot briefly say *what* he symbolizes, for that remains vague, and he is more potent in suggestion than symbolism. He owes a good deal to Hamlet.

He had first been seen outside Meaulnes's door, on the day after his arrival at the mysterious feast — a young man in a travelling-cloak, nervously whistling a sea-shanty, with a face of misery (surely Hamlet of Act V). He had next appeared at Ste Agathe, as a travelling gipsy with a bandaged head, in company with his faithful servant Ganache. There he had heard something of Meaulnes's mysterious adventure, for the other schoolboys were making fun of his strange absence. When they plotted to steal the map that Meaulnes was trying to construct of the way to the mysterious demesne, Frantz himself managed to steal it — and returned it to Meaulnes and François with a few corrections: by a schoolboy ritual (reminiscent of the cellarage scene) he made them swear to follow him, if he called on them for help. Before he left Ste Agathe he took off his bandages, revealing his identity to Meaulnes.

It was this promise, and a fault that he had to repair, that made Meaulnes hesitate to go to the newly found Yvonne de Galais — and on the evening of their marriage Frantz hooted from the edge of the wood; this time Meaulnes followed him.

The following chapters record the sickness of Yvonne, her recovery, her pregnancy and her death soon after her confinement — her body carried downstairs in the arms of François, because there was not room to carry down a coffin.

Henri Fournier had asked his sister's help: 'there are some very simple things, descriptions of familiar places . . . stories about little, everyday happenings that must be given absolutely clearly, with no admixture of symbolism . . . You would do this much better than me; you have a detailed memory, you knew it all with me, you would describe it all quite simply, as you recall it . . . And there are stories that you've told me that I want to use — like the day out by the Cher with the Groslins, which ended so badly with the accident to the horse that had been tethered too low, or Maria Bureau, whom a neighbour had to carry down dead in his arms because there was no room for a coffin to turn on the staircase.'

But Madame Rivière declines all the credit; it is her brother himself who achieved the purity and detachment for which he was striving, the faithful and humble rendering of small facts, and in the style of St. Matthew.

When Yvonne is dead, François goes through the papers in the house and finds a diary kept by Meaulnes. This contains some of the story of his attempts to live like other people in Paris. He falls in with Valentine, and she becomes his mistress — too late he discovers that he has not only betrayed Yvonne de Galais, but Frantz also; for he had never imagined that Valentine was the fugitive fiancée.

Valentine speaks of her former fiancé, and the promises he made her: 'we were to have had a house, like a cottage hidden in the country. It was quite ready, he said. We were to get there on the evening of our wedding-day, about this time — at night-fall, as if we were coming back from a long voyage. And on the way, and in the courtyard, and hidden in the trees, unknown children were to greet us, crying: "long live the bride!" '

There can be few novels of whose genesis so much is known. The happy appearance of a girl in a brown cloak as an 'objective correlative', the fusing of a calf-love, that became the love of a life-time, with Henri Fournier's love for Sologne: that is the history of *Le Grand Meaulnes*. But behind the nostalgia for *le domaine mystérieux* there is a very old nostalgia, once expressed by Henry Vaughan.

O how I long to travel back,
And tread again that ancient track!

That I might once more reach that plain
Where first I left my glorious train;
From whence th'enlightened Spirit sees
That shady City of Palm-trees.

III. THE RETREAT

The best thing ever said about Forrest Reid was said prophetically by his friend, Mr. E. M. Forster, before the publication of any of his major work. *Following Darkness* had been written, but with all the loose ends left that were to be tidied up when the book was reissued as *Peter Waring*. *The Bracknels*[1] and *The Spring Song* had been written, but they are both more subtle in feeling and experience than their texture indicates: their author was later to wish to rehandle them, as he had rehandled *Following Darkness*. There was not yet anything of the quality of *Apostate*, the autobiography, or of *Uncle Stephen*, his masterpiece.

Mr. Forster likened Forrest Reid to Wordsworth, who spent a lifetime in the recollection and expression of a vision that he had received in his youth. 'He is always harking back to some lonely garden or sombre grove, or to some deserted house whose entrance is indeed narrow but whose passages stretch to infinity, and when his genius gains the recognition that has so strangely been withheld from it, he will be ranked with the artists who have preferred to see life steadily rather than to see it whole, and who have concentrated their regard upon a single point, a point which, when rightly focused, may perhaps make all the surrounding landscape intelligible.'

In the opening lines of *Apostate* this is confirmed. 'The

[1] Later rewritten as *Denis Bracknel*.

primary impulse of the artist springs, I fancy, from discontent, and his art is a kind of crying for Elysium . . . Strangely different these Paradisian visions. For me it may be the Islands of the Blest "not shaken by winds nor ever wet with rain . . . where the clear air spreads without a cloud," for you the jewelled splendour of the New Jerusalem. Only in no case, I think, is it our own free creation. It is a country whose image was stamped upon our soul before we opened our eyes on earth, and all our life is little more than a trying to get back there, our art than a mapping of its mountains and streams.' He went on to say that he was speaking of a particular kind of art: Thackeray and Jane Austen loved this present world, and were not unique or even singular in this love.

In his dreams, he records, he visited the same spot night after night — he found himself on a grassy hill, sloping gently to the sea, and there he was waiting, never in vain, for what Corvo would have called 'the Divine Friend, much desired'. 'And presently, out from the leafy shadow he bounded into the sunlight. I saw him standing for a moment, his naked body the colour of pale amber against the dark background — a boy of about my own age, with eager parted lips and bright eyes . . . And from the moment I found myself on that hill-side I was happy. All my waking life, indeed, was blotted out. I had a sense of security, as if no doubt or trouble or fear could ever again reach me. It was as if I had come home; as if I were, after a long absence among strangers, once more among my own people. But the deepest well of happiness sprang from a sense of perfect communion with another being. Having tasted it, no earthly love could ever fill its place, and the memory of it was in my waking hours like a Fata Morgana, leading me hither and thither, wherever a faint reflection of it seemed for a moment to shine.'

A peculiar sympathy for the mysterious, because speechless, world of animals; a love for the drowsy, vague poetry of Poe, were also part of Reid's early, private world. Nor was this all: 'If you stand quite still in an ancient house, you will hear, even in broad daylight, strange sounds and murmurings. And so it was with me. I came on my mother's side, of a very old, perhaps too old a stock, one that had reached its prime four hundred years ago, and there were whisperings and promptings which when I was quite alone reached me out of the past. Very early I perceived that onc's mind was swarming with ghosts.'

Apostate, he named himself, for the same reason that the name was given to Julian: he preferred the ancient gods. 'The Divine Friend, much desired' was later given the name of Hermes. A lovely statue of Hermes from Magna Graecia stood in Uncle Stephen's bedroom, blessed and blessing. 'He is the God of sleep and dreams,' Uncle Stephen explains. 'The last libation of the day was made to him – a kind of "now I lay me down to sleep" ceremony. The Greeks would have found Doctor Watts's poem quite appropriate:

With cheerful heart I close my eyes,
Since Thou wilt not remove;
And in the morning let me rise
Rejoicing in Thy love.'

Reid owned, in *Private Road*, that he did not quite know why the Divine Friend should be identified with Hermes. 'I knew little of Hermes. The Homeric Hymn did not fit in with my conception of him, and there seemed indeed little to be known. He was the guide of souls; he was a God of dreams, and also a boy God – a protector of boys, whose image was set up in the corners of playgrounds and gymnasiums: there was the lovely statue of Praxiteles.' There seem also to have been recollections of Homer: Hermes with his golden wand 'disguised as a young man in the heyday of his youth and beauty with the down just coming on his face' – who met Odysseus on his way to Circe's palace, and gave him the saving herb, Moly. And he seems, in *Uncle Stephen*, to have acquired some of the characteristics of Asclepios, god of the dream oracle, who heals those who sleep in his sanctuary.

His cult of Hermes he called: 'the acceptance of an imaginative symbol projected from an unknown spiritual energy. It is not faith, because it will not bear the test of unhappiness: it comes, rather, *with* happiness, and in the hour of loneliness and loss would have no power to console . . . Nevertheless, the obstinacy with which it haunted my mind caused me to wonder if it had not its origin in some universal spiritual force from which Christianity and all religions had sprung'. He wrote to a friend, who obtained for him from an unnamed source what he quotes as 'the verdict of the Catholic church'.

'Your friend can find in his Hermes whatever spirit he likes to evolve out of his hungers and desires, and this ideal of his (in so far as it consorts with the ideals painted for us in the New Testament) is no doubt the same spiritual ideal as you have found in Christ, or rather one facet of it . . . it is clear that Christ is the fulfilment of all our earlier hopes and the reality of our later dreams, so that there, in Christ, all religions touch hands. . . .'

Forrest Reid took this answer to mean 'that to the Christian mind I was clinging obstinately and wilfully to an outworn creed, when all I had to do was to accept the light and the truth'. Possibly further contact between him and the unnamed author of 'the verdict of the Catholic church' might have produced closer sympathy, though they could never have been of one mind – Reid might have found more reverence than he expected for the 'other Old Testament', that of Hellenism – and his unknown critic might have seen in Hermes a figure not so remote from the Christ revealed in some writings of the saints. 'The statement that I must see him as Christ would, it seemed to me, be exactly paralleled were I to insist that the Christian must see Christ as him,' Reid complained. The parallel is not so exact as he thought – but early Christians had seen Christ as Orpheus. Reid, however, preferred to think of Hermes rather as the likeness of a semi-divine figure – something like the archangel Raphael when he accompanied the boy Tobias.

Elysium, and Hermes its messenger, are at the heart of all his best work. He is surely describing himself in his interesting portrait of the novelist, Linton, in *Brian Westby*: 'In that first story, you see, he's only feeling his way – pretty blindly too – yet there is something even in it, which he's trying to express. It's not exactly a meaning, or an idea, or a message: at least it's not quite any of these, though in a way it's all three. I don't know what to call it; but it's there, and with each book it ought to become clearer. Mind you, I don't say it *does* . . . Nobody can do more than feel his way till he's acquired a method, learned his job, so to speak; and Linton was uncommonly slow in learning his. Besides, he often chose the wrong kind of subject; and in the beginning the writing itself was often bad. Still, after a fashion the books do fit together. I mean, he's got an ideal; and each of his books is an attempt to express it. So far as it *is* his book, that is to say, for the subject sometimes won't allow it to be. That's what I meant when I said he chose the wrong subjects. There's only the faintest glimmer of what he's really after in op. one, for instance; and in none even of the latest books, perhaps, is it there all the time. If he *could* bring it off, *could* produce it naked and complete — then I should think he might make a bonfire of the earlier things. They'd be only sketches and studies for the finished work . . . Which *may* mean — you know — and I can't help thinking really *does* mean, that he isn't a novelist at all . . . Or do you think that's to take him quite too seriously?'

In the autobiography, *Apostate*, and in *Uncle Stephen* and *The Retreat* Reid has surely brought it off, has produced his ideal naked and complete — and they are important works of art. It is, however, a good thing that he could not make a bonfire of all his earlier work, and there is later work that is of value for a further revelation of his vision, or for a comment on it. Nevertheless, it is probably better for his final reputation to leave out of the canon those books 'breaking the sequence', as he says, in which there is no other-worldliness. *Brian Westby* is the exception — for it seems to be an earthly story with a heavenly meaning.

Into *Following Darkness* not more than a hint of the supernatural entered. In *The Bracknels* — surely an expansion and rehandling of the theme treated by Henry James in *The Pupil* — the supernatural is evil, and destroys the boy-hero Denis, as it threatens to destroy Grif in *The Spring Song*.

Reid expected more popular success for *The Spring Song*: 'either the tale never found its true public, or the public disapproved of my method of presenting children'. Perhaps the writing was not good enough to let the book reach its true public: there is some embarrassingly bad verse, and much very indifferent prose. The author is dead, and the book cannot now be rewritten, as it deserves to be, but the Cinema might yet give new life to this beautiful fantasy of childhood — it remains, indeed, with the sympathetic reader as a series of images, because the vision is so greatly superior to the writing: the comic play scenes, made by the children out of a sentimental novel by their governess; Grif's quest for his dog, stolen by the circus people, and the loosing of all their stolen dogs; the mad organist and his hallucinations; and his death, in a thunder of music, in the blazing church.

Uncle Stephen was first a dream story: 'from beginning to end, it was composed in sleep — or perhaps I should say "lived", for I undoubtedly was Tom'. Its first title was '*My* Uncle's a Magician' — and the source of the dream is not beyond conjecture. The boy Forrest Reid had been supposed to have as his true ancestor a great-uncle — 'Henry of Ashchurch' — one of the mysterious relations who hovered tantalizingly in the unknown. He looked him up in the Burke of 1863, in the article 'Parr of Parr', and found that he had lived as a recluse, shut up among his treasures, at Lathwood Hall in Shropshire: 'He was many years a grand juror of that county, but declined to act as a magistrate from his love of retirement. He formed a valuable collection of paintings, coins, and medals, all of which, together with his library, were dispersed by auction after his decease in 1847.' And another Irish writer, Le Fanu, had written that haunting story of another eremitical uncle who was a wicked magician — *Uncle Silas*. While the predicament of Tom at the beginning of the story is that fancied for himself by almost every sentimental schoolboy in love with one of his fellows — that each should lose a parent, and the survivors should marry, and make them brothers.

Tom, now completely orphaned, is bored and misunderstood by his dull but well-meaning step-relations. Uncle Stephen projects a telepathic message to Tom, who goes to him in answer to his call, to his old, quiet house in the country. In the strange and beautiful magic that follows, out of Tom's desire for a young companion, and Uncle Stephen's wish that he could sometimes be Tom's contemporary — the years roll away for the old man, and he appears as his youthful self Philip, the boy who ran away from home. The magic gains in power, and Uncle Stephen is unable to resume his own personality. Tom's panic, Philip's realization that he is a Rip van Winkle, and the return of Uncle Stephen, are all worked out with imaginative matter-of-factness.

Philip, with his unearthly quality, is like a manifestation of Reid's tutelary spirit — and his appearance on the first occasion is in accordance with this character, a boy looking down through a screen of green leaves. He is to Tom — though human and often tiresome — something of 'the Divine Friend, much desired' of Reid's boyhood.

But to Reid's maturity 'the Divine Friend, much desired' must have begun to put on the resemblance of a son, a nephew or a spiritual heir. Hermes could not have seemed quite the same to Socrates as to Alcibiades — and even the Christian, who has once imagined himself as a child among the Five Thousand, and later as St. Peter or St. John, may come to imagine himself as St. Joseph or St. Simeon.

The epigraph is taken from *Job VI.* 8: 'O that I might have my request; and that God would grant me the thing that I long for!' Reid has not given the verse reference, probably because his prayer was not at all the prayer of Job, which goes on: 'Even that it would please God to destroy me; that he would let loose his hand and cut me off!' He was surely longing that his call could produce a young companion and spiritual son — fashioned, perhaps, like Tom, partly out of his own past; even as Philip, fashioned out of Uncle Stephen's past, came as a companion to Tom. He was surely praying for that fulfilment, expressed at the beginning of the book in lines from Wordsworth's *Michael* — lines which are repeated, altered into prose rhythm, at the end of the book.

They were as companions . . .
Objects which the Shepherd loved before
Were dearer now . . . From the Boy there came
Feelings and emanations — things which were
Light to the sun and music to the wind;
And the old man's heart seemed born again.

Uncle Stephen, that lovely fusion of the old man's vision and the young man's dream, could not fail to reach a part of its true public — though it cannot yet have found its way to many who might greatly love and admire it.

Reid's prayer was partly answered: Tom never left him again.

The Retreat, the second novel of the trilogy, shows Tom a few years earlier, when both his parents were alive. The beautiful opening pages are the transcript of a dream: the boy apprentice of an old magician is alone and frightened in a large bare room — there is a knocking at the door; trembling, the boy opens it and lets in a young fawn, with whom he escapes into a world of running water and green leaves. 'I saw in this', says Reid, 'a kind of symbolism, a pledge of the alliance I had formed from the beginning with the animal world.'

Another fragment, this time a scene from waking life, had for some years been haunting Reid because of its strangeness and beauty. Mr. E. M. Forster had taken him for a walk in London, and they had visited a small park. 'This park, I suspect, must originally have been part of, or adjoined, a graveyard, for all along one side of it was a broken wall composed of ancient tomb-stones, and now, at the hour of our visit, seated on each of these tomb-stones was a cat. The path was deserted, the cats were motionless, and in the stillness and the fading autumn light, the whole picture seemed drenched in a kind of sorcery, which, partly perhaps because I was so little prepared for it, created an immediate response in my imagination.'

Reid seems to have felt that the episode and the dream were part of the same book, before he knew what the book was to be. This is probably not an infrequent experience with authors; it is very like Gide's experience recorded in *Le Journal des Faux-Monnayeurs* — he was haunted by several scattered happenings. Gide allowed his former hero, Lafcadio, to serve as a temporary link — but discarded him before he wrote the novel. Reid also turned back to a former hero of his own. 'The first step was to ask myself — who would have had the dream? The second was — who would have encountered the cats? . . . The pregnant answer to both questions was "Tom" — Uncle Stephen's Tom . . . only it must be Tom, as I promptly realized, at an earlier stage in his development . . . Tom, in fact, at a transition period, when everything that happened to him should be new and mysterious, and wishes and fears change unaccountably and involuntarily into realities.'

Much of the book came out of 'real life': schoolboys, dogs and cats whom Reid had known, needed little alteration — a shop in Belfast, a Donizetti air he had himself sung as a boy, all were put in. But through all the realistic, Northern Ireland setting, Tom comes, trailing clouds of glory.

To him appears an angel, under the name of Gamelyn — very like the Raphael of Tobias. Gamelyn helps him to dodge the flaming sword, and to trespass in Eden. Eden is wild and overgrown, populated by many of the first created animals, who have eaten of the tree of Life. Tom talks to Dog, the original dog; he is mothered by Albatross, the original albatross; and he is dangerously wooed by the serpent — who puts forward quite a new story of the Fall. The Temptation had been a plot on the serpent's part, to get rid of Eva, who bored him, and to have Adam, whom he loved, all to himself again — all this is worked out with serpentine plausibility and exquisite humour.

Tom thinks of eating of the Tree of Life — he admits that he would like to live for ever.

'It only means for ever in that body,' the serpent said. 'It would be a foolish choice. You will live for ever as it is, though it will not always be the same life. But that is better — '

'Do you think so?' Tom pondered doubtfully.

'Much better,' said the serpent. 'How do you know that your present life will not become a burden to you? I could show you lives you have already lived, and I don't think you would wish to return to them.'

And again Tom was in the large bare room, hung with decaying tapestries, attending on the old alchemist, his master.

Young Tom, the third book of the trilogy, follows Tom back to schoolroom days: it is a pleasant book, full of animals, and connected with the other world by a young ghost — but it is not much more than an excuse for the author and his readers to enjoy more of Tom's company.

Brian Westby, which appeared between *Uncle Stephen* and *The Retreat*, is altogether more interesting and important.

It is a rationalization of the theme of 'the Divine Friend, much desired', and told as a purely realistic story. A novelist, Martin Linton, has gone to Northern Ireland for convalescence — he is not a little reminiscent of some of the writers in Henry James's stories, and his work is that of his creator. He finds a boy reading one of his own books — the boy is his own son. Years ago his wife had left him, not telling him that she was pregnant — she gave birth to a son, but concealed this fact when she asked Linton for a divorce; and when she remarried, the boy was brought up under his step-father's name, as Brian Westby. Linton slowly woos the friendship of the boy, and when they try the experiment of writing a story together, he places some sheets of his own composition in the boy's hands, and lets him read on, and find his father revealed by the style. One is reminded of the scene in *Les Faux-Monnayeurs*, in which Edouard charges Georges with stealing, by showing him a passage in his novel referring to a theft by another boy — but the original of this scene is rather to be found in the great closing pages of *Apostate* when the fellow-apprentice, in whom for a long time the dream friend seemed to be merged, was given Reid's intimate journal of all his thoughts and longings to read.

This is the writer in whose work M. Mauriac found 'le vide effroyable que creuse dans les êtres l'absence de Dieu'. It is an astonishing judgment, for Forrest Reid, if anyone, has painted that subject, proposed by the good bishop of Angoulême and Laure de Rastignac to the all unworthy Lucien de Rubempré — 'L'âme qui se souvient du ciel.'

IV. A NOTE ON PROUST

Marcel Proust disliked the English title given to the translation of his work: *Remembrance of Things Past*. It did not express the quest implied in his own title; and it seems that it was not only time but also Eternity that was the object of this quest.

This is often forgotten by his readers, and yet it is clearly expressed in his great words about the novelist's vocation.

'How happy the man would be, I thought, who could write such a book; what a task before him! To give an idea of it, it is from the highest and the most different arts that one must borrow analogies — for that writer (who moreover must make the most opposed facets of each character appear, so that its volume may be felt as that of a solid), must prepare his book meticulously, continually regrouping his forces, as for an offensive; he must endure it, like a fatigue; accept it, like a rule; construct it, like a church; follow it, like a diet . . . create it, like a world; without leaving those mysteries on one side which have probably no explanation except in other worlds, the presentiment of which is perhaps that which most moves us in life and in art.'[1]

He had reached the conclusion 'that we are in no wise free in the presence of a work of art, that we do not create it as we please but that it pre-exists in us and we are compelled as though it were a law of nature to discover it because it is at once hidden from us and necessary. But is not that discovery, which art may enable us to make, most precious to us, a discovery of that which for most of us remains for ever unknown, our true life, reality as we have ourselves felt it and which differs so much from that which we had believed that we are filled with delight when chance brings us an authentic revelation of it'.[2]

This vocation of the artist had, in music, been magnificently fulfilled by Vinteuil, in his great septet.

'This song, different from those of other singers, similar to all his own, where had Vinteuil learned, where had he heard it? Each artist seems thus to be the native of an unknown country, which he himself has forgotten . . . When all is said, Vinteuil, in his latest works, seemed to have drawn nearer to that unknown country . . . This lost country composers do not actually remember, but each of them remains all his life somehow attuned to it; he is wild with joy when he is singing the airs of

[1] T.R., II, pp. 329-40. Apart from this passage, all others are quoted from the translation by C. K. Scott Moncrieff and Stephen Hudson; but it is assumed that those who require references will want them for the French text.

[2] T.R., II, pp. 27-8.

his native land....'[1] It was the mode in which Vinteuil 'heard' the universe, and expressed what he heard: 'This unknown quality of a unique world no other composer had ever made us see....'[2]

To Swann, a phrase in the sonata of Vinteuil had held out 'an invitation to partake of intimate pleasures — of whose existence, before hearing it, he never dreamed, into which he felt that nothing but this phrase could initiate him; and he had been filled with love for it, as with a new and strange desire.

'With a slow and rhythmical movement it had led him here, there, everywhere, towards a state of happiness noble, unintelligible, yet clearly indicated.'[3]

To the narrator, a motif in the septet was 'an ineffable joy which seemed to come from Paradise';[4] he connected it with other 'starting-points, foundation-stones for the construction of a true life' — his impressions at the sight of the steeples of Martinville, or of a row of trees near Balbec.

'Two hypotheses', he says, 'suggest themselves in all important questions, questions of the truth of Art, of the truth of the Immortality of the Soul . . . It is not possible that a piece of sculpture, a piece of music which gives us an emotion which we feel to be more exalted, more pure, more true, does not correspond to some definite spiritual reality. It is surely symbolical of one, since it gives that impression of profundity and truth. Thus nothing resembled more closely than some such phrase of Vinteuil the peculiar pleasure which I had felt at certain moments in my life, when gazing, for instance, at the steeples of Martinville, or at certain trees along a road in Balbec.—'[5] The other hypothesis being that we magnify the importance of impressions which we are not able to analyse.

[1] P., II, pp. 74-5. [2] Ibid., p. 235. [3] S., I, p. 301.
[4] P., II, p. 79. [5] Ibid., pp. 233-4.

There were 'privileged moments' in his life that Proust was able to analyse as no one else had analysed such moments — and the most famous is the wonderful moment of the *madeleine* and the cup of tea. His mother had persuaded him to have a cup of tea, and offered him a *madeleine*.

'And soon, mechanically, weary after a dull day with the prospect of a depressing morrow, I raised to my lips a spoonful of the tea in which I had soaked a morsel of the cake. No sooner had the warm liquid, and the crumbs with it, touched my palate than a shudder ran through my whole body, and I stopped, intent upon the extraordinary changes that were taking place. An exquisite pleasure had invaded my senses, detached, with no suggestion of its origin . . . Whence could it have come to me, this all-powerful joy? I was conscious that it was connected with the taste of the tea and the cake, but it infinitely transcended those savours . . . .'[1]

He tried again, and there was less power in the tea and the cake. He looked into his mind, and it told him nothing. Then he patiently cleared his mind of all other things.

'I place in position before my mind's eye the still recent taste of the first mouthful, and I feel something start within me, something that leaves its resting-place and attempts to rise, something that has been embedded like an anchor at a great depth; I do not yet know what it is but I can feel it mounting slowly; I can measure the resistance, I can hear the echo of great spaces traversed . . . And suddenly the memory returns.'

The narrator is in his Aunt Léonie's room at Combray.

'And just as the Japanese amuse themselves by filling a porcelain bowl with water and steeping in it little crumbs of paper which until then are without character or form, but, the

[1] S., I, p. 69.

moment they become wet, stretch themselves and bend, take on colour and distinctive shape, become flowers or houses or people, permanent and recognizable, so in that moment all the flowers in our garden and in M. Swann's park, and the water-lilies on the Vivonne and the good folk of the village and their little dwellings and the parish church and the whole of Combray and of its surroundings, taking their proper shapes and growing solid, sprang into being, town and gardens alike, from my cup of tea.'

The moment of the cup of tea was a moment in which a sense impression brought back the past with unusual power. Other 'privileged moments' were of this kind. Entering the courtyard of the Guermantes mansion the narrator had to step hurriedly out of the way of a carriage . . . 'Stepping backwards I stumbled against some unevenly placed paving-stones behind which there was a coach-house. As I recovered myself, one of my feet stepped on a flagstone nearer than the one next it. In that instant all my discouragement disappeared and I was possessed by the same felicity which at different moments of my life had given me the view of trees which seemed familiar during the drive round Balbec, the view of the belfries of Martinville, the savour of the madeleine dipped in my tea and so many of the other sensations of which I have spoken and which Vinteuil's last works seemed to synthesize . . . the sensation I had once felt on two uneven slabs in the Baptistery of St Mark had been given back to me.'[1]

On arriving at the musical-party given by the Princesse de Guermantes (formerly Madame Verdurin) the narrator had to wait for the end of an item in the programme. A servant brought him a glass of orangeade — and a noise the man made, knocking a spoon against a plate, caused in the narrator the

[1] T.R., II, pp. 7-9.

same sudden feeling of happiness as that in which the uneven paving-stones brought back Venice to him.

'This time my sensation was quite different, being that of heat accompanied by the smell of smoke tempered by the fresh air of a surrounding forest, and I realized that what appeared so pleasant was the identical group of trees I had found so tiresome to observe and describe when I was uncorking a bottle of beer in the railway carriage, and, in a sort of bewilderment, I believed for the moment, until I had collected myself, so similar was the sound of the spoon against the plate to that of the hammer of a railway employee who was doing something to the wheel of the carriage while the train was at a standstill facing the group of trees, that I was actually there.'[1]

On the same occasion the feel of a napkin brought back Balbec, and the sound of a water-pipe was like the scream of an excursion steamer there.

'Yes, if a memory, thanks to forgetfulness, has been unable to contract any tie, to forge any link between itself and the present, if it has remained in its own place, of its own date, if it has kept its distance, its isolation in the hollow of a valley or on the peak of a mountain, it makes us suddenly breathe an air new to us because it is an air we have formerly breathed, an air purer than that the poets have vainly called Paradisiacal, which offers that deep sense of renewal only because it has been breathed before, inasmuch as the true paradises are paradises we have lost.'[2]

And yet, though the cup of tea and the madeleine brought back Aunt Léonie's room at Combray; though the tapping of a spoon against a plate brought back the row of trees; though the feel of a napkin and the noise of a water-pipe brought back Balbec; though the uneven paving-stones brought back Venice;

[1] T.R., II, pp. 9-10. [2] Ibid., p. 13.

and though many of these 'privileged moments' seemed to be synthesized in the later works of Vinteuil — this is not all. The peculiar joy which the trees at Balbec gave to the narrator remains unexplained, and so does his happiness at the sight of the towers of Martinville.

'In ascertaining and noting the shape of their spires, the changes of aspect, the sunny warmth of the surfaces, I felt that I was not penetrating to the full depth of my impression, that something more lay behind that mobility, that luminosity, something which they seemed at once to contain and to conceal. . . .'[1]

It seems at least a possibility that the pleasure given by the trees at Balbec, and by the towers at Martinville, since we are told that it was comparable with the pleasures of an involuntarily recalled memory, arose from the narrator's involuntary recollections of that unknown country which, as Wordsworth says, we forget at birth, but never wholly forget.

And perhaps we may refer to the narrator's joy at 'singing the airs of his native land', and neither to perversity, nor to a natural pleasure at seeing bits of a pattern fit together, the especial pleasure with which he finds a unity in his worldly experiences. It may be human wickedness which has caused the convergence of the different bits of the pattern, but the resulting unity may nevertheless reflect an other-worldly unity, remembered from that imperial palace whence he came.

There are several moments of this sort. For example, in the musical party at Madame Verdurin's, to which M. de Charlus invites the guests, *le petit clan* of the Verdurins and the world of Guermantes meet. Sodom and Gomorrah also shake hands: the efficient cause of the meeting is the friendship, now pure and exalted, between Mademoiselle Vinteuil and her friend —

[1] S., I, pp. 258-9.

the latter has laboriously deciphered Vinteuil's posthumous work: the final cause is the friendship between Charlus and Morel – Charlus hopes to get his young friend decorated. For the narrator Swann's way, in Mademoiselle Vinteuil, who came from Montjouvain on the way to Méséglise, here unites with the Guermantes way – and M. de Charlus connects both with Balbec.

(It would be tempting to compare Combray, crowned with its church of S. Hilaire, and Guermantes, on the Vivonne, with the Jerusalem and Babylon of patristic writers – so immortally a part of French thought since Pascal and Bossuet. The objection is that Proust would have delighted to make this comparison if he had intended it – he is not likely to have implied it in silence.)

Another occasion, in which Swann's way and the Guermantes way meet, is the *faire-part* sent out on the death of Marie-Antoinette d'Oloron, marquise de Cambremer.[1] She was Jupien's niece, adopted by M. de Charlus – therefore almost all the mediatized princes of Europe were put in mourning by her death. So also was the Comte de Méséglise – none other than Legrandin, of Combray and of Swann's way, the brother of Marie-Antoinette's mother-in-law, who had given himself this sham title. Swann himself is represented, for the Forchevilles' names are there – Odette de Forcheville, Swann's widow, was a cousin of Jupien. Balbec mourns, in the Cambremer family; Sodom is represented by Jupien, by M. de Charlus and by the widower; Gomorrah is represented by Odette, who also represents Mme Verdurin's little group.

All the threads are gathered together at the end of the book. Madame Verdurin is now the second Princesse de Guermantes; the Duc de Guermantes is, in old age, the lover of Odette de

[1] A.D., II, pp. 182ff.

Forcheville. Gilberte, daughter of Swann and Odette, is now widow of Robert de St Loup, and the intimate friend of Albertine's friend Andrée. Gilberte's daughter is daughter of Guermantes and Méséglise, of Sodom and Gomorrah. Already, in a previous volume, the narrator has visited Gilberte at Swann's house, Tansonville, and she has shown him that Swann's way and the Guermantes way are not geographically opposed as they had been in his childhood fancy – one can go to Guermantes by way of Méséglise.[1]

It is difficult not to see in this reception of the Princesse de Guermantes an illustration of 'the philosophy of Hermes that this visible world is but a picture of the invisible, wherein, as in a portrait, things are not truly but in equivocal shapes, as they counterfeit some real substance in that invisible fabrick'.

In short, *A la Recherche du Temps Perdu* appears to be less a Human than a Divine Comedy. The *Inferno* is terribly and unsparingly described – but the *Paradiso* is not completely absent. And though M. Mauriac has said that in all this vast novel God is absent, and it is true that no character in it troubles to perform what He commands – M. Mauriac is right in saying that the grandmother and mother of the narrator are pure and good on no supernatural principle – yet at least Swann and the narrator desire what He promises, and this is perhaps an even rarer sign of grace in the twentieth century. They not only have immortal longings, but they recognize that they have them.

[1] A.D., II, p. 206.

INDEX

INDEX

INDEX

INDEX

INDEX